# SUCCESSFUL
# ACADEMIC WRITING

PEARSON
Education

We work with leading authors to develop the strongest educational materials in academic writing, bringing cutting-edge thinking and best learning practice to a global market.

Under a range of well-known imprints, including Longman, we craft high quality print and electronic publications which help readers to understand and apply their content, whether studying or at work.

To find out more about the complete range of our publishing, please visit us on the World Wide Web at www.pearsoned.co.uk

# INSIDE TRACK

# SUCCESSFUL ACADEMIC WRITING

Andy Gillett, Angela Hammond
and Mary Martala

University of Hertfordshire

PEARSON
Longman

Harlow, England • London • New York • Boston • San Francisco • Toronto
Sydney • Tokyo • Singapore • Hong Kong • Seoul • Taipei • New Delhi
Cape Town • Madrid • Mexico City • Amsterdam • Munich • Paris • Milan

**Pearson Education Limited**

Edinburgh Gate
Harlow
Essex CM20 2JE
England

and Associated Companies throughout the world

*Visit us on the World Wide Web at*:
www.pearsoned.co.uk

First published 2009

ISBN: 978-0-273-72171-0

**British Library Cataloguing-in-Publication Data**
A catalogue record for this book is available from the British Library

**Library of Congress Cataloging-in-Publication Data**
Gillet, Andy.
   Writing academic essays / Andy Gillet, Angela Hammond and Mary
Martala-Lockett.
      p. cm. – (Inside track)
   ISBN 978-0-273-72171-0 (pbk.)
   1. English language–Rhetoric–Study and teaching (Higher) 2. Academic
writing. I. Hammond, Angela. II. Martala-Lockett, Mary. III. Title.
   PE1408.G5584 2009
   808'.0420711–dc22

                                                         2009008664
                     Page 1

10 9 8 7 6 5 4 3 2 1
13 12 11 10 09

Typeset in 9/12.5 pt Helvetica Neue by 3
Printed in Great Britain by Henry Ling Ltd., at the Dorset Press, Dorchester, Dorset

*The publisher's policy is to use paper manufactured from sustainable forests.*

# BRIEF CONTENTS

# GET THE INSIDE TRACK TO ACADEMIC SUCCESS

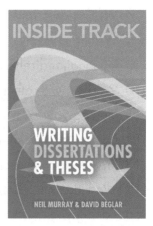

# CONTENTS

Contents

# Contents

Contents

# ABOUT THE AUTHORS

The authors all work in the School of Combined Studies at the University of Hertfordshire where they teach academic writing, research and study skills as well as a range of language and education courses at undergraduate and postgraduate level. They have a wide range of experience working in universities, colleges, as well as private and government organisations and companies both in the UK and abroad.

## Acknowledgements

The authors would like to thank Ian, James, Kay, Neil, Philip, Paissia, Shigeko and Simon for putting up with missed meals and lonely evenings and weekends during the time in which the book has been in development.

We would also like to thank our colleagues in the School of Combined Studies at the University of Hertfordshire for their sustained interest and also for trying out our materials and giving us valuable feedback.

Without Pearson Education, this publication would not exist. So we would like to thank Steve, Katy, Linda and Joy for keeping us on target and making our manuscript into the book you see before you.

## Publisher's acknowledgements

*We are grateful to the following for permission to reproduce copyright material:*

**Figures**
Figure 4.2 from *Accounting: An Introduction*, 4th ed., Harlow: Pearson Education (McLaney, E. and Atrill, P. 2008); Figure 7.1 from *Fundamentals of Nursing: Concepts, Procedures & Practices*, 7th ed., Pearson Education, Inc. (Kozier, Barbara J.; Glenora, Erb.; Berman, Audrey J.; Snyder, Shirlee. 2004) p. 722; Figure 7.2 from *Hughes' Electrical and Electronic Technology*, 10th ed., Harlow: Pearson Education (Hughes, E., Hiley, J., Brown, K. and McKenzie-Smith, I. 2008) p. 812; Figure 7.3a from *Operations Management*, 5th ed., Harlow: Pearson Education (Slack, N., Chambers, S. & Johnston, R. 2007); Figure 7.3b from *Operations Management*, 5th ed., Harlow: Pearson Education (Slack, N., Chambers, S. & Johnston, R. 2007) 18.12; Figure on page 124 from *The Penguin Book of the Physical World*, London: Penguin (1976)

**Tables**
Table on page 149 from *Hughes' Electrical and Electronic Technology*, 10th ed., Harlow: Pearson Education (Hughes, E., Hiley, J., Brown, K. and Mckenzie-Smith, I.

2008) p. 814; Table on page 150 from *Principles of Marketing*, 4th ed., Harlow: Pearson Education (Brassington, F and Pettit, S. 2006)

**Text**

Extract 4.3 from *Accounting: An Introduction*, 4th ed., Harlow: Pearson Education (McLaney, E. and Atrill, P. 2008) p.iv; Extracts 4.4, 4.5, 4.6 from *Accounting: An Introduction*, 4th ed., Harlow: Pearson Education (McLaney, E. and Atrill, P. 2008); Example on page 79 from *Principles of Marketing*, 5th ed., Harlow: Pearson Education (Kotler, P., Armstrong, G., Wong, V. and Saunders, J. 2008) pp. 530-3; Activity 5.5 from *English Legal System*, 9th ed., Harlow: Pearson Education (Elliot, C. and Quinn, F. 2009) pp. 161-2; Activity 5.6 from *Accounting: An Introduction*, 4th ed., Harlow: Pearson Education (McLaney, E. and Atrill, P. 2008) pp. 19-21; Activity 5.7 from *Accounting: An Introduction*, 4th ed., Harlow: Pearson Education (McLaney, E. and Atrill, P. 2008) p. 222; Activity 5.9 from *English Legal System*, 9th ed., Harlow: Pearson Education (Elliot, C. and Quinn, F. 2009) p. 169; Activity 5.10 from *English Legal System*, 9th ed., Harlow: Pearson Education (Elliot, C. and Quinn, F. 2008) pp. 94-6; Activity 5.11 from *English Legal System*, 9th ed., Harlow: Pearson Education (Elliot, C. and Quinn, F. 2008) pp. 171-2; Extract on page 95 from *Principles of Marketing*, 5th ed., Harlow: Pearson Education (Kotler, P., Armstrong, G., Wong, V. and Saunders, J. 2008) p. 77; Extract on page 115 from *Principles of Marketing*, 5th ed., Harlow: Pearson Education (Kotler, P., Armstrong, G., Wong, V. and Saunders, J. 2008) p. 737; Extract on page 115 from *Accounting: An Introduction*, 4th ed., Harlow: Pearson Education (McLaney, E. and Atrill, P. 2008) p. 578; Extract on page 116 from *Accounting: An Introduction*, 4th ed., Harlow: Pearson Education (McLaney, E. and Atrill, P. 2008) p. 582; Extract on page 117 from *Psychology*, 3rd ed., Harlow: Pearson Education (Martin, Neil, Carlson, N.R. and Buskist, W. 2007) p. 120; Extract on page 117 from *Psychology*, 3rd ed., Harlow: Pearson Education (Martin, N., Carlson, N.R and Buskist, W. 2006) p. 146; Extract on page 118 from *English Legal System*, 9th ed., Harlow: Pearson Education (Elliot, C. and Quinn, F. 2008) pp. 76-7; Extract on page 121 from *Operations Management*, 5th ed., Harlow: Pearson Education (Slack, N., Chambers, S. & Johnston, R. 2007); Extract on page 122 from *Fundamentals of Nursing*, 1st ed., Harlow: Pearson Education (Kozier et al. 2008) p. 214; Extract on page 128 from *English Legal System*, 9th ed., Harlow: Pearson Education (Elliot, C. and Quinn, F. 2008) p. 2; Extract on page 128 from *Accounting: An Introduction*, 4th ed., Harlow: Pearson Education (McLaney, E. and Atrill, P. 2008) pp. 49-50; Extract on page 130 from *English Legal System*, 9th ed., Harlow: Pearson Education (Elliot, C. and Quinn, F. 2008) p. 74; Worked Example 7.3 from *Fundamentals of Nursing*, 1st ed., Harlow: Pearson Education (Kozier et al. 2008) p. 276; Worked Example 7.4 from *Hughes' Electrical and Electronic Technology*, 10th ed., Harlow: Pearson Education (Hughes, E., Hiley, J., Brown, K. and McKenzie-Smith, I. 2008) p. 812; Worked Examples 7.5, 7.10 from *Fundamentals of Nursing*, 1st ed., Harlow: Pearson Education (Kozier et al. 2008) p. 214; Worked Example 7.6 from *The Penguin Book of the Physical World*, London: Penguin (1976) p. 52; Worked Example 7.9 from *Business Law*, 8th ed., Harlow: Pearson Education (Keenan, D. and Riches, S. 2007) p. 13; Extract on page

139 from *Psychology*, 3rd ed., Harlow: Pearson Education (Martin, N, Carlson, N.R. and Buskist, W. 2007) p. 385; Extract on page 142 from *Psychology*, 3rd ed., Harlow: Pearson Education (Martin, N., Carlson, N.R. and Buskist, W. 2007) p. 491; Extract on page 145 from *English Legal System*, 9th ed., Harlow: Pearson Education (Elliot, C and Quinn, F 2008) p. 5; Extract on page 145 from *English Legal System*, 9th ed., Harlow: Pearson Education (Elliot, C and Quinn, F. 2008) p. 6; Extract on page 145 from *English Legal System*, 9th ed., Harlow: Pearson Education (Elliot, C. and Quinn, F. 2008) p. 5; Extract on page 146 from *English Legal System*, 9th ed., Harlow: Pearson Education (Elliot, C. and Quinn, F. 2008) pp. 184-6; Extract on page 147 from *English Legal System*, 9th ed., Harlow: Pearson Education (Elliot, C. and Quinn, F. 2008) p. 185; Extracts on page 147, page 156 from *Psychology*, 3rd ed., Harlow: Pearson Education (Martin, N., Carlson, N.R. and Buskist, W. 2007) p. 376; Extract on page 148 adapted from *Hughes' Electrical and Electronic Technology*, 10th ed., Harlow: Pearson Education (Hughes, E. Hiley, J., Brown, K. and McKenzie-Smith, I. 2008) p. 824; Extract on page 151 from *Accounting: An Introduction*, 4th ed., Harlow: Pearson Education (McLaney, E. and Atrill, P. 2008) p. 119; Extracts on page 155, page 158 from *Social Work*, 1st ed., Harlow: Pearson Education (Wilson, K., Ruch, G., Lymbery, M. and Cooper, A. 2008) p. 540; Extract on page 156 from *Physical Geography and the Environment*, 2nd ed., Harlow: Pearson Education (Holden, J. 2008) p. 381; Extract on page 157 from *The Essential Guide to Teaching*, 1st ed., Harlow: Pearson Education (Davies, S. 2006) pp. 36-7; Extract on page 157 from *Social Work*, 1st ed., Harlow: Pearson Education (Wilson, K., Ruch, G., Kymbery and Cooper, A. 2008) p. 556; Extract on page 158 from *Business Law*, 8th ed., Harlow: Pearson Education (Keenan, D. and Riches, S. 2007) p. 3; Activity 8.1 from *Psychology*, 3rd ed., Harlow: Pearson Education (Martin, N., Carlson, N.R. and Buskist, W. 2007) p. 385; Worked Example 8.2 from *Physical Geography and the Environment*, 2nd ed., Harlow: Pearson Education (Holden, J. 2008) p. 458; Worked Example 8.3 from *Principles of Marketing*, 5th ed., Harlow: Pearson Education (Kotler, P., Armstrong, G., Wong, V. and Saunders, J. 2008) pp. 552-3; Activity 8.4 from *Psychology*, 3rd ed., Harlow: Pearson Education (Martin, N., Carlson, N.R. and Buskist, W. 2007) p. 486; Worked Example 8.5a from *The Essential Guide to Teaching*, 1st ed., Harlow: Pearson Education (Davies, S. 2006) p. 130; Worked Example 8.5b from *Psychology*, 3rd ed., Harlow: Pearson Education (Martin, N., Carlson, N.R. and Buskist, W. 2007) p. 491; Worked Examples 8.5c, 8.15 from *Physical Geography and the Environment*, 2nd ed., Harlow: Pearson Education (Holden, J. 2008) p. 59; Worked Examples 8.5d, 8.6a from *Accounting: An Introduction*, 4th ed., Harlow: Pearson Education (McLaney, E. and Atrill, P. 2008) p. 119; Worked Example 8.6b from *Social Work*, 1st ed., Harlow: Pearson Education (Wilson, K., Ruch, G., Lymbery, M. and Cooper, A. 2008) p. 514; Worked Example 8.6c from *Psychology*, 3rd ed., Harlow: Pearson Education (Martin, N. Carlson, N.R. and Buskist, W. 2007) p. 532; Worked Examples 8.6d, 8.17 from *Principles of Marketing*, 5th ed., Harlow: Pearson Education (Kotler, P., Armstrong, G., Wong, V. and Saunders, J. 2008) p. 326; Activity 8.7a from *English Legal System*, 4th ed., Harlow: Pearson Education (Elliot, C. and Quinn, F. 2008) p. 185; Worked Example 8.7a from *English Legal System*, 4th ed., Harlow: Pearson Education (Elliot, C. and

Quinn, F. 2008) p. 185; Activity 8.7b from *Psychology*, 3rd ed., Harlow: Pearson Education (Martin, N, Carlson, N.R and Buskist W 2007) p. 376; Worked Example 8.7b from *Psychology*, 3rd ed., Harlow: Pearson Education (Martin, N., Carlson, N.R. and Buskist, W. 2007) p. 376; Worked Example 8.7c from *Social Work*, 1st ed., Harlow: Pearson Education (Wilson, K., Ruch, G., Lymbery, M. and Cooper, A. 2008) p. 540; Worked Examples 8.8a, 8.8a from *Social Work*, 1st ed., Harlow: Pearson Education (Wilson, K., Ruch, G., Lymbery, M. and Cooper, A. 2008) p. 566; Worked Examples 8.8b, 8.8b from *Physical Geography and the Environment*, 2nd ed., Harlow: Pearson Education (Holden, J. 2008) p. 480; Activity 8.9 from *Hughes' Electrical and Electronic Technology*, 10th ed., Harlow: Pearson Education (Hughes, E., Hiley, J., Brown, K. and McKenzie-Smith, I. 2008) p. 818; Worked Example 8.9 from *Hughes' Electrical and Electronic Technology*, 10th ed., Harlow: Pearson Education (Hughes, E., Hiley, J., Brown, K. and McKenzie-Smith, I. 2008) p. 818; Worked Example 8.10 from *Hughes' Electrical and Electronic Technology*, 10th ed., Harlow: Pearson Education (Hughes, E., Hiley, J., Brown, K. and McKenzie-Smith, I. 2008) p. 814; Worked Example 8.11 from *Principles of Marketing*, 4th ed., Harlow: Pearson Education (Brassington, F. and Pettit, S. 2006); Activity 8.12 from *Psychology*, 3rd ed., Harlow: Pearson Education (Martin, N, Carlson, N.R. and Buskist, W. 2007) p. 486; Worked Example 8.12 from *Psychology*, 3rd ed., Harlow: Pearson Education (Martin, N., Carlson, N.R and Buskist, W. 2007) p. 486; Worked Example 8.13 from *Social Work*, 1st ed., Harlow: Pearson Education (Wilson, K., Ruch, G., Lymbery, M. and Cooper, A. 2008) p. 566`; Activity 8.13a from *Social Work*, 1st ed., Harlow: Pearson Education (Wilson, K., Ruch, G., Lymber, M. and Cooper, A. 2008) p. 566; Activity 8.13b from *Principles of Marketing*, 5th ed., Harlow: Pearson Education (Kotler, P., Armstrong, G., Wong, V. and Saunders, J. 2006) p. 326; Activity 8.15 from *Physical Geography and the Environment*, 2nd ed., Harlow: Pearson Education (Holden, J. 2008) p. 59; Worked Example 8.16a from *Physical Geography and the Environment*, 2nd ed., Harlow: Pearson Education (Holden, J. 2008) p. 406; Activity 8.16a from *Physical Geography and the Environment*, 2nd ed., Harlow: Pearson Education (Holden, J. 2008) p. 406; Worked Example 8.16b from *Physical Geography and the Environment*, 2nd ed., Harlow: Pearson Education (Holden, J. 2008) p. 302; Activity 8.16b from *Physical Geography and the Environment*, 2nd ed., Harlow: Pearson Education (Holden, J. 2008) p. 302; Activity 8.17 from *Principles of Marketing*, 5th ed., Harlow: Pearson Education (Kotler, P., Armstrong, G., Wong, V., and Saunders, J. 2008) p. 326; Activity 8.18 from *Hughes' Electrical and Electronic Technology*, 10th ed., Harlow: Pearson Education (Hughes, J., Hiley, J., Brown, K. McKenzie-Smith, I. 2008) p. 810; Worked Example 8.19 from *The Essential Guide to Teaching*, 1st ed., Harlow: Pearson Education (Davies, S. 2006); Extract on page 164 from *Fundamentals of Nursing*, 1st ed., Harlow: Pearson Education (Kozier et al. 2008) p. 140; Activity 9.2 from *Psychology*, 3rd ed., Harlow: Pearson Education (Martin, N., Carlson, N.R. and Buskist, W. 2007) p. 298; General Displayed Text on page 183 from *Business Law*, 8th ed., Harlow: Pearson Education (Keenan, D. and Riches, S. 2007) p. 114; Extract on page 186 from *Physical Geography and the Environment*, 2nd ed., Harlow: Pearson Education (Holden, J. 2008) p. 57; Activity 10.5 from *Physical Geography and the Environment*, 2nd ed.,

# Acknowledgements

Harlow: Pearson Education (Holden, J. 2008) pp. 612-13; Activity 10.6 from *English Legal System*, 9th ed., Harlow: Pearson Education (Elliot, C. and Quinn, C. 2008) p. 413; Activity 10.7 from *Fundamentals of Nursing*, 1st ed., Harlow: Pearson Eduction (Kozier et al. 2008) p. 489; Activity 10.10a from *Social Work*, 1st ed., Harlow: Pearson Education (Wilson, K., Ruch, G., Lymbery, M. and Cooper, A. 2008) p. 502; Activity 10.10b from *Principles of Marketing*, 5th ed., Harlow: Pearson Education (Kotler, P., Armstrong, G., Wong, V. and Saunders, J. 2008) p. 693; Example on page 213 from *Psychology*, 3rd ed., Harlow: Pearson Education (Martin, N., Carlson, N.R. and Buskist, W. 2007) p. 491; Activity 11.1a from *Psychology*, 3rd ed., Harlow: Pearson Education (Martin, N., Carlson, N.R and Buskist, W. 2007) p. 420; Activity 11.1b from *Social Work*, 1st ed., Harlow: Pearson Education (Wilson, K., Ruch, G., Lymberty, M. and Cooper, A. 2008) p. 324; Activity 11.3 from *Psychology*, 3rd ed., Harlow: Pearson Education (Martin, N., Carlson, N.R. and Buskist, W. 2007) p. 420; Activity 11.5 from *Psychology*, 3rd ed., Harlow: Pearson Education (Martin, N., Carlson, N.R. and Buskist, W. 2007) p. 491; Activity 11.8 from *Psychology*, 3rd ed., Harlow: Pearson Education (Martin, N., Carlsson, N.R and Buskist, W. 2007) p. 486; Worked Example 11.8 from *Psychology*, 3rd ed., Harlow: Pearson Education (Martin, N., Carlson, N.R. and Buskist, W. 2007) p. 486; Box on page 277 from *Business Law*, 8th ed., Harlow: Pearson Education (Keenan, D. and Riches, S. 2007) p. 29; Activity 15.3 from *Social Work*, 1st ed., Harlow: Pearson Education (Wilson, K., Ruch, G., Lymbery, M. and Cooper, A. 2008) p. 310.

In some instances we have been unable to trace the owners of copyright material, and we would appreciate any information that would enable us to do so.

# INTRODUCTION

## Writing in higher education

You would probably accept that you have to write in different ways throughout your lives. But why do you need to learn about academic writing? Considering one of the main ways you are assessed in higher education is through your writing, either by coursework or exams, knowing how to express yourself well, in good, written academic English is crucial. When you are a student, you will find that your tutors use your writing to gauge how much you have learned and understood about a particular subject and to judge the quality of your thinking. But you should not only see academic writing as an assessment tool. Writing is also indirectly encouraging you to read widely, think critically, improve your communication skills and develop a certain level of competence and professionalism needed for your future career.

In academic writing it is often assumed that by the time students have finished secondary school education, they already possess the skills to write at a level appropriate to higher education, but this is not always the case. As a result, when students are faced with written assignments of anything upward of 1500 words they may find the whole process daunting. The aim of this book is to provide tools to address this.

 Academic writing is a social practice. This means that you always write with a readership in mind and you always write with a purpose, for example to explain or to persuade. It also means that what is right and wrong, appropriate or inappropriate is defined by the users in the social community. In your case these are other students, lecturers or examiners. There is nothing natural about the organisation and the way language is used in a scientific report, for example. It is as it is because that is the way it has developed through centuries of use by practitioners. For that reason it has to be learned. No-one speaks (or writes) academic English as a first language (Bourdieu and Passeron, 1994: 8). It must be learned by observation, study and experiment.

In higher education, you will be required to complete a wide range of writing tasks, some which will be familiar to you, but some which will not. You may, for example, have written essays before, but never completed a reflective log. Whatever the task, remember that writing is a process which leads to a final product. It starts from understanding what you have to do and planning your work. It then goes on to doing the reading and any necessary research. The next stage is writing various drafts. This is followed by proof-reading and editing. All this, taking into account the feedback you may receive, should lead to the final text.

# How this book is organised

In this book, we are addressing various aspects of writing in higher education and trying to answer two main questions:

1 What kinds of texts are expected of students in higher education and what sort of language is used in them?
2 How should students go about preparing for, researching and writing these texts?

We know the process of academic writing is complicated and not necessarily straightforward. You may be very good at planning but you may have trouble writing in the correct style, for example. For this reason, we do not necessarily expect you to work through the book chapter by chapter. To help you decide on which aspects you need, we have included both a section with questions that you may like answered, and a flow chart (see p. xxiv) to guide you through the various chapters of the book. This approach will allow you to dip in and out of the book as and when you need help.

Our approach in this book is to show you examples of the kind of writing we want you to do and help you to notice the relevant features of it. We then give you activities to try and offer you some feedback. Some activities will help you to notice the kind of language or skill we hope you will develop. Other activities will ask you to write something. It is very difficult for us to give you useful feedback in these freer writing situations. We hope, though, that by giving a suggested solution to the activity, you will:

- look at what we have offered
- compare it to what you have written
- notice something that we have done but you have not done yourself, and
- possibly use it next time you write.

# The chapters

The book begins with a chapter which looks at the major features you will find in the rest of the book. It explains how academic writing is different from other forms of writing and introduces various styles of academic writing, or genres, that may be used in a range of disciplines.

Chapter 2 works on the principle that when you are given an assignment to write, you might have initial doubts as to how to approach this task. The chapter offers you some tools to help you overcome that beginning stage of apprehension.

Chapter 3 addresses the process of planning and preparation that is integral to successful academic writing. It covers looking behind an assignment, deciding upon preparatory work and planning your time.

Chapter 4 helps you research your topic. It suggests ways in which you can find information and ideas from other sources that you could then bring in to your own work.

Chapter 5 asks you to consider effective reading strategies, before moving on to looking at keeping a record of what you read by using various note-taking methods.

Chapter 6 covers the style conventions of an academic text, developing paragraphs and turning them into organised and cohesive text, writing plans and writing drafts.

Chapter 7 focuses on descriptive writing. It includes defining a topic, describing an object, system or process. It also includes categorising and classifying as well as reporting past events.

Chapter 8 focuses on writing critically. This is broken down by looking at texts that explain and justify and then move on to texts that analyse and evaluate.

Chapter 9 looks at the type of language that is used to write reflectively and suggests some frameworks to help you develop this way of writing.

Chapter 10 helps you use other people's ideas to support the points that you make or the arguments that you raise in your assignments.

Chapter 11 looks at the place of the writer in a piece of academic writing and highlights that apart from including the work of others, it is essential to keep your own ideas clear.

Chapter 12 focuses on providing advice on how to use different genres. It points out that most genres of writing use a range of text types for their purpose.

Chapter 13 considers ways of presenting your work. This includes effective use of computers, writing by hand and adapting a text for use in oral presentations and the writing of posters.

Chapter 14 looks at ways in which you can make the best use of the feedback you receive from your lecturers in order to improve your marks.

Chapter 15 looks at the final stage of the writing process, the stage of proof-reading, editing and presentation. It emphasises the importance of this stage in helping you to make a good impression.

We strongly believe that as well as knowing their subject, professionals need to be able to communicate clearly, accurately and appropriately. Communication is more than just providing ideas and information: it is an essential feature of being a professional. Writing well is part of this and we hope we can help you achieve this skill.

## The example texts

We believe that you learn to write by reading and noticing features of written texts in that reading and then trying, with help, to produce similar texts yourself. One feature of this book is the number of examples we have used of the kinds of text that you will be expected to write. Some of these we have written ourselves, some are from our students but most of them have been adapted by us from a range of Pearson's undergraduate textbooks. We know the readers of this book will be studying a wide range of subjects so we have tried to give examples from a similar wide range of topics. We have also used the following books for reading and other activities.

Brassington, F. and Pettitt, S. (2006) *Principles of Marketing* (4th edn). Harlow: Pearson Education.

Davies, S. (2006) *The Essential Guide to Teaching*. Harlow: Pearson Education.

Elliott, C. and Quinn, F. (2008) *English Legal System* (9th edn). Harlow: Pearson Education.

Holden, J. (ed.) (2008) *Physical Geography and the Environment* (2nd edn). Harlow: Pearson Education.

Hughes, E. (2008) *Hughes Electrical and Electronic Technology* (10th edn). Harlow: Pearson Education.

Keenan, D. and Riches, S. (2007) *Business Law* (8th edn). Harlow: Pearson Education.

Kotler, P., Armstrong, G., Wong, V. and Saunders, J. (2008) *Principles of Marketing* (5th edn). Harlow: Pearson Education.

Kozier, B., Erb, G., Berman, A., Snyder, S., Lake, R. and Harvey, S. (2008) *Fundamentals of Nursing: Concepts, Process and Practice*. Harlow: Pearson Education.

Martin, G.N., Carlson, N.R. and Buskist, W. (2007) *Psychology* (3rd edn). Harlow: Pearson Education.

McLaney, E. and Atrill, P. (2008) *Accounting: An Introduction* (4th edn). Harlow: Pearson Education.

Slack, N., Chambers, S. and Johnston, R. (2007) *Operations Management* (5th edn) Harlow: Pearson Education.

Wilson, K., Ruch, G., Lymbery, M. and Cooper, A. (2008) *Social Work: An Introduction to Contemporary Practice.* Harlow: Pearson Education.

**Note**: When we have used or adapted extracts from these books, the references have been highlighted in a specific way, for example:

(Brassington and Pettitt, 2006: 343)

# Reference

Bourdieu, P. and Passeron, J.-C. (1994) 'Introduction: Language and the relationship to language in the teaching situation', in P. Bourdieu, J.-C. Passeron and M. de Saint Martin (eds) pp. 1–34, *Academic Discourse*. Cambridge: Polity Press.

# Frequently asked questions

| Questions | Advice | Key chapters |
|---|---|---|
| **Reading** | | |
| How do I find sources? | Libraries, assignment briefs, internet, keyword searches. | Chapter 4 |
| How do I know the sources are relevant? | Evaluate them. | Chapter 4 |
| Why do I need sources? | To give weight to your arguments. | Chapter 10 |
| What should I do with sources? | Read and make notes from them. Use them in your writing. | Chapters 5 and 10 |
| What should I read? | Textbooks, journal articles and items suggested on your reading list. | Chapter 5 |
| How should I read effectively? | Read efficiently, critically, interactively and purposefully. | Chapter 5 |
| How much should I read? | This will depend on your plan. | Chapter 2 |
| **Planning** | | |
| How do I know what I have to do? | You need to understand the genre. Read the assignment brief thoroughly. | Chapter 1 Chapter 3 |
| Where do I begin? | Deconstruct the title. | Chapter 2 |
| How do I plan my time? | Use the charts provided to help you. | Chapter 3 |
| How do I plan my writing? | Make sure you have covered all the vital areas before you start planning. | Chapter 6 |
| How can I plan to improve the standard of my writing? | Check lecturers' feedback from previous assignments. | Chapter 14 |

→

| Questions | Advice | Key chapters |
|---|---|---|
| **Text organisation** | | |
| How do I structure my writing? | This will depend on the genre you are writing. | Chapter 12 |
| How do I organise my ideas? | Match relevant ideas from your notes to your plan. Develop each main idea into a paragraph. | Chapter 6 |
| How do I develop my paragraphs? | Start with a topic sentence and build on that. | Chapter 6 |
| How do I link my paragraphs? | Use signalling words and phrases to connect them. | Chapter 6 |
| **Writing** | | |
| How do I write a report? | This has to be written following a very clear structure. | Chapters 1 and 12 |
| How do I write an essay? | There are many kinds of essays but they have a common format. | Chapters 1 and 12 |
| What does being critical mean? | It means you need to analyse and evaluate sources, and then use them to support your points. | Chapter 8 |
| How do I write descriptively? | You need to define, categorise and classify a topic. | Chapter 7 |
| What does being analytical mean? | It means you examine and break information into parts. | Chapter 8 |
| What does being reflective mean? | It means you analyse actions or events and consider consequences. | Chapter 9 |
| **Language** | | |
| What is academic language? | It is language which is formal, objective and cautious. | Chapters 6 and 11 |

| | | |
|---|---|---|
| How can I express my opinion in my writing? | By looking at our suggested words and phrases. | Chapter 11 |
| When can I use 'I'? | When you are writing reflectively. | Chapter 9 |
| **Using sources** | | |
| How do I use the ideas I find in the sources? | You can summarise, synthesise and acknowledge the sources. Your own voice must also come through. | Chapter 10 Chapter 11 |
| How do I refer to authors I use in my writing? | You can either cite the author(s) or quote from their work. | Chapter 10 |
| How do I avoid over-quoting? | Use a summary or paraphrase instead. Use quotations as evidence to support your own points. | Chapter 10 |
| How do I write a reference list? | You need to follow a set format and give full information on the source. | Chapter 10 |
| **Look and feel** | | |
| How can I make my work look good? | Make use of white space and page layout; order and number your pages; use an appropriate font. | Chapters 13 and 15 |
| What must I check before I hand the work in? | Check for structure, relevance, communication, bias, economy, ownership and referencing. | Chapter 15 |
| Why is layout important? | It helps clarify meaning and it creates an impression of professionalism. | Chapter 13 |

Finding your way around the book

**GETTING INFORMATION**

Carrying out the research
Chapter 4
Reading and note-taking
Chapter 5

**LANGUAGE**

Features of academic writing
Chapter 6
Personal and reflective writing
Chapter 9
Using your own voice
Chapter 11

**PLANNING**

Understanding the task
Chapter 1
Overcoming the blank page
Chapter 2
Planning your work
Chapter 3

**USING INFORMATION**

Working with other
people's ideas and voices
Chapter 10
Finding your own voice
Chapter 11

FEEDBACK
Chapter 14

FEEDBACK
Chapter 14

FEEDBACK
Chapter 14

FEEDBACK
Chapter 14

**WRITING:**
descriptively, critically,
analytically and
reflectively
Chapters 7, 8, 9

**TEXT ORGANISATION**

Features of academic writing
Chapter 6
Genre and discipline-specific
writing
Chapter 12

**LOOK AND FEEL**

Presenting your work
Chapter 13
Editing your work
Chapter 15

# 1 UNDERSTANDING THE TASK

This chapter touches on many of the major features of the book but does not address them in detail. Instead it looks forward and gives you an idea of what to find in the rest of the book. It will explain how academic writing is different from other forms of writing as well as present various styles of academic writing, or genres, across a range of disciplines.

This chapter will cover:

- common reasons for why we write
- how academic writing differs from other forms of writing
- the basic structures of an essay and a report
- different disciplines and their favoured forms.

## USING THIS CHAPTER

# INTRODUCTION

Writing is one of the main ways that human beings communicate: it is a social practice. The reasons for and purpose of any piece of writing will vary, depending upon situations, relationships and events. Sometimes people write purely for themselves, for example to record their thoughts and events in a diary or to remind themselves of things they have to do. Some people write poetry or short stories, perhaps with a view to being published but also to express their ideas and inner thoughts. Sometimes the communication is a two-way process, for example an exchange of emails leads to a business transaction. At other times the communication is only one way – a letter goes unanswered or is never received by the person it is intended for.

It would not take long to think of 10 different kinds of writing that most people produce in a year: they write letters, emails and text messages; they write instructions and requests; they send invitations and fill in forms; they scribble down recipes they hear on the radio; they send cards to friends and relatives. In one sense, academic writing is just another form of writing, another way of communicating with fellow human beings. But it has certain qualities that mark it out and make it quite different from the rest of writing.

# ACADEMIC WRITING

One of the main ways that academic writing is different from other forms of writing is in its relationship with its audience – that is to say the reader. For most students that reader is one of their lecturers or tutors, although it could also be fellow students. Whoever it is, the reader will be concerned with whether the piece of writing has reached a certain standard and will use those standards to judge the quality of the writing. Furthermore, the judgement will be made formally, with a mark or grade and perhaps some written comments. People might make judgements privately about the quality of a letter they receive from a friend or business associate but there is no need or expectation that they will record their verdict.

The judgements that are made about a piece of academic writing are part of the whole process of deciding upon the quality of a person's learning and, in turn, the class of degree they should be awarded at the end of their studies. The standards that are used to form those judgements may be expressed in different ways according to the subject of study or institution but they will always be concerned with structure, clarity and accuracy. There will also be an expectation that the writing will demonstrate an objective approach and explore the subject matter thoroughly, resulting in a careful analysis.

Whatever your level of study it is important to be critical when you write an academic piece of work. This does not mean finding fault with something, as it can mean in everyday life. In the context of academic writing being critical includes:

- showing an understanding and knowledge of theory
- demonstrating an awareness of what has been written or said about the subject
- taking into consideration different points of view
- using reason to make a judgement
- not accepting ideas until they have been examined closely (and then maybe rejecting them)
- coming to your own conclusions
- using your own voice.

You might think this looks like a tall order, but hopefully there is nothing in the list that you would disagree with. The same approach is used in reading an academic text, where you need to:

- identify the line of reasoning or argument
- look for hidden assumptions
- decide if the evidence used to support the argument is good enough.

A useful framework to think about academic writing can be found in a theory about the process of learning and study called Bloom's (1956) Taxonomy of Learning. It presents six stages that a learner goes through, each one becoming more complex and building on the last. Starting with the simple mastery and recall of facts (*Knowledge*) the learner moves through rephrasing, applying and breaking down that knowledge before finally being able to manipulate and evaluate it (*Synthesis* and *Evaluation*). The taxonomy is often used to write instruction words in essay titles, so knowing something about it can help you understand what lecturers expect to see in your writing. However you also need to get familiar with the particular characteristics of your discipline.

---

## BLOOM'S TAXONOMY – WHAT THE LEVELS MEAN

1 **Knowledge** – the recall of facts
2 **Comprehension** – rephrasing what has been understood
3 **Application** – applying new knowledge to a situation
4 **Analysis** – breaking information down
5 **Synthesis** – putting the parts together to create meaning
6 **Evaluation** – deciding on the worth of something

How are these terms useful when you are trying to understand the task you have been given? They can be translated into essay titles as follows.

### Sample titles for essays about the World Wide Web

- **Knowledge** – *Describe the history of the World Wide Web*.
  A simple account is required, tracing a timeline and detailing facts.

- **Comprehension** – *What effect has the World Wide Web had on the way people communicate?*
  The writer needs to show an understanding of cause and effect in this answer.

- **Application** – *Explain how the World Wide Web works*.
  The writer must use knowledge of the system to demonstrate how it works in practice.

→

- **Analysis** – *How have methods of communication changed since the development of the World Wide Web?*
  Comparisons must be drawn, methods must be defined and examined in detail.

- **Synthesis** – *How could the World Wide Web be used to develop new ways of learning?*
  This essay calls for the writer to bring together ideas to create fresh understanding.

- **Evaluation** – *Comment on the value of the World Wide Web for society.*
  The writer must stand back from the subject and make a judgement.

## Disciplines and their differences

Academic subjects are classified into different disciplines that have evolved over time and have their own traditions and conventions. Generally speaking, a discipline is a broad area into which certain subjects are slotted. For example History is classified as a Humanities discipline, and Business as a Social Sciences discipline. Each discipline has its own approach to academic study, its own discourse and its own favoured ways of writing about its subject. A very basic division of the disciplines (http://www.intute.ac.uk) puts them into four main areas:

See
Chapter 4

- Arts and Humanities
- Science, Engineering and Technology
- Health and Life Sciences
- Social Sciences.

While this is not a universally recognised way of dividing up subjects, it is a useful way of thinking about the differences between them, and this chapter will use it as a model for discussion.

### Arts and Humanities

This category includes subjects that relate to the cultural life of people and society, foregrounding interpretation and expression of events and ideas. Visual and creative subjects such as Music or Architecture fall into this area along with, for example:

- Literature
- Philosophy
- Theology.

This discipline relies heavily on the essay, which as an extended piece of writing becomes a dissertation. Other forms you might often come across in Arts and Humanities are a critique or a book review.

### Science, Engineering and Technology

Included in this category are any subjects that study the laws and structures of the natural world, both the physical environment (e.g. Astronomy) and the built environment (e.g. Engineering). Other examples are:

- Physics
- Geography
- Mathematics.

You could expect a report to be very common in these disciplines, with an extended piece of writing being a project. Another example would be some form of research proposal.

## Health and Life Sciences

Subjects that study the physical condition of people, animals and the land fall into this category, so they include Medicine, Veterinary Science and Agriculture. Other examples are:

- Biology
- Zoology
- Physiotherapy.

Again a report would dominate in this area, more specifically an experimental type of report, documenting a process such as an experiment or laboratory procedure.

## Social Sciences

This final category includes subjects that relate to the way people live in and use society. Business, Law and Education come into this area as well as, for example:

- Anthropology
- Politics
- Sports Studies.

The type of report common in these disciplines would be an investigative or project report. The case study is also a frequent genre, especially in Business.

## Activity 1.1 Your subjects of study

Which of these four main areas do your current subjects of study fall into?

# GENRES OF WRITING

oter 12

Different types of academic writing are known as genres. They have distinct purposes, forms and recognised structures. Common examples are essays, reports, case studies and projects. Although certain genres seem more suited to certain disciplines than others, you could well be asked to write in any of the above genres during your study. The clue to this will be in your assignment brief, and it is worth spending time to make sure you know exactly what type of writing you have got to produce. Whatever the genre, there are certain things that are common to all. All academic writing:

- uses evidence to support the points it makes
- uses structure and order to guide the reader through the writing
- contains references for anyone else's ideas or work used.

# LEARNING OUTCOMES AND ASSESSMENT CRITERIA

Two things you always need to check whenever you are given an assignment brief are:

- what the assignment will test and measure, often called the *learning outcomes*
- how it will do this, known as the *assessment criteria*.

## Learning outcomes

Learning outcomes state what a student should learn and be able to demonstrate by studying a particular course or module. They are often written in ways that refer to understanding, knowledge, skills and abilities. Most modules or courses will have several learning outcomes and an assignment will be set to see how well you have achieved one or all of them. For example an assignment may state that it will assess:

- your *ability* to analyse an argument
- your *skills* in communicating your ideas
- your *understanding* of different concepts or theories.

### Activity 1.2 Understanding learning outcomes

Find one of your assignments and check what it says it will be testing. Do you understand all the terminology?

## Assessment criteria

Any assignment should include information on how your work will be judged and where marks will be awarded. For example you may be marked on:

- the quality of your explanation and analysis
- your style
- your use of theory
- the scope of your research.

The assessment criteria might be a series of statements or benchmarks that describe the different levels of achievement and explain the range of marks each level falls into. Alternatively, it may be a tick list or grid that classifies the piece of work. Whatever form they take, assessment criteria need to be transparent and clearly understood, so that you know in advance how your work will be judged and can keep this information at the front of your mind as you write. For example, if you know that 10 per cent of the marks are reserved for references and you forget to include any, you will miss out on those marks.

## Activity 1.3 Understanding the assessment criteria

Find one of your assignments and look at how it says you will be tested. How are the marks divided?

# THE ASSIGNMENT TITLE

One thing in the assignment title that you have to be very careful about is any 'instruction' words. They provide a clue to the approach you should adopt. Look at the examples of instruction words and an explanation of their meanings shown in Table 1.1.

**Table 1.1 Examples of instruction words and their meanings**

apter 2

| Word | Definition |
|---|---|
| Analyse | Consider all the relevant factors and answer in a methodical and logical way. |
| Compare | Discuss the similarities and differences. Write a balanced (fair, objective) answer. |
| Criticise | Point out the strengths and weaknesses. Write a balanced answer. |
| Discuss | Give both points of an argument, with implications, before reaching a conclusion. |
| Explain | Give detailed reasons for a situation. |
| Outline | Give the main points in a concise manner. Leave out details. |
| Summarise | Give the main points in a concise manner. Leave out details. |

Failure to write in this way (e.g. comparing, explaining, describing) will result in loss of marks *as you will not have answered the question or met your tutor's expectations*.

# BASIC STRUCTURES

Structure is of major importance in a piece of academic writing and is one of the key ways that it differs from other forms of writing. There is an expectation that the writing will take the reader through the different stages or sections of the work, including clear signposts along the way. Assessment criteria will almost always include how well a piece of work has been structured. An assignment brief may give you advice on this and you should follow it carefully.

Although different disciplines will rely on and prefer different types of writing, there are two that are common to almost all: the essay and the report. It is worth understanding and knowing the accepted structure of each.

# Essay

The essay has been described as 'the default genre' (Andrews, 2003) and as such cuts across all disciplines. It is used to ask you to discuss and explore something in depth – for example the reasons for a particular event in history, the advantages and disadvantages of a theory, the impact of a new law on society. It will usually expect you to indicate your point of view or judgement on the topic.

Usually you will be given an essay title to answer, with an instruction word to give you an idea of the angle you should take in your essay. It is usually the first word, as in the following examples:

Discuss the following question: why are comparatively few older people the subjects of fictional coverage in televison drama?

(Wilson *et al*., 2008: 651)

Explain how criminal cases are allocated for trial between magistrates' courts and the Crown Court.

(Keenan and Riches, 2007: 71)

Outline the powers available to protect consumers.

(Keenan and Riches, 2007: 430)

## Typical essay structure

See
Chapter 12

An essay normally follows this structure:

1 Introduction
2 Development
3 Conclusion
4 References.

See
Chapter 6

The four areas play very different parts. The *Introduction* acts as a way in to the main section, providing some background information on the topic and explaining which particular aspects of it will be covered in the essay. It is normally one or two paragraphs long. The *Development* section builds up the writer's main ideas in a series of paragraphs. These paragraphs must be linked to one another so that anyone reading the essay can follow the line of argument and thread of the discussion. The *Conclusion* draws together the main point of each of the paragraphs and can include a statement on the opinion of the writer. Finally the *References* section gives full details of any sources (books, journals, websites, etc.) that have been mentioned, cited or quoted in the essay.

**TIP** *Most exam questions call for an essay in a shorter form, so you can use the model structure to answer an exam question as well.*

## Report

A report is usually the result of some kind of investigation of a situation, event or series of events. It is very common to working life so if you become familiar with its structure and use it well you will find you are developing an important skill for future employment. Some common examples of reports are:

- a market research report, explaining trends and consumer behaviour
- an annual report from a company, documenting performance
- a survey report, presenting findings on opinions, preferences or behaviour.

### Typical report structure

Unlike an essay, a report will have sections and headings to guide the reader through the document. Like an essay, it has a beginning, middle and end.

- **first part**: title page; summary; list of contents
- **middle part**: introduction; methodology; findings/results; discussion; conclusion
- **last part**: references; bibliography; appendices.

The *first* part presents your work to the audience, rather like the opening credits of a film or play. The summary (or abstract) is particularly useful here as it gives a condensed version of the entire report. The *middle* part is where the material is developed. Each section has a heading and takes the reader through the investigation, analysis and discussion. The *last* part contains all the supporting material that has been used in the report, for example any outside sources, the raw data or questionnaires, if used.

# OTHER TYPES OF ACADEMIC WRITING

Although essays and reports are generic terms, there are many other types of academic writing or genres (Gillett and Hammond, in press). Guidance is offered here on some of the most common and they are linked to the four main subject areas mentioned earlier:

- **Arts and Humanities**: essay; critique or review
- **Science, Engineering and Technology**: report; research proposal
- **Health and Life Sciences**: lab report; reflective account
- **Social Sciences:** project: case study.

## 1 Understanding the task

It is important to remember that no genre belongs exclusively to one particular discipline or subject area.

**Table 1.2 Academic writing styles**

See
Chapter 12

| Genre | Used for |
|---|---|
| Essay | Exploration of an issue. |
| Critique/review | Critical appraisal of a piece of writing. |
| Report | Written account of an investigation. |
| Research proposal | Suggestions for research. |
| Lab report | Write-up of an experiment. |
| Reflective account | Personal account of an event, experience, etc. |
| Project | Investigation with stages, targets and deadlines. |
| Case study | In-depth analysis of an organisation or situation. |

## Critique/review

A critique (or review) is used to make a judgement about a book or article. It calls upon a number of academic skills, including summary, analysis and evaluation. While it is commonly used in the Arts and Humanities it is useful for any student who has to evaluate sources as part of an assignment.

## Research proposal

A research proposal is used to put forward ideas for future research. It has to justify the proposed research, explain how the work will be done and what the research is expected to show, and include a time-frame.

## Lab report

Many science subjects will use a lab report in which a student will write up the results of an experiment, reporting findings and interpreting results. Usually, a lab report follows a set structure in which the results are presented before any analysis or discussion.

See
Chapter 9

## Reflective account

It is becoming more and more common for reflective accounts to be used in all disciplines as a way of helping students develop their professional and employment skills. Reflective accounts are characterised by a personal view of events, with an explanation of how the writer reacted to and acted upon those events.

## Project

This is taken to mean both the activity – again perhaps an investigation – that takes place over an extended period of time and the written account once the project is completed. A project includes tasks, stages, deadlines and timings.

## Case study

Case studies are frequently used to analyse a situation, place or organisation in order to draw some general conclusions that could then be applied elsewhere. It is very useful for developing an understanding of the working environment.

# SUMMARY

Understanding how academic writing differs from other forms of writing is a key part of being an effective student, as is becoming familiar with the genres that are common to your discipline. Whenever you produce a piece of academic writing you need to ensure that you follow the recommended structure, tailoring your work to the assessment criteria and producing a polished finished product.

## References

Andrews, R. (2003) 'The end of the essay?', *Teaching in Higher Education*, 8(1), pp. 117–28.

Bloom, B. S. (ed.) (1956) *Taxonomy of Educational Objectives: The Classification of Educational Goals. Handbook: Cognitive Domain.* New York: David McKay.

Gillett, A. and Hammond A. (in press) 'Mapping the maze of assessment: an investigation into practice', *Active Learning in Higher Education*.

**Details of highlighted references can be found in the Introduction on page xxii.**

# 2 ▶ OVERCOMING THE BLANK PAGE

When you are given an assignment to write, you may have initial doubts as to how to approach this task. The aim of this chapter is to offer you some tools to help overcome that initial stage of apprehension. It suggests ways of deconstructing the assignment title, offers advice on talking to your lecturer and takes you through the first stages of writing.

This chapter will cover:

- understanding the assignment title
- approaching your lecturer
- starting to write.

## USING THIS CHAPTER

# INTRODUCTION

How many times have you found yourself staring at an assignment title willing yourself to understand it? You may even think you know what the title is asking but how can you be sure? And what do you do beyond understanding the title? How do you begin to fill enough pages to fulfil the requirement of your lecturer? Writing between 1500 and 3500 words can seem daunting, especially when faced with the title of a subject you have only spent a few weeks studying. The solution is to treat it as a learning opportunity and take it one step at a time. Try not to feel inundated with the amount of work you will need to do, and just concentrate on that next step. The first one to deal with is understanding the requirements of the title. You should then consider what you already know about the subject, draw up a skeleton plan of the points you will address, add more information from your reading and gradually build this jigsaw into an academic piece of work. This chapter will attempt to help you in this step-by-step approach as far as putting thoughts on paper. Later chapters help you put your ideas together into a cohesive whole.

# UNDERSTANDING THE ASSIGNMENT TITLE

One of the first hurdles you need to overcome before you can start writing anything is to make sure that you have understood the title you have been given. You may otherwise spend hours writing what you feel is the perfect answer only to be told that you have not answered the question. So what does understanding the title actually involve?

Assignment titles tend to include instructions such as *analyse*, *discuss*, *consider*, *evaluate* and other such specific terms (see page 19 for a fuller list). Lecturers' expectations when setting these terms are outlined later, but you also need to look at the title further. For example, when you are asked to 'discuss' you know that your lecturers want you to consider different sides of an argument before reaching a conclusion. This, however, is not the full requirement of the title. Part of your job is to identify all the parts of the title which will need to be addressed, whether you are writing a report or essay, or answering an examination question.

One way of making sure you answer all parts of the title is to draw attention to the key words. Another way of tackling the title is to change the points into questions. You may try some or all of the following suggestions and see which method works for you.

## Drawing attention to the key words

By *key* words here we mean (a) *instruction* words such as 'discuss' and 'evaluate', and (b) *content* words, those words or phrases which you will need to address in your writing.

Below is a title with the instruction word in a box and its content words highlighted. This approach, which draws attention to the key words in the title, may help you identify what is significant and relevant for you to concentrate on in your essay:

Discuss the impact of culture on marketing using an example of a business you are familiar with.

Highlighting or drawing a box around the key words in this way will help focus your eyes on what is important and hopefully the more you look at the key words the more sense the title will make. Instead of highlighting you may choose to underline, circle or even rewrite the title and use linking lines with arrows to join points together:

Whatever method you choose, make sure it helps *you* focus on the key words. Think about how these words link to the content of your lectures and the reading you have done.

### What is this title asking you to do?

Once you have accentuated the key words, you need to interpret them. It seems that in order to fulfil the requirements of this assignment you need to:

- identify a business as your example
- provide information on the marketing of that business
- describe what is meant by marketing
- describe what is meant by 'culture' in this context
- discuss the impact of culture: consider and show how culture will affect the future marketing of your chosen business.

## Turning the title into a series of questions

Another strategy you could try is forming questions using the key words. Trying to answer questions such as these will help you focus on the relevant areas to research.

- Which business shall I choose?
- How is this business currently marketing its products and services?
- What is meant by marketing?
- What is meant by 'culture'?
- What are the potential challenges that 'culture' will bring to the future marketing of the business?

The following example is taken from an actual essay title given to business students. This may seem like a long title at first, but when you read the second sentence you realise in fact that it provides further helpful details rather than an added requirement.

> Using a global corporation/organisation discuss the impact of a macro factor on the business process of marketing its products and services. You are expected to discuss the potential challenges this macro factor will make to the organisation's future marketing strategies, i.e. the impact on people and products/processes.

This title may seem more complex than the earlier one at first, but the same strategies could be applied here.

> Using a global corporation/organisation discuss the impact of a macro factor on the business process of marketing its products and services. You are expected to discuss the potential challenges this macro factor will make to the organisation's future marketing strategies, i.e. the impact on people and products/processes.

## What is this title asking you to do?

This time it seems that in order to fulfil the requirements of this assignment you need to:

- identify a global organisation
- provide information on the organisation's marketing strategies. (You should show knowledge of elements of marketing strategy, i.e. segments/markets, products, promotion, distribution, market entry, pricing and so on.)
- identify a (one) macro factor. (From your knowledge of the subject you will know that this factor comes from what is known as PEST, STEEPLE or STEP – a variation on political, legal, econonic, sociocultural and technological factors.) You are expected to give details about this macro factor, not just provide a name
- consider and show how this macro factor will affect the organisation's future marketing strategies
- include the impact of this macro factor both on people (within and outside the organisation, i.e. employees and customers) and on the organisation's products and processes
- discuss the impact of this macro factor.

## Forming questions

Once again, the following questions could be formed using the key words:

- Which global organisation should I choose?
- Which macro factor should I consider?
- How is this business currently marketing its products and services?
- What areas of marketing do I need to take into account when talking about the organisation's marketing strategies?
- What are the potential challenges this macro factor will bring to the organisation's future marketing strategies?

■ How will the macro factor impact on the people within and outside the organisation?

Try out these techniques with future assignments. For further practice you can work on the following activities.

## Activity 2.1 Understanding the title (1)

Work with the following assignment title and follow the steps below: 'Choose an English language test you are familiar with in your teaching context. Use relevant background theories to evaluate this test'. Write a 1500 to 2000 word report.

(a) Draw attention to the key words in the title. (You may experiment with some or all of the methods outlined earlier.)

(b) Turn the key words into questions. The first one is given as an example.

What is the teaching context that I am familiar with?

_____

_____

_____

_____

_____

(c) Decide which of the following you would include in answer to this title. Tick all the relevant ideas:

☐ language learning theories

☐ a description of your chosen teaching context

☐ test design theories

☐ an outline of different test design methods

☐ a description of the test

☐ a list of the different teaching contexts

☐ a copy of the test

☐ a review of existing English language tests

☐ an answer key for the test

☐ a decision on the usefulness of this test in your teaching context.

## Activity 2.2 Understanding the title (2)

Work with the following assignment title and follow the steps below: 'Critically evaluate the term "Resource Utilisation". What strategies can a business pursue to enhance its ability to create value through utilising its financial resources? Illustrate your answer with any relevant case materials'.

(a) Draw attention to the key words in the title. (If you did the earlier exercise, now try experimenting with a different method to the one you have already used.)

(b) Turn the key words into questions. The first one is given as an example.

_What does 'resource utilisation' mean?_

_____

_____

_____

_____

(c) Decide which of the following you would include in answer to this title. Tick all the relevant ideas:

- [ ] an explanation of the term 'resource utilisation'
- [ ] an assessment of how valuable the term 'resource utilisation' is
- [ ] a short description of the different kinds of resources a business can draw on
- [ ] details of the various ways a business can create value
- [ ] an outline of the financial resources available to a business
- [ ] an in-depth discussion of the different strategies available to a business
- [ ] examples of specific cases which can be used as evidence.

# Instruction words

You may now have a better understanding of how to break down a title and decide on the general content of the assignment, but what do instructions such as 'describe' and 'discuss' mean? The following examples may help:

**Example 1: Describe the relationship between Parliament and the judiciary in respect of Acts of Parliament.**

In this examination title, 'describe' is quite straightforward as it requires you to say how something works. You are expected to write about the relationship between Parliament and the judiciary. Your answer may be something like:

Parliament's job is to enact law by passing Acts of Parliament. The role of the judiciary is to apply the legislation to real-life situations. In so doing the judges will be required to interpret the words of the Acts using statutory rules and common law approaches to interpretation, such as the mischief rule and the purposive approach. (Keenan and Riches, 2007)

**Example 2: Solar energy is the only energy of the future. Discuss.**

Clearly, a description of what solar energy is would be relevant when answering this title. That would only form a small part of the answer, however. The instruction word 'discuss' expects you to put forward arguments for and against this statement and to conclude one way or the other. You may be forming questions in your plan such as: is solar energy a good alternative to other sources of energy? Why? What are the benefits? What about other forms of energy? What is wrong with them? As you answer these and other questions you set yourself, you are *discussing* the topic. Failure to do so would result in your essay being marked down for being too descriptive.

Below you will find a list of the most common instruction words used in assignment and examination titles with a definition for each. The definitions are only meant as a rough guide and it is important that the instructions are considered within the whole context of the title.

## Table 2.1 Examples of instruction words and their meanings

| Instruction word | Definitions |
| --- | --- |
| Account for | Give reasons for ... |
| Analyse | Consider all the relevant factors and answer in a methodical and logical way. |
| Assess | Examine the value of the subject looking at the positives and negatives before reaching a decision. |
| Comment on | Give your opinion. Back up your views with evidence from your reading. |
| Compare | Discuss the similarities and differences. Write a balanced (fair, objective) answer. |
| Consider | Give your views. Back up your points with evidence from your reading. |
| Contrast | Discuss the differences between subjects. |
| Criticise | Point out the strengths and weaknesses. Write a balanced answer. |
| Define | Explain the meaning of the concept concisely. |
| Demonstrate | Use examples to show something. |
| Describe | Explain how something works or what it is like. |
| Discuss | Give both points of an argument, with implications, before reaching a conclusion. |

$\rightarrow$

| Evaluate | Examine the value of the subject looking at the strengths and weaknesses before reaching a decision. |
|---|---|
| Explain | Give detailed reasons for a situation. |
| Explore | Examine the topic thoroughly and consider it from a variety of viewpoints. |
| Identify | Recognise and list. |
| Illustrate | Show with examples. |
| Justify | Give reasons for or against an argument. |
| Outline | Give the main points in a concise manner. Leave out details. |
| Prove | Show a proposition is true through evidence. |
| Report | Give an account of… |
| Review | Examine the topic critically and consider whether it is adequate or accurate. |
| State | Express relevant points briefly and clearly without minor details. |
| Summarise | Give the main points in a concise manner. Leave out details. |
| Trace | Outline the development of a theme in a logical or chronological order. |
| To what extent is X true? | Discuss and explain in what ways X is and is not true. |

Below are some other common words used in assignment and examination titles. You may find them within the title and you should also view them as important. Here are two examples of titles containing such words (underlined):

Example 1: What factors would you consider when selecting materials for the manufacture of a simple set of weighing scales?

Example 2: What were the implications of the poor methods of communication in the mobilisation of armies at the beginning of WWI?

Table 2.2 Other common words and their meanings

| Word | Definition |
|---|---|
| Concept | An important idea. |
| Concise | Short, brief. |
| In the context of | Referring to, inside the subject of… |
| Criteria | The standards you would expect. |
| Deduction | The conclusion/generalisation you come to after examining the facts. |

| Factor(s) | The circumstances bringing about a result. |
|---|---|
| Function | The purpose or activities of something. |
| Implications | Long-term, suggested results which may not be obvious. |
| Limitations | Explain where something is not useful or irrelevant. |
| With/by reference to X | Make sure you write about X. |
| In relation to X | You need to focus your answer on X. |
| Role | What part something plays/how it works, in cooperation with others. |
| Scope | The area where something acts or has influence. |
| Significance | Meaning and importance. |
| Valid/validity | Is there evidence and are there facts to prove the statement? |

The next time you look at an assignment title, remember to break it down into sections taking the following into consideration:

- content words (verbs or nouns carrying meaning)
- instruction words (the essay requirement, such as 'analyse' or 'explore')
- other common words.

Once you have identified all the important words, ask questions which include the key words and construct a list of what the title is expecting you to do.

## Activity 2.3 Understanding your own title

Working with an assignment title relevant to your course, follow the same format as Activities 2.1 and 2.2. You could try working with a fellow student to check whether you have both arrived at the same title expectations.

# APPROACHING YOUR LECTURER

Having identified the key elements of the title, you may have a good understanding of the points you should look to include in your assignment. If you are still unsure, or even if you just need reassurance that you are on the right path, you should visit your lecturer. Most students with questions tend to ask fellow students for help. Many students choose not to contact lecturers for fear they will be imposing on them or interrupting their work. Others are anxious that lecturers may feel students are not coping and so refrain from contacting them. In fact, most lecturers complain that students are not making enough use of their time! Most would like to see or hear more of you. Your fellow student may have misunderstood the question. Each lecturer knows what to expect as an answer, so go to the one who has set the assignment and discuss your thoughts. You should approach your lecturer with a specific question. 'I don't understand this title' is not appropriate as it may indicate that you have not spent time looking at it. 'I understand this title to mean X, Y and Z. I think therefore that A, B and C should be included. Is that right?' will be far more productive because even if you are not entirely right, it shows your lecturer you have spent time on the question and are not merely looking to be spoon-fed.

# STARTING TO WRITE

When it is time to start writing your assignment, make sure you are in the type of environment you find works best for you, whether this is at a clear desk in the early evening with a cup of hot chocolate, or first thing in the morning after a good break-fast. People are all different in the way they approach writing but this starting point – the first mark on the page – can be quite tough. There are people who spend time thinking everything through in their head first, and then just start writing it all down. There are people who need to be clear what their goal is and need a complete picture to help them get organised. There are others who just start to put down ideas onto paper straightaway. Others still like to use diagrams, spidergrams or brainstorming maps. You may identify with one of these descriptions through your experiences of writing. Take time to reflect on the techniques you have used and assess how effective they have been. If you feel they can be improved, try to think what changes you can make. The suggestions offered below are meant to help encourage you to get started.

See
Chapter 3

## Tackling the blank page

You have been given a title for an assignment. You have deconstructed this title perhaps by using the techniques discussed earlier in the chapter. You have understood the instruction in the title. You have been attending lectures, written some notes, looked at lecturers' slides and handouts and read some articles and chapters from books on the reading list. You are now going to use all this knowledge to write your assignment. Admittedly, at this stage you will not have sufficient information to tackle the title fully, but this should not stop you from writing what you already know about the subject. You should not worry at this stage about the *product* – the final essay or report. You should concentrate on the *process* – the development of the small elements on which you can build and which will finally grow into your product. The most important point to remember is that you have plenty of time to turn this work in progress into a well-organ-ised, spell-checked, edited and proof-read text. At this stage, do not worry about your style, your spelling, your seemingly haphazard thinking or your lack of reading. If you try the following suggestions, which work around the principle of writing down anything you know about the subject, you may find that you can conquer the blank page and you have found gaps in your knowledge which you can easily address with further focused reading. Look at Chapters 4 and 5 for help on research and reading.

See
Chapter 15

Here are some suggestions.

## Plan your writing

Clearly, you do not have enough information to write a full plan at this stage, but it is still a valuable experience to make a skeletal plan. It may only be three or four lines but if you make sure you space them out enough, you can return to your plan later and add or remove points as you feel appropriate. Many students tend to ignore planning altogether. If you compare lack of planning in your writing to lack of planning in your life in general you may learn to appreciate it more. After all, getting to university required some planning. How often do you open your front door to leave your house without having planned where you are going? If you did not plan when or where you would meet your friends, you would reduce your chances of seeing them. Sending text messages, making phone calls or thinking where you are going – these are all plans which you frequently make in your everyday life. Planning your writing needs more effort perhaps, but in your academic life it is just as important.

Imagine you are planning an essay which would follow the standard format: intro-duction, development and conclusion. In order to write your plan you need to gather your notes and group them into specific sections. The main ideas will be grouped in the development section, the introduction will include background information and how you intend to develop the essay, and the conclusion will summarise your points. Below is an example of a plan which we used to help in the writing of this chapter.

---

### PLAN OF CHAPTER 2

**Introduction**

    What's the problem with the blank page?

    How will this chapter help?

**Main part**

    Understanding the assignment title (activities throughout)

        Draw attention to key words

        Turn title into questions

        Provide instruction word glossary

    Approaching your lecturer

        Why is this important?

    Starting to write (activities throughout)

        Ways of tackling the blank page

        Planning

        Subheadings into computer file

        Brainstorm (alone or with friends)

→

---

---

Mindmaps

Using notes

**End**

Summary

---

## Activity 2.4 Evaluating plans

Look at the following skeletal plan and identify its strengths and weaknesses in the table below. (Leave the third column blank for this activity.) The essay title is 'Describe the effect the World Wide Web has had on the way people communicate'.

**PLAN**

Key words: WWW; effect; people communicate

Instruction word: describe

**Introduction** – 2 paragraphs:

The development of WWW

History of the internet

Functions of WWW

**Central section**

1 para on e-commerce and e-learning

3 paras (1 each) on chat rooms, message boards, emails

**Conclusion**

1 para on web accessibility and security

1 para personal view of WWW, how it is a good thing

**Resources**

None – just a few pages off Google to show what WWW can do

| Strengths | Weaknesses | Changes |
|-----------|------------|---------|
|           |            |         |
|           |            |         |
|           |            |         |
|           |            |         |
|           |            |         |

## Activity 2.5 Improving the plan

Using the plan and table in Activity 2.4, fill in the third column (Changes) showing how you would improve this plan. You may find it easier to rewrite the plan instead.

**TIP** *Remember that once you have created a plan you may need to return to it and make appropriate adjustments.*

## Put subheadings straight into a computer document

As you are deciding on the key words of the title, you could use those key words to act as subheadings. Type them onto a document and leave enough space between them for notes. You may also find it useful to break the subheadings down into more manageable points. Now choose the ones you immediately have something to say about and start writing.

## Brainstorm on a piece of paper or a computer page

Using the key words of the title to help you focus, put down on paper any thoughts that come to mind as long as they are relevant. You can choose any format you like. For example you could write a list, you could spread your ideas all across the page, or you could write in columns. You may be surprised at how much you can already say on the given subject.

## Use an A3 sheet of paper and create mind-maps

Mind-maps can help you focus your ideas. You can use a large A3 sheet but if that seems too daunting at this stage, start with an A4 page in landscape. You can always then expand it by gluing it onto an A3 page! Using the key words of the title as your starting point, write these key words on the page, and circle them or draw a square around them to mark them as your central points. Then think of anything you can which relates to each key word and, drawing a line from each circle, write your thought along that line. You can then continue drawing lines which either link to each central point, or which link to other points you have thought about. In effect you are creating branches going off in various directions on the page. Figure 2.1 shows an example of such an activity using this chapter as the topic.

**TIP** *Did you know that there are mind-mapping computer packages available on the Internet?*

## Brainstorm with other students on your course

You may find that doing the earlier brainstorming or mind-mapping exercises works better with other students. That way you all pool your knowledge together in an attempt to identify gaps. You may then take this group work further by allocating specific chapters or articles to different people to read and then regrouping to brainstorm once more on the information you have each gathered. That way you will not feel alone in this initial task.

## Use your notes first

Gather your notes and, as you read through them, write the main point of your sentence or paragraph in the margin on the left-hand side of the page. Continue until

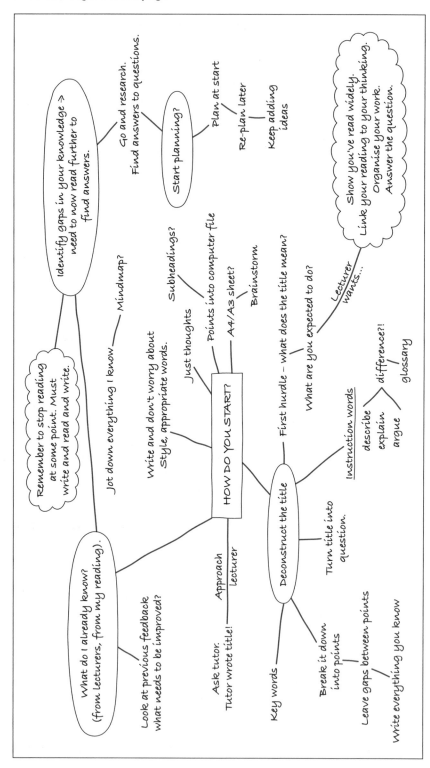

**Figure 2.1 Creating a mind-map**

the end of your notes. If you now look down the summarised notes in the margin, you should be able to identify points which can be grouped together. Perhaps you can use a numbering system, or different colour highlighters or pens, to group similar ideas together. In turn, these groups can be turned into subheadings which you can expand on.

### Do not start at the beginning

Surprising though this may seem to some of you, it is better to start with the middle of your essay – the main content. Ignore the introduction until you have finished working on the middle section. After all, part of the introduction is dedicated to the structure of your middle section, and until you have written that middle section you may not have a clear idea of the content or the organisation.

Remember, brainstorming or mind-mapping and writing is a process. Once you have identified the gaps in your knowledge and researched appropriate texts to find answers, go back to your chosen format for tackling the blank page and keep adding points. It is vital that you keep a record of the sources you are using for referencing purposes. See Chapters 4 and 10 to help you.

Look through all your notes and identify any links. Do you have evidence to back up your arguments? Read further if you need to, but remember that there will have to come a time when you must stop reading. Further reading can often act as an excuse for not writing.

### Activity 2.6 Experimenting with blank pages

Using the earlier title 'Describe the effect the World Wide Web has had on the way people communicate', try jotting down some ideas, adopting the above suggested techniques.

### Activity 2.7 Evaluating techniques

Using the titles you have been given on your course, try out the different approaches suggested in this chapter and evaluate which ones work best for you. Remember you may need to try out different approaches a few times in order to familiarise yourself with them before drawing any conclusions.

## Examination questions

The advice on starting to write assignments can easily be transferred to answering examination questions. The only difference with examinations is that there is no further time to read and add to your notes. In an examination, you need to identify quickly the relevant information to answer the set question based on all the knowledge you have gathered during your studies. The techniques covered in the chapter may help you to write a plan which can prove particularly valuable because you are writing against the clock.

# SUMMARY

This chapter has provided you with suggestions on how to approach an assignment. Remember to look at the assignment instruction words carefully and use the guide on pages 19–20 to help you understand the requirements of the title. Underlining key words in the title and turning them into questions are useful strategies to help you decide on the content of your work. Try out the activities offered in the chapter to help you tackle the blank page when working with your assignments, and remember to plan your work. Finally, make sure you approach your lecturers as this activity is currently an underused but valuable tool.

## References

Details of highlighted references can be found in the Introduction on page xxii.

This chapter will address the process of planning and preparation that is integral to successful academic writing. We suggest that you find one assignment that you have to do in the near future and work through the different activities in this chapter, using the charts, checklists and tips to guide you in the planning process.

This chapter will cover:

- looking behind an assignment
- deciding upon preparatory work
- planning your time.

## USING THIS CHAPTER

# INTRODUCTION

You might turn to this chapter and ask yourself why it is relevant when this is a book about writing, but we hope not. We hope instead that it will persuade you that spending time planning an assignment is worth it, to give you a better chance of doing a good piece of work and getting a satisfactory mark for your efforts. To be successful, an assignment needs to be thought out carefully. You may be the type that likes to do this in a very formal way, with a plan set out on paper – or you may just turn ideas over in your mind without actually writing anything down. Whatever you prefer, this chapter suggests that there are seven main areas to think about when planning your work. Each area is discussed below, with activities and check-lists to help you.

# THE LANDSCAPE OF AN ASSIGNMENT

When you start work on an assignment it is important to think about the *structure* of what you need to write and your *time management* strategy. One of the first things you need to know is:

- What kind of assignment is this (e.g. essay, report, project)?

See
Chapter 12

This information will be in the assignment brief, that is to say the information that tells you what you need to do. When you first look at your assignment brief there will almost certainly be a clue in the instructions about exactly what kind of writing you have to produce. For example, there might be a sentence that begins 'write an essay' or 'prepare a report' or 'produce a reflective account of'. Sometimes, though, the wording is less clear and will use a more academic term. For example, you might be asked to write an evaluation, an analysis or a critical review of something. In many cases the assignment brief will give advice on the format to use, so make sure you follow it closely. If there is no guidance it is better to follow the generic structures of either the essay or the report, depending upon which you think is more suitable for the assignment you have been given.

Other things that you need to know are:

- How many marks is this assignment worth?
- When is the deadline?
- How does it fit into what I am learning on this course?
- How much do I know about the subject?

## Activity 3.1 Understanding the assignment brief

Find an assignment and go through the brief, checking that you understand it fully.

## Practicalities

Having got a broad overview of your assignment and a sense of where it fits into your overall studies, you now need to look at some basic housekeeping issues. Use this list to ask yourself:

- What is the word length? Is there a minimum and maximum length?
- When is the hand-in date? Are there penalties for handing it in late?
- How many copies must I give in?
- Where must I hand it in?
- How must I submit the work – electronically or as hard copy?

## Activity 3.2 Practicalities

Use the same assignment to ask yourself the questions above.

# ASSESSMENT CRITERIA

It is important to find out right at the beginning how a piece of work will be marked, to help you do the work as well as possible and guide you in the areas you need to concentrate on. For example, if some of the marks are for including references and you do not give any you are likely to be marked down. As well as subject-specific criteria, here are some areas that might be included in any mark scheme:

pter 1

- appendices
- grammar
- layout
- references
- spelling
- style
- word length.

It is also worth asking yourself how many marks you want for this assignment. Do you want really high marks or are you happy just to pass? This will help you decide on how much time and effort you need to put in.

Use the same assignment as before to look at the assessment criteria and check you know what you will be marked on.

# WHAT TO INCLUDE

Knowing exactly what type of assignment you have to write and how it will be marked is the first step in deciding what needs to go in it. The structure of an essay differs from a report, which in turn differs from a research proposal. How you organise your work will depend on the accepted structure of each.

Activity 3.4 **Checklist**

Choose one of your assignments and place a tick against anything you think will be needed.

| Sources | Yes | No | Perhaps | Organisation | Yes | No | Perhaps |
|---|---|---|---|---|---|---|---|
| books | | | | abstract/summary | | | |
| journals | | | | appendices | | | |
| newspapers | | | | chapters | | | |
| reference material | | | | charts/diagrams | | | |
| existing data | | | | footnotes | | | |
| primary research | | | | headings | | | |
| company reports | | | | references | | | |
| government publications | | | | table of contents | | | |
| websites | | | | title | | | |

# YOUR EXISTING KNOWLEDGE OF THE SUBJECT

Linked in to the research that you have to do for this assignment is your existing level of knowledge about the subject. You need to think about this in order to plan your time effectively.

## Activity 3.5 Needs analysis

Using the same assignment as before, make notes for the following areas:

| | |
|---|---|
| **What I know already about the subject** | |
| **What I need to know for this assignment** | |
| **What I need to do to find the information out** | |

# RESEARCH

Any assignment will call for some research before you can begin to write. This part of the preparation often consists of filling in certain gaps. The research you do could be:

- using your existing notes
- making new notes
- using outside sources
- carrying out primary research.

They will all need to have time allocated to them, either for any reading and note-taking you will need to do or for any primary research.

## Using your existing notes

Look through the notes you have on the subject of the assignment, either from your own reading or from lectures and seminars. They will be useful in helping you plan what you are going to say. Make sure they are in good order and that you can understand them. If you find any problems with them, you might have to make new notes or at least tidy up your existing ones.

## Making new notes

If you want to do a good assignment and get as many marks as you can you will need to make new notes on the subject you are going to write about. Ways that you can do this include:

- taking apart the assignment title and making notes on the different aspects you find in it
- working through additional material suggested on your reading list and making notes from that
- following up specific chapters you have been advised to read and making notes from them
- making notes from any other sources you use as part of your research.

See
Chapter 4

You might also have missed a key lecture, in which case you need to find relevant handouts, either from a fellow student or from your lecturers. Whatever it is, make sure that you know where to go to get the information and that you build in time for this aspect of your preparation.

## Using outside sources

Does the assignment brief give you any advice on which sources to use? Does it state a particular number of sources you should use? What types of sources are advised (internet, books, journals, etc.)?

## Carrying out primary research

You might be told that you have to do some primary research as part of the assignment. For example, you may have to collect data through questionnaires or interview, or you may be asked to research an organisation for a case study. The process of gathering, collating and analysing the data takes time and must be built in to your planning.

# RESOURCES

Look back at Activity 3.4. You need to be clear about exactly what kinds of resources you need to use for each assignment. They may be:

- books
- journals
- the internet
- companies or other organisations
- published research
- existing studies
- other sources.

Whatever kind of resource you use (and it is likely to be more than one) make sure you allow enough time for the process of finding or borrowing material as well as absorbing the information and making good notes from it.

# TIME MANAGEMENT

Time management is an essential part of planning an assignment, both so that you clear space in the week for the reading, research and drafting that you need to do as well as deciding when to start work and when to try to finish it by. In a sense, you need to think of any assignment as a small project, with tasks, stages and milestones to help you monitor your progress. If you are familiar with Gantt charts, you could draw up one for yourself or you could use some of the charts in this section.

However you do your planning, first ask yourself:

- How much time can I give to this piece of work?
- Does the assignment brief have any guidance on how long it should take?
- How long do I think it will take?
- How do I prefer to work?
- What other assignments have I got to do?

## Activity 3.6 Prioritising your work

If this is one of several assignments you have to do, try to put your work in order of importance.

| Assignment name | Deadline | Prioritise dates | Re-order assignment list |
| --- | --- | --- | --- |
| | | | |
| | | | |
| | | | |
| | | | |
| | | | |

## Activity 3.7 Planning your week

Block out periods when you can spend concentrated time on your assignment during the week. For example:

| | 8–10 | 10–12 | 12–2 | 2–4 | 4–6 | 6–8 | 8–10 |
|---|---|---|---|---|---|---|---|
| Monday | | | | | | | |
| Tuesday | | | | | | | |
| Wednesday | | | | | | | |
| Thursday | | | | | | | |
| Friday | | | | | | | |
| Saturday | | | | | | | |
| Sunday | | | | | | | |

## Activity 3.8 Planning the tasks

Now draw up a chart to help you plan the tasks, adding detail under each main heading. Suggestions for the first one (Preparation) have been included.

| Tasks | Estimate of time needed | Start date | End date |
|---|---|---|---|
| **Preparation** | | | |
| Understanding the assignment | | | |
| Sorting through notes | | | |
| Initial reading | | | |
| | | | |
| **Research and further reading** | | | |
| | | | |
| | | | |
| | | | |
| **Writing the assignment** | | | |
| | | | |
| | | | |
| **Assignment deadline** | | | |

# SUMMARY

Making sure that you understand an assignment fully and prepare carefully for it will help you do a good piece of work. There are stages you need to go through and key areas to consider before you start writing. This chapter has given you ideas for planning your time according to the different stages of preparation. The next chapter goes into more detail on one of those stages – the process of research.

Chapter 3 covered planning your work and included research as one of the things you need to do to prepare for an assignment. You may feel you know a lot about the subject already, but whatever kind of assignment you are asked to write for your studies you will also need to find information and ideas from other sources that you then bring in to your own work.

This chapter will cover:

■ understanding what you need to do to carry out effective research for an assignment
■ using key words to search for information
■ deciding how to choose good sources for an assignment.

## USING THIS CHAPTER

# INTRODUCTION

The word *research* in academic study can cover many activities: here it is used to mean the process of looking for and choosing your sources so that they help you write a good assignment. You could liken this to choosing good-quality ingredients for a meal you are about to cook for friends. And to carry the comparison further, just as you would presumably want to give those friends a good meal that you had put time and effort into making, so you should do the same for all your assignments, to ensure that you achieve to the best of your ability.

## Six questions to ask

You might know these four lines that are from 'The Elephant's Child' in the *Just So Stories* by Rudyard Kipling:

> *I keep six honest serving-men*
> *(They taught me all I knew);*
> *Their names are What and Where and When*
> *And How and Why and Who.*

They can serve as a useful reminder when you are starting out on your research and the six question words are used as headings in this chapter, appearing in a slightly different order from the poem.

# *WHY* DO YOU NEED TO DO ANY RESEARCH?

Research is an important activity in any study and helps develop your learning and knowledge of your subject. Whatever type of writing you have to do as part of that study (essay, report, case study, etc.), there is an expectation that what you create has not come entirely from ideas in your head. Sources that you bring in can be used in many ways: for example to provide background information, to support your arguments, as evidence or to give a fuller explanation. If used properly they will improve the quality of your work, showing that you are aware of the wider context you are writing in and that you understand the depth and complexity of academic study.

# *WHAT* RESEARCH DO YOU NEED TO DO?

It may be that you know quite a bit about the subject of the assignment already – perhaps it is something you are very interested in or have studied before. However you will need to find and use additional sources to any existing material you have.

# Sources

There are usually three main source areas for any assignment:

1 material you already have
2 libraries (for traditional sources)
3 online (for electronic sources).

## Material you already have

This could, for example, be:

- lecture, tutorial or seminar notes
- notes from textbooks
- course reading list(s).

Check how useful the material will be for your assignment. Notes will help provide a broad understanding of the topic you are going to write about but are unlikely to be in sufficient detail.

## Libraries

Your assignment brief may recommend material to use for your research in addition to your textbooks and recommended books on your reading lists. These are unlikely to be sufficient and you will almost certainly need to look further afield. Start with your university library catalogue, using the classification numbers for the subject(s) you are researching or to look for work by particular authors. Printed copies of journals are another important source to use, although it is often more convenient to search for journal articles online.

## Online resources

While computers mean you can access an enormous amount of material at speed and with ease that facility can at times seem overwhelming. There is a place for printed material in any research you do, from the textbook that gives a comprehensive overview of your subject to the useful book you come across by chance when browsing the subject shelves in your university library. You can work backwards and forwards in a book, marking pages with a bookmark or adhesive note in a way that is not possible with an electronic source. Many books and textbooks are now of course also available as e-books, allowing you to search the text for specific information. However access to them is restricted in various ways (e.g. the time you are allowed to browse the book or the number of pages you can copy).

Journals should be of major importance in your research. They can provide up-to-date articles on a specific aspect of the subject you are writing about. A peer-reviewed journal means the article will have been written by someone who knows about the subject and is then put through a quality vetting process by other experts in the field. Both journals and newspapers can be searched easily through electronic databases. If you find a good article it is certainly much faster and easier to access it online than to have to borrow and photocopy it from your library.

## Activity 4.1 Sources you have used before

Place a tick against any of the following that you have used in preparing previous assignments. Are you clear about the different uses they have? Do you avoid using print-based sources? Could you have used a greater variety of sources?

| | Notes | Books | Journals | Newspapers | Reports | Reference material |
|---|---|---|---|---|---|---|
| Traditional | | | | | | |

| | Websites | Books | Journals | Newspapers | Reports | Reference material |
|---|---|---|---|---|---|---|
| Electronic | | | | | | |

## Primary vs. secondary sources

Sometimes an assignment will specify whether you should use either primary or secondary sources, or may ask you to use both. If the information you find out about your topic comes from the writings of other people this is a secondary source (e.g. what historians have written about the Industrial Revolution). If the information is from someone who lived in that time (e.g. the diary of a factory owner) this is a primary source.

## Electronic sources

One of the biggest problems in being able to access so much information through computers is deciding which sources are reliable and useful and which can be ignored. Search engines such as Google or online encyclopedias such as Wikipedia can be useful at the very beginning of your research in pointing you towards sources and helping you decide the parameters of the subject you are writing about. Google Scholar will help you find academic, peer-referenced journals. However you cannot rely on these sources alone for your research, they will not be comprehensive enough and many sources will lack authenticity. You may find that they will be discounted as credible sources if you include them in your references, so you need to check your institution or department's policy on this. You also need to ensure that any sources you use are correctly and fully referenced.

See
Chapter 10

## Types of websites

The two or three letters that you see towards the end of a website address can be very useful when you are searching as they tell you what kind of website it is. Some of the most common you are likely to see in your searches are:

.ac   = academic institution
.co   = a commercial organisation (note this is usually .com in the USA)
.gov = government organisation
.org = other kind of organisation
.net = for networks, internet service providers
.uk  = an example of a country code.

## Electronic databases

Electronic databases are the best places to go for good-quality material for your research and you should make sure you get to know those that are relevant to your subject area. They store information from a range of sources and allow you to construct targeted searches. Authorised access is needed, normally via your place of study.

## Subject gateways

One way of helping you locate good sources is to use subject gateways. Two that are very useful and are maintained by universities are Pinakes and Intute. Pinakes (**www.hw.ac.uk/libwww/irn/pinakes/pinakes.html**) offers a selection of databases across a range of subjects. Intute (**www.intute.ac.uk/**) has a subject gateway for each of the four broad divisions it uses: Science, Engineering and Technology; Arts and Humanities; Health and Life Sciences; and Social Sciences. Any of these subject gateways will point you in the direction of good-quality resources, ranging from reports to journals to conferences to government publications.

## Activity 4.2 Investigating your subject gateway

Log on to Pinakes. What kind of links can you find?

Log on to Intute. Type in the words 'essay writing' into the search box and confirm. Can you find resources for all four main subject areas?

Now try using the words 'report writing'. Scroll through and explore those that are relevant to your own subject area.

# *HOW* SHOULD YOU DO THE RESEARCH?

This will depend in part upon the way you like to study and work, but it is best to try to carry out your research in a systematic way. Decide first which sources you are going to use, taking notes as you read and keeping thorough records of those sources to help you write your references. How you decide which sources to use is linked to your understanding of the assignment and how you develop the topic and the key words in the assignment title.

## Understanding an assignment

See Chapter 2

The title of any assignment is of major importance in directing you in your research. Whether you are given the assignment title or able to decide it yourself, you need to pick out those words in the title that are about the concepts and ideas you will write about. These are known as *key words*. Look at this sample question taken from a law textbook:

**Discuss the extent to which lay magistrates are representative of society.**

An essay on this topic would need to be built around a discussion of how far (*Discuss the extent* ...) lay magistrates reflect the mix (*are representative of* ...) of society. You could expect a student answering this question to have covered the magistrate system in their studies so they could turn first to their notes. If their notes included recommendations for sources to look at they could go there next and to any textbooks they had.

However this is not likely to be enough. There is a judgement to be made here, something which a student answering the question could only do after they had explored the topic in detail. The sample guidance for an answer in the textbook is as follows:

---

Lay magistrates deal with ninety-five per cent of all criminal trials and are appointed by the Lord Chancellor in the name of the Queen, on the advice of local Advisory Committees (comprised mostly of existing magistrates). The only formal requirement is that an applicant should be under 65 and live within 15 miles of the commission area to which they will be appointed (although appointments are now made on a national basis). There is an expectation that they will be able to devote one half day per week to acting as a magistrate. There is no minimum educational qualification or requirement of legal knowledge, but they receive only expenses and a small allowance.

Research by Morgan and Russell found that while the percentage of magistrates from the ethnic minorities was increasing, magistrates remained predominantly professional or managerial, middle-aged (or older) and so increasingly unrepresentative of the community they served. One explanation might be the employers' reluctance to give paid time off work, thus effectively facilitating the appointment of the self-employed and those in senior positions. **(Elliott and Quinn, 2008: 244–5)**

---

Although not a full essay the sample answer includes:

- an *explanation* of what magistrates do
- *information* on qualifications needed to be a magistrate
- *statistics* (it mentions the percentage of criminal trials covered by lay magistrates and while not giving actual figures cites research to show that the percentage of magistrates from ethnic minorities is increasing).

In terms of searching for information to complete this assignment, the key words for the student to research are *magistrate* and *society*. They would need to go to reference books or good-quality websites for the statistics and to other textbooks or journal articles for views on this question. They might decide to include the opinion of experts, other magistrates or the population in general, all of which would require research beyond what they had in their notes.

Now look at this sample case study assignment:

> Develop a case study on an organisation of your choice. The case study should examine how the organisation uses environmentally friendly policies in its operations to comply with current legislation. The case study should be no longer than 5000 words.

This is clearly a substantial piece of work that would call for careful research including:

- selecting an organisation
- finding out about its environmentally friendly policies
- deciding which policies to look at
- deciding how to find out the information (e.g. interviews, company reports, questionnaires)
- finding out about current legislation concerning the environment.

Once you have chosen the organisation you could contact it for information but would also need to use published material from other sources, to ensure you produced a balanced and objective view.

## Activity 4.3 Deciding the type of sources

Make a list of sources you could use to research this case study assignment.

# Developing your topic

Before you can start looking for information you need to break down your title. Imagine you have been set the following assignment:

> Examine the influence of sporting personalities on public attitudes towards overall fitness.

### 4 Carrying out the research

This is quite an open-ended title that you would need to put some boundaries around in order to search effectively for information. Some suggestions for those boundaries (or parameters) are:

■ Sport: which one(s) would you look at?
■ Sporting personalities: who would you choose?
■ Population: what age range or gender will you look at?

These decisions are important so that you know where and when to search. You then need to develop your key words.

## Keyword searches

Keywords are those words in a title that tell you what the concepts or ideas are. They help you focus your thinking. Once decided, you can use them to carry out keyword searches (usually only electronically). If you do them in a structured way you will maximise the quality of your results.

The flow chart below shows the steps to go through:

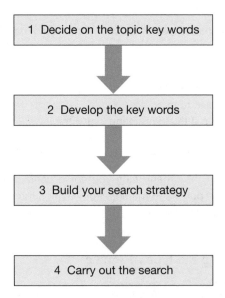

### Decide on the topic key words

◀ See Chapter 2

Key words are those that indicate major ideas or concepts in a title. For example:

**Discuss the relationship between diet and obesity in the population.**

Key words here are 'diet', 'obesity' and 'population'. They define the boundaries of your search.

## Activity 4.4 **Deciding the topic key words**

Use the assignment title to pick out the key words. Place a tick against any of the following words that you think are key words.

**Examine the influence of sporting personalities on public attitudes towards overall fitness.**

Examine ☐

Influence ☐

Sporting personalities ☐

Public attitudes ☐

Overall ☐

Fitness ☐

## Develop the key words

While you could carry out a search simply using key words and find a lot of information you might find that it is not specific enough to the boundaries you have given your topic. You also need to think of alternative key words, known as synonyms.

Sporting personalities – e.g. **sportsmen; sportswomen; athletes**
Public – e.g. **popular; social**
Attitudes – e.g. **opinions; views**
Fitness – e.g. **exercise.**

## Build your search strategy

Now that you have your key words and your synonyms, you need to decide how to use them in your search. Boolean logic uses three words to do this: 'and'; 'or'; 'not'.

**AND** between two key words will only find a record if it contains both the key words. It is therefore useful for narrowing down results to get more specific information. For example:

**sporting AND personalities**

will ensure you avoid being given information on sporting equipment.

**OR** will find either of the key words (or both), so is useful if you want to widen your search. For example:

**sportsmen OR sportswomen**

will ensure you get information about both male and female sporting personalities

**NOT** will exclude any examples that have the key word in them. You can use it to eliminate material. For example:

sportsmen NOT sportswomen

will ensure you get information that excludes female sporting personalities.

One other useful tool for key word searches is truncation, where you take the root of the word and add an asterisk to it. In this example, writing sport* would also find articles with the words 'sportsmen' and 'sportswomen'.

### Carry out the search

This is a complex process that will vary from one database to the other. However there are some general rules you can follow:

- Set the parameters for your search (e.g. include dates, state the type of source you are looking for, name a specific author if you know of one).
- Save the search strategy and keyword construction if you think you will need to come back to it at a later date.
- Use the facility that most databases give you of marking and then viewing your list so that you can look through an overall view of results before you print or save.
- Print or email the results of the search so that you have a record and can print out details in your own time.

Time spent on defining topics, deciding key words and then searching for information is time well spent. It allows you to gain a deeper knowledge and understanding of your topic and to develop your ideas to the full.

# *WHEN* SHOULD YOU DO THE RESEARCH?

See
Chapter 3

Most advice will tell you to do the research before you start to write and although this is good advice there will be times when you discover that you need to do more research, for example if you realise as you write that you do not know enough about a particular area of the subject you are writing about. However, you should try to do as much of the research as you can before you start planning and drafting your work.

# *WHERE* SHOULD YOU DO THE RESEARCH?

This goes back to the pros and cons of traditional and electronic methods of research mentioned earlier – should you use the library to look for books, journals, etc. or should you sit at your computer and rely on the internet to get everything you need? Usually you will do both, depending upon what stage you are at with your research; if your library offers internet access it becomes easier in some ways for you to move between the two types of source.

# *WHO* SHOULD YOU RESEARCH?

The answer to this question will usually come from your lecturer(s), fellow students and colleagues as well as from the assignment brief. Deciding which sources to use requires careful judgement as to what is relevant and what is not. Once you have made your choices you need to bring those ideas into your writing, being careful to use your own words at all times.

## Navigate the sources

Most of your research will be on textbooks, journal articles and other academic texts which you will need to read closely and carefully in order to understand specific information. However, you cannot read every word in every book or journal. It is important therefore to learn reading techniques that help you quickly assess material, decide if it is useful and, if so, which parts need to be read more carefully. It is also much easier to read the text in detail when you have a rough idea of what it is about: what the author's purpose is, what is at the beginning of the text and what is at the end.

Whatever you read, it is useful to look at the layout and organisation of the text as this is part of the overall meaning. The following table shows what might be included in your text, although it will vary depending upon what you are reading.

| | Textbook | Journal article |
|---|---|---|
| **Title (plus maybe a subtitle)**<br>Sometimes, you need to make quick decisions on the basis of the title alone. The title can give you a clue as to whether the text is relevant for your purpose and what sort of information you can expect to get from it. | ✓ | ✓ |
| **Details about the author or authors**<br>It can be helpful to know about the author or authors: what their job is, where they work, what their position is, what experience they have had. | ✓ | ✓ |
| **Date of publication and edition**<br>This helps you to decide whether or not the book or article is up to date. It is worth checking whether or not there is a more recent edition of a book. | ✓ | ✓ |
| **Abstract**<br>An abstract is usually a single paragraph at the beginning of a journal article. It normally summarises the different sections of the text and draws attention to the main conclusions. Reading the abstract will help you to decide whether or not the text is relevant for your purpose. | ✗ | ✓ |

→

|  | Textbook | Journal article |
|---|---|---|
| **Preface, Foreword or Introduction**<br>These come at the beginning and explain the purpose and organisation of the book along with any features you should especially notice. Read it carefully. The author is explaining how to get the most out of the book. | ✓ | ✓ |
| **Table of contents**<br>This gives an overall view of the material in the book. Looking at this is a quick and easy way to see if the book includes information you need. | ✓ | ✓ |
| **Text**<br>Textbooks are organised into chapters that have titles and section headings. Very often each chapter will start with an introduction of what is in the chapter and a summary at the end. Journal articles and textbooks usually have subheadings to help you find your way around the text. | ✓ | ✓ |
| **Reference list**<br>An alphabetical list of books and articles which have been referred to is included either at the end of each chapter or at the end of a book or article. Looking through the list of references will give you some idea of the author's background. Looking at the dates of the articles and books referred to will help you decide if the information is up to date.<br><br>Note that a **Bibliography** is similar to the list of references but also includes books or journals that are of interest to the reader but which may not have been specifically referred to in the text. | ✓ | ✓ |
| **Index**<br>One of the most important sections of any textbook is the index at the end. This is a fairly detailed alphabetical listing of all the major people, places, ideas, facts or topics that the book contains, with page references. The index can give you information about the topics covered in the book and the amount of attention paid to them.<br><br>Some journals (e.g. law journals) put together an index after a certain number of issues have been produced. | ✓ | ✓ |
| **Blurb**<br>The blurb is the publisher's description of what the book is about, usually on the back cover. | ✓ | ✗ |
| **Reviewers' comments**<br>These are opinions of people who have read or used the book. They are usually on the back cover of a book. | ✓ | ✗ |
| **Glossary**<br>Many textbooks have a list of important terms with definitions. | ✓ | ✗ |
| **Appendix**<br>Both textbooks and journal articles can have appendices with supplementary information such as further reading or more data. | ✓ | ✓ |

## Activity 4.5 **Identifying extracts from a text**

Look at the text extracts on the following pages and identify which of these elements are included.

| | |
|---|---|
| Abstract | |
| Acknowledgments | |
| Appendix | |
| Author | |
| Blurb | |
| Date of publication | |
| Details about author | |
| Edition | |
| Foreword | |
| Glossary | |
| Index | |
| ISBN | |
| List of contents | |
| List of references | |
| Place of publication | |
| Preface | |
| Publisher | |
| Reviewers' comments | |
| Sub-title | |
| Title | |

**Fourth Edition**

# Accounting
## An Introduction

**Eddie McLaney**
**Peter Atrill**

Text extract 1

**Pearson Education Limited**

Edinburgh Gate
Harlow
Essex CM20 2JE
England

and Associated Companies throughout the world

*Visit us on the World Wide Web at:*
www.pearsoned.co.uk

———————————————

First published 1999 by Prentice Hall Europe
Second edition published 2002
Third edition published 2005
**Fourth edition published 2008**

© Prentice Hall Europe 1999
© Pearson Education Limited 2002, 2005, 2008

ISBN 978-0-273-71136-0

**British Library Cataloguing-in-Publication Data**
A catalogue record for this book is available from the British Library

10  9  8  7  6  5  4  3  2
11   10   09   08

Typeset in 9.5/12.5pt Stone Serif by 35
Printed and bound by Mateu Cromo Artes Graficas, Spain

*The publisher's policy is to use paper manufactured from sustainable forests.*

**Text extract 2**

## Brief contents

**Text extract 3**

# Accounting
## An Introduction

**Eddie McLaney  Peter Atrill**

Fourth Edition

*Accounting: An Introduction* 4th edition is renowned for its clear, accessible and uncluttered style. It provides a comprehensive introduction to the main principles of financial accounting, management accounting, and the core elements of financial management. With a clear and unequivocal focus on how accounting information can be used to improve the quality of decision making by managers, combined with a strong practical emphasis, this book provides the ideal grounding for a career in management.

### Audience

Suitable for all those studying an introductory course in accounting, who are seeking an understanding of basic principles and underlying concepts without detailed technical knowledge.

### Authors

**Eddie McLaney** is Visiting Fellow in Accounting and Finance at the University of Plymouth.

**Peter Atrill** is a freelance academic and author working with leading institutions in the UK, Europe and SE Asia. He was previously Head of Business and Management at the University of Plymouth Business School.

Visit the companion website at **www.pearsoned.co.uk/mclaney**

### Features

- Progress checks: numerous activities and exercises enable you to constantly test your understanding and reinforce learning.

- Lively and relevant examples from the real world demonstrate the practical application and value of concepts and techniques learnt.

- Interactive 'open learning' style is ideal for self study.

- Decision making focus on the use of accounting information rather than its preparation is highly appropriate for tomorrow's business managers.

- Fully incorporates International Financial Reporting Standards, which are crucial in the European and world business arena.

- Key terms, glossary and bulleted summaries are excellent revision aids.

- Clearer distinctions between process costing and job order costing.

- More extensive coverage of corporate governance and ethics issues.

The text is supported by MyAccountingLab, a completely new type of educational resource. MyAccountingLab complements student learning by presenting the user with a study plan that adapts and customises to the student's individual requirements as they progress through online tests. Students can also practice problems before taking tests, and because most of these are algorithmically driven, they can practice over and over again without repetition. Additionally, students have access to an eBook, animated guides to various key topics, and guided solutions, all of which are designed to help them overcome the most difficult concepts. Both students and lecturers have access to gradebooks that allow them to track progress, and lecturers will have the ability to create new tests and activities using the large number of problems available in the question database.

**Text extract 4**

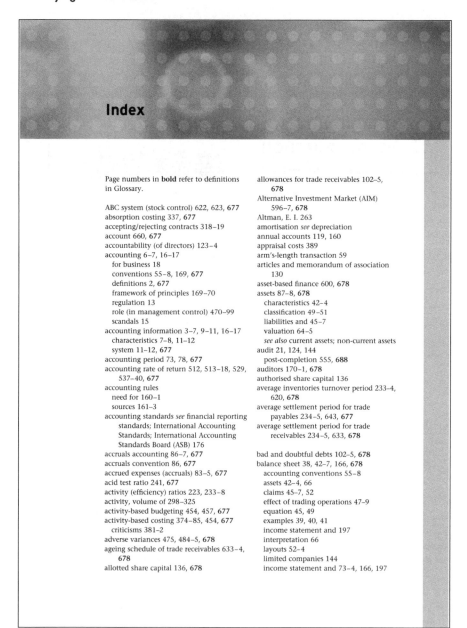

## Index

**Text extract 5**

## Activity 4.6 Looking at your own material

Look at a textbook or journal article that you are using for your writing. Which of the sections are included?

## Activity 4.7 Using the index

Look at the index on page 56, and answer the following question.

Which of the following subjects are treated in detail?

- accounting scandals
- auditors
- balance sheets
- classification of assets
- E. I. Altman.

In each case, which pages would you look at for a definition and the most information?

# Evaluate the sources

Once you have found your sources you need to decide upon how useful they will be to your assignment. Divide the criteria you use into external and internal criteria.

### External criteria

This relates to an overall judgement you will make on the value of the source and might include:

- **Currency**, i.e. the date the source was published. This may or may not be important and will depend on the topic, how much material you have found as well as the dates you set for your searches.
- **Relevance to your topic**. Use details in the abstract of a journal, the blurb on the back of a book or any general information you have about the source to decide this. At this stage you just need to make a yes/no decision.
- **Author(s)**, i.e. how well-known they are in their field. You may have heard of the author or authors already. They might have written a chapter in one of your textbooks. Or you may just keep noticing a particular name coming up again and again as you search.
- **Reputation.** You need to establish the credibility of the source. Questions you can ask yourself are:
  - Have I heard of this journal before?

- Has it been recommended to me?
- How many years has it been around?
- How well-known is the publisher?
- Is it a peer-reviewed journal?

### Internal criteria

➡
See
Chapter 5 This relates to your critical judgement about the content and ideas in the source.

- **Relevance to your topic**. You now need to look more closely at the source. Examples of questions you could ask to help decide relevance are:
  - Is it of major importance or does it just give you background information?
  - Does it support or contradict your arguments?
  - Is the data useful?
- **Quality of the content**. Ask yourself:
  - Is the subject matter discussed fully enough?
  - Is evidence given to support the points made?
- **Strength of the argument.** Examples of questions to ask here are:
  - Is the argument well-constructed?
  - Are alternative points of view given?
  - Is there a clear conclusion?

# SUMMARY

This chapter has considered the research processes that are part of academic writing and has addressed some basic questions of 'how' 'why', 'when', 'what', 'where' and 'who'. It has shown you how to plan your searches in a methodical way to ensure you find the best sources you can to write your assignment. The next chapter takes you through the process of effective reading and note-taking before you begin to write.

## References

Details of highlighted references can be found in the Introduction on page xxii.

## Further reading

Blaxter, L., Hughes, C. & Tight, M. (2006) *How to research* (3rd edn). Maidenhead: OUP.

Rumsey, S. (2008) *How to find information* (2nd edn). Maidenhead: OUP.

The content of this chapter will focus on the final areas to consider in the preparatory process. It will ask you to think about and develop effective reading strategies (e.g. reading for a general idea, reading for specific information and content) before moving on to look at how to keep a record of what you read (i.e. effective note-taking methods). It will suggest models for you to adopt (e.g. mind-maps, linear notes, spider diagrams) as well as presenting worked examples of texts with different methods of taking notes from text.

This chapter will cover:
- reading efficiently and critically for writing
- taking notes for writing.

## USING THIS CHAPTER

## Activity 5.1 What do you read?

Before you start this chapter, take a few minutes to think about the kind of reading you do every day. What kinds of things do you read? How often do you read these kinds of texts? You could put the information in a table like this:

| What do I read? | How often do I read it? |
| --- | --- |
|  |  |
|  |  |

# INTRODUCTION

In previous chapters, we have covered understanding your task, planning your writing, and finding the information you need. So now that you know what information you need, you need to start reading. There are many reasons for reading, but in higher education, one main purpose of reading is to collect information and ideas that you can use in your writing. You will gather this information from reading textbooks, magazines and journal articles, some of which will be given to you on reading lists, and some you will find for yourself. This kind of reading is what we will focus on in this book on writing. In your course, there will be a lot of reading to do and you probably will not have time to read everything you want to. You therefore need to develop effective reading strategies.

Effective reading means reading purposefully, efficiently, interactively and critically.

- **Purposeful reading**. Reading for writing needs to be purposeful. You should always know why you are reading. You will have questions to be answered and information to collect.
- **Efficient reading**. This means reading selectively and not wasting time on texts or parts of texts that are not relevant to your purpose. It also means varying your reading speed depending on the task, sometimes reading fast and sometimes reading in more detail.
- **Interactive reading**. Reading is an interactive, two-way process. As a reader you are not passive, just taking in the facts that your eyes pass over, but active. You need to construct the meaning of your text from what you see on the printed page, making use of your knowledge of the world and your subject, what you know about the texts in your field and the language (see the box opposite). When you read, you use your eyes and your brain. In order to read effectively, you need to use your brain more.

■ **Critical reading**. It is important to read critically when you are reading in order to write. Critical reading requires you to evaluate the arguments in the text. You need to distinguish fact from opinion, and evaluate the evidence given to support the various points.

---

### INTERPRETIVE FRAMING

MacLachlan and Reid (1994) talk about *interpretive framing*, which influences your understanding. They discuss four types of framing:

1 Extratextual framing – using information from outside the text (your background knowledge and experience) to understand texts.
2 Intratextual framing – making use of cues from the text, such as headings and subheadings and referential words such as 'this' and 'that' to understand texts.
3 Circumtextual framing – using information from the cover of the book, title, abstract, etc. to understand the text.
4 Intertextual framing – making connections with other texts you are reading to help understand your text.

---

# Purposeful reading

You read different texts in different ways depending on what you want from the text. In everyday life, you usually know why you are reading; you have a question and you read to find the answer. You usually know your way around your favourite newspaper, so if you want to know the sports results, you go straight to the correct page, or if you want to know what is on television tonight, you go straight to the TV listings. You do not, of course, start on the first page and read every word. When you read a novel, it is different. You probably start at the beginning and slowly move towards the end. In academic reading, you need to be flexible when you read: you may need to read quickly to find relevant sections that deal with particular points, and then read carefully when you have found what you want.

Always ask yourself:

■ Why am I reading this text?
■ What do I want to get from this text?
■ How can this text help me with my task?
■ Where in the text might I find what I am looking for?

**TIP** *Always think about why you are reading a text before you start reading.*

# Efficient reading

The amount of text in the world, both paper and electronic, is increasing every day. There are now millions of books in English available. If you add web-based material, the number is massive. You certainly cannot read all of it or even everything in the library on your topic. You probably cannot even read everything on your reading lists. So in order to survive in higher education, you need to read efficiently. This means only reading what you need to read, and then reading it efficiently by using contents pages, indexes, summaries and reviews.

Before you read, ask yourself:

- Do I need to read this?
- Will it help me?
- Do I need to read all of it?
- Which parts can I leave out?

# Interactive reading

You need to be active all the time when you are reading and use all the information that is available. It is useful, therefore, before you start reading to try actively to remember what you know, and do not know, about the subject and as you are reading to formulate questions based on the information you have. You will also find learning about how texts are structured in your subject can help you to find your way around them.

Before reading ask yourself:

- What do I know about the topic?
- What do I want to know from this text?
- What is the source of the text and how do such sources present information?
- What do I know about texts in my field?
- What language is used in such texts?

This should help you to interact with the text and thus to understand it better.

**TIP** *Keep questioning as you read.*

# Critical reading

It is important to read critically when you are reading in order to write. Critical reading requires you to evaluate the arguments in the text. You need to see if the conclusions are justified in the light of the evidence that is presented. You need to distinguish fact from opinion, and look at arguments given for and against the various points. You also need to check that nothing is taken for granted in the text.

To help you read critically, ask the following questions:

- Is there a clear distinction between fact and opinion?
- Is the text giving me different points of view or simply giving me one-sided infor-mation?
- What evidence is used to support arguments?
- What conclusions are drawn? Are they justified?
- Are alternatives considered?

## Activity 5.2 **How do you read?**

You might now like to complete the table you started in Activity 1 by adding a column with notes about why and how you read different texts.

| What do I read? | How often do I read it? | What is my purpose in reading the text? | In what way do I read the text? |
|---|---|---|---|
| | | | |
| | | | |

# EFFECTIVE READING STRATEGIES

Useful strategies (in no particular order depending on your purpose and the text type) are:

- using the title – sometimes you have to make quick decisions based on the title
- using text structure to help understanding
- scanning to locate specifically required information
- skimming a text to get an overall impression.

TIP *You cannot read every book on your reading list. Read selectively.*

## Using the title

The title can be seen as a summary of the text. Sometimes you will have to make quick decisions based only on the title. Therefore it is useful to try to understand it well. This may mean looking up unfamiliar words in a dictionary.

It is a good idea to ask yourself the following questions, based on the title.

- Is this text relevant to my needs? Is it related to the subject I am studying?
- What do I expect to learn from the text? (Ask yourself some questions that you expect the text to answer.)

## Activity 5.3 Exploring titles

Look at the titles of any text – books or articles – that you have close by and then ask three questions that you hope the text will answer. Read the texts aiming to see if they answer your questions.

## Activity 5.4 Using titles

You are trying to answer a question about the value of brands in marketing. Which of the following texts might be worth looking at?

Brassington, F. and Pettitt, S. (2006) *Principles of Marketing* (4th edn). Harlow: Pearson Education.

Davies, S. (2006) *The Essential Guide to Teaching.* Harlow: Pearson Education.

Elliott, C. and Quinn, F. (2008) *English Legal System* (9th edn). Harlow: Pearson Education.

Holden, J. (ed.) (2008) *Physical Geography and the Environment* (2nd edn). Harlow: Pearson Education.

Keenan, D. and Riches, S. (2007) *Business Law* (8th edn). Harlow: Pearson Education.

Kotler, P., Armstrong, G., Wong, V. and Saunders, J. (2008) *Principles of Marketing* (5th edn). Harlow: Pearson Education.

Martin, G.N., Carlson, N.R. and Buskist, W. (2007) *Psychology* (3rd edn). Harlow: Pearson Education.

McLaney, E. and Atrill, P. (2008) *Accounting: An Introduction* (4th edn). Harlow: Pearson Education.

Wilson, K., Ruch, G., Lymbery, M. and Cooper, A. (2008) *Social Work. An Introduction to Contemporary Practice.* Harlow: Pearson Education.

# Using your knowledge of text structure to understand a text

Most of the time you will be reading serious academic textbooks, journal articles and other academic texts. These texts are well organised with clear structures. You can use your knowledge of this structure to understand the texts.

For example, if you know that paragraphs usually have a main theme and that theme is often summarised in a topic sentence which appears at the beginning of a paragraph, then it makes sense to read the text by only reading the first sentences of each paragraph. Similarly if you know that subheadings are 'paragraph titles', you can get an understanding of the text by just reading the subheadings. (See Chapter 6 for more on this.)

In the same way, the more you know about the structure of the whole text, the better. For example, you may know – and you certainly will when you finish this book – that reports are often written with the following sections: Introduction, Methods,

Results and Discussion. This knowledge should help you to find your way round a report. Chapters 7, 8, 9 and 12 will help you to make sense of the overall text structure.

Whatever you need to read, it is useful to have a quick look at it all first to get an idea of the layout of the text and what is included.

**TIP** *Always try to see patterns and structure in anything you read.*

## Activity 5.5 Making use of text structure

Read the title of the following text. It is about the training and qualifications of solicitors. You can imagine, then, that it will describe in chronological order how solicitors are trained. So if you want to know what education you need to get started, you will look at the beginning of the text and if you want to know what the final stages of training are, you will look at the end of the text.

Read the text to answer two questions:

1 What sort of qualifications do you need to start training as a solicitor?
2 What are the final stages of a solicitor's training?

> ### Qualifications and training
>
> Almost all solicitors begin with a degree, though not necessarily in law. A number of law schools introduced an admissions test in 2004, the National Admissions Test for Law, to help select students onto their popular law degrees. Although no minimum degree classification is laid down, increased competition for entry to the profession means that most successful applicants now have an upper second class degree, and very few get in with less than a lower second.
>
> Students whose degree is not in law have to take a one-year course leading to the Common Professional Examination (CPE). It is possible for non-graduate mature students, who have demonstrated some professional or business achievements, to enter the profession without a degree. They take a broad two-year, CPE course. Only a very small number of people take this route and it is not a route the Law Society encourages – they suggest that, for most people, it is worth putting in the extra year to do a law degree and enter in the conventional manner, especially bearing in mind that many universities and colleges now offer mature students law degrees which can be studied part time, so that students do not have to give up paid employment. It is also possible for legal executives (discussed at p. 188) to become solicitors without first taking a degree course.
>
> The next step, for law graduates and those who have passed the CPE, is a one-year Legal Practice Course, designed to provide practical skills, including advocacy, as well as legal and procedural knowledge. Fees for the LPC are between £5,000 and £9,000, yet both the CPE and the Legal Practice Course are eligible only for discretionary LEA grants, and are not covered by the Government's student loan scheme. The Law Society provides a very small number of bursaries, and has also negotiated a loans scheme with certain high street banks, which offers up to £5,000, that students do not begin paying back until they

have finished studying; a few large London firms also offer assistance to those students they wish to attract into employment. The vast majority of students, however, are obliged to fund themselves or rely on loans.

After passing the Legal Practice exams, the prospective solicitor must find a place, usually in a firm, to serve a two-year apprenticeship. There can be intense competition for these places, especially in times of economic difficulty when firms are reluctant to invest in training; in 1995–96, there were only 4,170 traineeships on offer, for the almost 7,000 LPC students. Formally known as articles, the two-year period is now called a training contract, and includes a 20-day practical skills course, building on subjects studied during the Legal Practice Course. The work of a trainee solicitor can be very demanding, and a survey carried out for the Law Society found that a third work more than 50 hours a week. Trainee solicitors should receive a minimum salary of £15,332 outside London and £17,110 in London. In practice, the average salary for a trainee solicitor is £20,925.

It is possible to become a solicitor without a degree, by completing the one-year Solicitors' First Examination Course, and the Legal Practice Course, and having a five-year training contract. Legal executives (see p. 188) sometimes go on to qualify in this way.

The majority of solicitors qualifying each year are still law graduates – in 1993–94, 64 per cent of those admitted to the Law Society Roll had a law degree, with only 19 per cent being graduates in subjects other than law. However, the Law Society say that the non-law degree and CPE route is becoming more popular, with a third of places on Legal Practice Courses currently being taken by people aiming to qualify this way. Legal academics have expressed some concern about this, but the Law Society point out that, in some years, pass rates for non-law graduates in Solicitors' Finals have been higher than those for law graduates. Making up the remaining 17 per cent are Fellows of the Institute of Legal Executives, lawyers from overseas, solicitors transferring from Scotland or Northern Ireland and ex-barristers.

All solicitors are required to participate in continuing education throughout their careers. They are required to do 16 hours a year, with the subjects covered depending on each individual's areas of interest or need. Records must be kept of courses attended. Lord Woolf has observed that the solicitor profession is becoming 'increasingly polarised' depending on the nature of the work carried out, with lawyers working in City firms earning significantly more than those in high street practices. Specialist LPC courses are now being offered for City law firms. Lord Woolf has criticised this development, as he fears it could undermine the concept of a single-solicitor profession with a single professional qualification. Such courses may, over time, create a barrier which prevents students from other colleges from entering a big commercial practice. Lord Woolf has observed that, given the quality of the trainees attracted by the City firms, it should be possible for them to provide any enhanced training they require after the end of the Legal Practice Course.

Certain lawyers qualified abroad, particularly Europe, and English barristers can convert to become English solicitors by passing the Qualified Lawyers Transfer Test (QLTT).

(Elliott and Quinn, 2008: 161–2)

# Scanning to locate specifically required information

When you look for a telephone number or a name in an index, your eyes tend to move quickly over the words until you find the particular information you are looking for. You do not read every word – you ignore everything except the specific information you want. Scanning is directed and purposeful and should be extremely fast. When you are reading to write an assignment, you need to scan texts to find the information you need.

## Activity 5.6 **Scanning a text**

Read the following text quickly and then answer the following questions.

1 What kinds of businesses are there?
2 Can you find a definition for each of these?
3 What kind of businesses are the following: electrical repair shops, solicitors, easyJet?

> ### What kinds of business ownership exist?
>
> The particular form of business ownership has important implications for accounting purposes and so it is useful to be clear about the main forms of ownership that can arise.
>
> There are basically three arrangements:
>
> - sole proprietorship
> - partnership
> - limited company.
>
> Each of these is considered below.
>
> **Sole proprietorship**
> Sole proprietorship, as the name suggests, is where an individual is the sole owner of a business. This type of business is often quite small in terms of size (as measured, for example, by sales revenue generated or number of staff employed), however, the number of such businesses is very large indeed. Examples of sole-proprietor businesses can be found in most industrial sectors but particularly within the service sector. Hence, services such as electrical repairs, picture framing, photography, driving instruction, retail shops and hotels have a large proportion of sole-proprietor businesses. The sole-proprietor business is easy to set up. No formal procedures are required and operations can often commence immediately (unless special permission is required because of the nature of the trade or service, such as running licensed premises). The owner can decide the way in which the business is to be conducted and has the flexibility to restructure or dissolve the business whenever it suits. The law does not recognise the sole-proprietor business as being separate from the owner, so the business will cease on the death of the owner.
>
> Although the owner must produce accounting information to satisfy the taxation authorities, there is no legal requirement to produce accounting information relating to the business for other user groups. However, some user groups may demand accounting information about the business and may be in a position to have their demands met (for example, a bank requiring accounting information on a regular basis as a condition of a

loan). The sole proprietor will have unlimited liability which means that no distinction will be made between the proprietor's personal wealth and that of the business if there are business debts that must be paid.

### Partnership

A partnership exists where at least two individuals carry on a business together with the intention of making a profit. Partnerships have much in common with sole-proprietor businesses. They are often quite small in size (although some, such as partnerships of accountants and solicitors, can be large). Partnerships are also easy to set up as no formal procedures are required (and it is not even necessary to have a written agreement between the partners). The partners can agree whatever arrangements suit them concerning the financial and management aspects of the business, and the partnership can be restructured or dissolved by agreement between the partners.

Partnerships are not recognised in law as separate entities and so contracts with third parties must be entered into in the name of individual partners. The partners of a business usually have unlimited liability.

### Limited company

Limited companies can range in size from quite small to very large. The number of individuals who subscribe capital and become the owners may be unlimited, which provides the opportunity to create a very large scale business. The liability of owners, however, is limited (hence 'limited' company), which means that those individuals subscribing capital to the company are liable only for debts incurred by the company up to the amount that they have agreed to invest. This cap on the liability of the owners is designed to limit risk and to produce greater confidence to invest. Without such limits on owner liability, it is difficult to see how a modern capitalist economy could operate. In many cases, the owners of a limited company are not involved in the day-to-day running of the business and will invest in a business only if there is a clear limit set on the level of investment risk.

The benefit of limited liability, however, imposes certain obligations on such a company. To start up a limited company, documents of incorporation must be prepared that set out, among other things, the objectives of the business. Furthermore, a framework of regulations exists that places obligations on the way in which such a company conducts its affairs. Part of this regulatory framework requires annual financial reports to be made available to owners and lenders and usually an annual general meeting of the owners has to be held to approve the reports. In addition, a copy of the annual financial reports must be lodged with the Registrar of Companies for public inspection. In this way, the financial affairs of a limited company enter the public domain. With the exception of small companies, there is also a requirement for the annual financial reports to be subject to an audit. This involves an independent firm of accountants examining the annual reports and underlying records to see whether the reports provide a true and fair view of the financial health of the company and whether they comply with the relevant accounting rules established by law and by accounting rule makers.

All of the large household-name UK businesses (Marks and Spencer, Tesco, Shell, BSkyB, BA, BT, easyJet and so on) are limited companies.

(McLaney and Atrill, 2008: 19–21)

**TIP** *Do not waste time on text that you do not need.*

# Skimming to get an overall impression

Skimming is useful when you want to survey a text to get a general idea of what it is about. In skimming you ignore the details and look for the main ideas. Most academic texts are well organised with a clearly distinguishable structure. They start with introductions and finish with conclusions. Details are in the middle. Main ideas are usually found in the first and last paragraphs and in the first sentences of each paragraph.

Even if you know you will need to read the text in detail, before you start reading intensively it is useful to skim the text to get a feel for the main points and the text organisation. Skimming a text for gist can help you formulate questions. You can then read the text more slowly and carefully to find the answers, and this will help you to keep interacting with the text.

## Skimming a text using first lines of paragraphs

In most academic writing, the paragraph is a coherent unit, about one topic, connected to the previous and next paragraphs. Paragraphs are organised internally and the first sentence of each paragraph – normally called the topic sentence – is often a summary of, or an introduction to, the paragraph. You can therefore get a good idea of the overall content of a text by reading the first sentence of each paragraph. This should help you get a feeling for the structure of the text and is very useful when you are summarising. In many cases that will be enough, but if it is not, you will now have a good idea of the text structure and find it easier to read in detail. Familiar texts are easier to read.

## Activity 5.7 Skimming a text (1)

Read the first sentence of each paragraph in the following text. You will then have a broad understanding of the content of the text.

### Financial ratios

Financial ratios provide a quick and relatively simple means of assessing the financial health of a business. A ratio simply relates one figure appearing in the financial statements to some other figure appearing there (for example, operating profit in relation to capital employed) or, perhaps, to some resource of the business (for example, operating profit per employee, sales revenue per square metre of selling space, and so on).

Ratios can be very helpful when comparing the financial health of different businesses. Differences may exist between businesses in the scale of operations, and so a direct comparison of, say, the operating profit generated by each business may be misleading. By expressing operating profit in relation to some other measure (for example, capital [or funds] employed), the problem of scale is eliminated. A business with an operating profit of, say, £10,000 and capital employed of £100,000 can be compared with a much larger business with an operating profit of, say, £80,000 and sales revenue of £1,000,000 by the

→

use of a simple ratio. The operating profit to capital employed ratio for the smaller business is 10 per cent (that is, $(10,000/100,000) \times 100\%$) and the same ratio for the larger business is 8 per cent (that is, $(80,000/1,000,000) \times 100\%$). These ratios can be directly compared whereas comparison of the absolute operating profit figures would be less meaningful. The need to eliminate differences in scale through the use of ratios can also apply when comparing the performance of the same business over time.

By calculating a small number of ratios it is often possible to build up a good picture of the position and performance of a business. It is not surprising, therefore, that ratios are widely used by those who have an interest in businesses and business performance. Although ratios are not difficult to calculate, they can be difficult to interpret, and so it is important to appreciate that they are really only the starting point for further analysis.

Ratios help to highlight the financial strengths and weaknesses of a business, but they cannot, by themselves, explain why those strengths or weaknesses exist or why certain changes have occurred. Only a detailed investigation will reveal these under-lying reasons. Ratios tend to enable us to know which questions to ask, rather than provide the answers.

Ratios can be expressed in various forms, for example as a percentage or as a proportion. The way that a particular ratio is presented will depend on the needs of those who will use the information. Although it is possible to calculate a large number of ratios, only a few, based on key relationships, tend to be helpful to a particular user. Many ratios that could be calculated from the financial statements (for example, rent payable in relation to current assets) may not be considered because there is no clear or meaningful relationship between the two items.

There is no generally accepted list of ratios that can be applied to the financial statements, nor is there a standard method of calculating many ratios. Variations in both the choice of ratios and their calculation will be found in practice. However, it is important to be consistent in the way in which ratios are calculated for comparison purposes. The ratios that we shall discuss here are those that are widely used. They are popular because many consider them to be among the more important for decision-making purposes.

(McLaney and Atrill 2008: 222)

## Activity 5.8 Skimming a text 2

Take any text you have. Read the title and ask a question that you think may be addressed in the text. Read the first sentence of each paragraph in the text. You will then have a broad understanding of the content of the text. Does it answer your question?

## Skimming a text using first and last paragraphs

In most academic writing, the text is organised clearly with an introduction and a conclusion. The introduction gives you an idea of what the text is going to be about and the conclusion shows what it has been about. You can therefore get a good idea of the overall content of a text by reading the first and last paragraphs.

## Activity 5.9 **Skimming a text (3)**

Read the first and last paragraphs in the following text. Reading these sentences gives you a good idea about the meaning of the text. If you need to introduce the Queen's Counsel as one of the different legal professionals at the beginning of an assignment, this may be enough. However, if you have to do an in-depth comparison of the different members of the profession, it will not be.

### Queen's Counsel

After ten years in practice, a barrister may apply to become a Queen's Counsel, or QC (sometimes called a silk, as they wear gowns made of silk). This usually means they will be offered higher-paid cases, and need do less preliminary paperwork. The average annual earnings of a QC are £270,000, with a small group earning over £1 million a year. Not all barristers attempt or manage to become QCs — those that do not are called juniors, even up to retirement age. Juniors may assist QCs in big cases, as well as working alone. Since 1995, solicitors can also be appointed as QCs, but there are currently only eight QCs who come from the solicitor profession.

The future of the QC system was put in doubt when the Office of Fair Trading in 2001 suggested the system was merely a means of artificially raising the price of a barrister's services. The Bar Council counter-argued that, actually, the system was an important quality mark which directs the client to experienced, specialist lawyers where required.

In the past the appointment process for QCs was similar to that for senior judges, including the system of secret soundings, and with civil servants, a Cabinet Minister and the Queen all involved. In 2003 the appointment process was suspended, following criticism of the QC system. Appointments were recommended in 2004 but relying on a new appointment process. The Government is no longer involved. Instead, responsibility for appointments has been placed in the hands of the two professional bodies: the Bar Council and the Law Society. They select candidates on the basis of merit, following an open competition. The secret soundings system has been abolished and replaced by structured references from judges, lawyers and clients who have seen the candidate in action. A wider diversity of people are expected to be appointed, including more solicitor-advocates. The title of QC has been retained for the time being, though the Law Society would like to see it replaced with another name, to mark a clean break from the past, when the system clearly favoured barristers. Commenting on the new appointment procedures, the Law Society president stated:

> Consumers can be assured that holders of the QC designation under the new scheme have been awarded it because of what they know not who they know, and that their superior expertise and experience has been evaluated by an independent panel on an objective basis.

The Government's current view is that the badge of QC is a well-recognised and respected 'kitemark' of quality both at home and abroad. The existence of QCs helps enhance London's status as the centre of international litigation and arbitration.

**(Elliott and Quinn, 2008: 169)**

## Skimming a text, using section headings

In much academic writing, the text is organised through the use of headings and subheadings. You can therefore get a good idea of the overall content of a text by reading the headings and subheadings first.

The title, subtitles and section headings can help you formulate questions to keep you interacting with the text.

## Activity 5.10 Skimming a text (4)

Read the headings in the following text and answer the following question:

Which of the following determine whether custom can be a source of law?

(a) applies everywhere
(b) consistent and clear
(c) optional
(d) reasonable
(e) recent
(f) written down.

---

### When can custom be a source of law?

To be regarded as conferring legally enforceable rights, a custom must fulfil several criteria.

**'Time immemorial'**

It must have existed since 'time immemorial'. This was fixed by a statute in 1275 as meaning 'since at least 1189'. In practice today claimants usually seek to prove the custom has existed as far back as living memory can go, often by calling the oldest local inhabitant as a witness. However, this may not always be sufficient. In a dispute over a right to use local land in some way, for example, if the other side could prove that the land in question was under water until the seventeenth or eighteenth century, the right could therefore not have existed since 1189. In *Simpson* v *Wells* (1872), a charge of obstructing the public footway by setting up a refreshment stall was challenged by a claim that there was a customary right to do so derived from 'statute sessions', ancient fairs held for the purpose of hiring servants. It was then proved that statute sessions were first authorised by the Statutes of Labourers in the fourteenth century, so the right could not have existed since 1189.

**Reasonableness**

A legally enforceable custom cannot conflict with fundamental principles of right and wrong, so a customary right to commit a crime, for example, could never be accepted. In *Wolstanton Ltd* v *Newcastle-under-Lyme Corporation* (1940) the lord of a manor claimed a customary right to take minerals from under a tenant's land, without paying compensation for any damage caused to buildings on the land. It was held that this was unreasonable.

**Certainty and clarity**

It must be certain and clear. The locality in which the custom operates must be defined, along with the people to whom rights are granted (local fishermen, for example, or tenants

---

of a particular estate) and the extent of those rights. In *Wilson* v *Willes* (1806) the tenants of a manor claimed the customary right to take as much turf as they needed for their lawns from the manorial commons. This was held to be too vague, since there appeared to be no limit to the amount of turf which could be taken.

### Locality
It must be specific to a particular geographic area. Where a custom is recognised as granting a right, it grants that right only to those specified — a custom giving fishermen in Lowestoft the right to dry their nets on someone else's land would not give the same right to fishermen in Grimsby. Custom is only ever a source of local law.

### Continuity
It must have existed continuously. The rights granted by custom do not have to have been exercised continuously since 1189, but it must have been possible to exercise them at all times since then. In *Wyld* v *Silver* (1963), a landowner, wishing to build on land where the local inhabitants claimed a customary right to hold an annual fair, argued that the right had not been exercised within living memory. The court nevertheless granted an injunction preventing the building.

### Exercised as of right
It must have been exercised peaceably, openly and as of right. Customs cannot create legal rights if they are exercised only by permission of someone else. In *Mills* v *Colchester Corporation* (1867) it was held that a customary right to fish had no legal force where the right had always depended on the granting of a licence, even though such licences had traditionally been granted to local people on request.

### Consistency
It must be consistent with other local customs. For example, if a custom is alleged to give the inhabitants of one farm the right to fish in a lake, it cannot also give the inhabitants of another the right to drain the lake. The usual course where a conflict arises is to deny that the opposing custom has any force, though this is not possible if it has already been recognised by a court.

### Obligatory
Where a custom imposes a specific duty, that duty must be obligatory – a custom cannot provide that the lord of a manor grants villagers a right of way over his land only if he likes them, or happens not to mind people on his land that day.

### Conformity with statute
A custom which is in conflict with a statute will not be held to give rise to law.

(Elliott and Quinn, 2008: 94–6)

This chapter has only been able to deal with the kind of reading you need to do for your writing. You will also read for many other purposes: see Chapter 3 of Price and Maier (2007) for more information.

# READING AND NOTE-TAKING

## Taking notes

Taking notes is an important part of the life of every student who has to do background research in order to write. There are two main reasons why note-taking is important:

1 When you are reading, taking notes helps you concentrate and understand. In order to take notes – to write something sensible – you must understand the text. As reading is an interactive task, taking notes helps you make sense of the text. Taking notes does not mean writing down every word you read: you need actively to decide what is important and how it is related to what you have already written and – importantly – what else you need to find out.

2 Notes help you to maintain a record of what you have read. This is essential when you come to do your writing, or for revising in the future for examinations or other reasons.

Good notes should be accurate, clear and concise. They should show the organisation of the text, and this should show the relationship between the different ideas.

## How to take notes

When you are reading, there are several things that you need to do: you need to survey the text to see how it is organised and you need to find the main points and see how they are related. You also need to read for the subsidiary points and observe how they are related to the main points and to each other. As well as this, you need to reduce the points to notes, making sure that you make links to show the relationships between the ideas.

**TIP** *You cannot take good notes if you do not understand the structure of the text and the relationships in it.*

Good notes need to be organised appropriately. There are two main methods for this – lists and diagrams.

### Lists

The topic is summarised one point after another, using numbers and letters and indentation to organise information in order of importance. The numbers and letters can be used by themselves or in combination:

I, II, III
A, B, C, D
1, 2, 3
(i), (ii), (iii)
a, b, c

or using decimals:

1.1, 1.2, 1.2.1, 1.2.2, 1.3, 2.1, 2.2, 2.3

For example:
1. XXXX
2. XXXX
   a. XXXX
   b. XXXX
   c. XXXX
3. XXXX
   a. XXXX
   b. XXXX
      i. XXXX
      ii. XXXX
4. XXXX
   a. XXXX
   b. XXXX
5. XXXX

Notes are a summary and should therefore be much shorter than the original. Thus, abbreviations and symbols can be used whenever possible. Table 5.1 shows some conventional English symbols and abbreviations. You will need specific ones for your own subject.

Table 5.1 **Symbols and abbreviations**

| Full version | Symbol/abb. | Full version | Symbol/abb. | Full version | Symbol/abb. |
|---|---|---|---|---|---|
| and | & | government | govt. | pages | pp. |
| and others (people) | et al. | greater than | > | per cent | % |
| and other things | etc. | grows, increases | ↗ | plus | + |
| answer | A | important | N.B. | possibly | poss. |
| approximately | ≈ , approx., c. | in one year | p.a. | probably | prob. |
| at | @ | information | info. | proportional to | ∝ |
| because | ∵ | kilogram | kg | question | Q |
| before example | : | less than | < | results from | ← |
| centimetre | cm | male | ♂ | results in, leads to | → |

→

## Table 5.1 continued

| Full version | Symbol/abb. | Full version | Symbol/abb. | Full version | Symbol/abb. |
|---|---|---|---|---|---|
| century | C | maximum | max. | same as above (ditto) | " |
| chapter | ch. | minimum | min. | similar to | ≈ |
| compare | cf. | minus | – | that is to say, in other words | i.e. |
| correct | ✓ | much greater than | >> | therefore | ∴ |
| decreases, falls | ↘ | much less than | << | south | S |
| degrees | ° | multiplied by | × | unlikely | ?? |
| department | dept. | north | N | uncertain, not sure | ? |
| divided by | ÷ | not come from | ↚ | very | v. |
| east | E | not equal to | ≠ | with reference to | re. |
| equal to | = | not lead to | ↛ | wrong | ✗ |
| equivalent to | ≡ | not proportional to | ∝̸ | west | W |
| especially | esp. | not similar to | ≠ | year | yr. |
| female | ♀ | number | No. or # | | |
| for example | e.g. | page | p. | | |

**TIP** *Use your own symbols for regularly occurring words and phrases in your own subject.*

## Example

Read the following text and notice how notes have been taken in list format.

## Brand development

A company has four choices when it comes to developing brands. It can introduce *line extensions, brand extensions, multibrands* or *new brands.*

### Line extensions

Line extensions occur when a company extends existing brand names to new forms, colours, sizes, ingredients or flavours of an existing product category. Thus, after generations of keeping true to the original format of KitKat, Nestle's top chocolate bar, it successfully extended the two and four finger range to KitKat Chunky in 1999. This success was soon followed by repeated extensions including KitKat Low-Carb, KitKat Minis and KitKat Ice Cream. Finding their number two bar brand Aero was losing sales, in 2006 the brand was boosted by Aero Bubbles, a new line extension designed to compete with Mars's Maltesers.

A company introduces line extensions as a low-cost, low-risk way to introduce new products, or it might want to meet consumer desires for variety, to use excess capacity or simply to command more shelf-space from resellers. However, line extensions involve some risks. An overextended brand might lose its specific meaning, falling into the 'line-extension trap'. Heavily extended brands can also cause consumer confusion or frustration. A consumer buying cereal at a supermarket might be confronted by more than 150 brands, including up to 30 different brand flavours and sizes of oatmeal. Quaker alone offers its original Quaker Oats, several flavours of Quaker instant oatmeal, and several dry cereals such as Oatmeal Squares, Toasted Oatmeal and Toasted Oatmeal-Honey Nut.

Another risk is that sales of an extension may come at the expense of other items in the line. A line extension works best when it takes sales away from competing brands, not when it 'cannibalises' the company's other items.

### Brand extensions

A brand extension (or brand stretching) extends a current brand name to new or modified products in a new category. For example, Victorinox extended its venerable Swiss Army brand from multi-tool knives to products ranging from cutlery and ballpoint pens to watches, luggage and clothing. Swatch spread from watches into telephones. And Honda stretched its company name to cover different products such as its cars, motorcycles, lawnmowers, marine engines and snowmobiles.

A brand-extension strategy offers many advantages. A well-regarded brand name helps the company enter new product categories more easily as it gives a new product instant recognition and faster acceptance. For example, Sony puts its name on most of its new electronic products, creating an instant perception of high quality for each new product. A brand extension also saves the high advertising costs usually required to build a new brand name.

At the same time, a brand-extension strategy involves some risk. Brand extensions such as Bic pantyhose and fragrances, Heinz pet food and Cadbury soup and synthetic meat met early deaths. The extension may confuse the image of the main brand. And if a brand extension fails, it may harm consumer attitudes towards the other products carrying the same brand name.

Further, a brand name may not be appropriate to a particular new product, even though it is well made and satisfying. Would you consider buying a Harley-Davidson cake-decorating kit or an Evian water-filled padded bra (both tried and failed)? A brand name may lose its special positioning in the consumer's mind through overuse. *Brand dilution* occurs when consumers no longer associate a brand with a specific product or even highly similar

→

products. Companies that are tempted to transfer a brand name must research how well the brand's associations fit the new product.

## Multibrands

Companies often introduce additional brands in the same category. Thus, companies such as Unilever and Procter & Gamble market many different brands in each of their product categories. Multibranding offers a way to establish different features and appeal to different buying motives. It also allows a company to secure more reseller shelf-space. Or the company may want to protect its major brand by setting up *flanker* or *fighter brands*. Seiko uses different brand names for its higher-priced watches (Seiko Lasalle) and lower-priced watches (Pulsar) to protect the flanks of its mainstream Seiko brand. Further, companies such as Unilever, Nestle, Masterfoods and Procter & Gamble create individual brand identities for each of their products. Unilever's line of laundry detergents – Persil/Omo, Surf, etc. – have distinct labels, with the corporate name hardly featured. Similarly, Procter & Gamble produces at least nine brands of laundry products – Ariel, Bold, etc.

These manufacturers argue that a multibrand strategy permits finer segmentation of the market, with each brand name suggesting different functions or benefits appealing to different buying motives of different customer segments.

Some companies develop multiple brands, not for individual products but for different families of products. For example, the Japanese electronics group Matsushita uses range branding – it develops separate range names for its audio-hifi product families (Technics, National, Panasonic and Quasar).

A major drawback of multibranding is that each brand might obtain only a small market share, and none may be very profitable. The company may end up spreading its resources over many brands instead of building a few brands to a highly profitable level. These companies should reduce the number of brands they sell in a given category and set up tighter screening procedures for new brands.

The multibranding approach contrasts with the corporate branding strategy. In corporate branding, the firm makes its company name the dominant brand identity across all of its products, as in the case of Mercedes-Benz, Philips and Heinz. The main advantages are economies of scale in marketing investments and wider recognition of the brand name. It also facilitates the launch of new products, especially when the corporate name is well established.

Other companies have used a company and individual branding approach. This focuses on both the corporate and individual brand names. Kellogg's (e.g. Cornflakes, Just Right, Raisin Bran, Rice Krispies, Coco Pops, Nutri-Grain, etc.), Nestlé (KitKat, Nescafé, Coffee-Mate, etc.) and Cadbury's (e.g. Dairy Milk, Roses, Milk Tray) are supporters of this branding strategy.

## New brands

A company might believe that the power of its existing brand name is waning and a new brand name is needed. Or it may create a new brand name when it enters a new product category for which none of the company's current brand names are appropriate. Thus, Toyota established a separate family name — the Lexus — for its new luxury executive cars in order to create a distinctive identity for the latter and to position these well away from the traditional mass-market image of the Toyota brand name. And Siemens introduced a new line of upmarket, fashion mobile phones in 2003 under a new brand name — Xelibri — to create a distinctive identity for these phones.

As with multibranding, offering too many brands can result in a company spreading its resources too thinly. In some industries, such as consumer-packaged goods, consumers and retailers have become concerned that there are already too many brands, with too few differences between them. Thus, Lever Brothers, Procter & Gamble and other large consumer product marketers are now pursuing *megabrand* strategies — weeding out weaker brands and focusing their marketing dollars only on brands that can achieve the number-one or number-two market-share positions in their categories.

(Kotler *et al.* 2008: 530–3)

NOTES

<u>Develop brands</u> (Kotler, Armstrong, Wong & Saunders, 2008, pp. 530-533)
4 ways: line extension, brand extension, multibrands, new brands:

<u>Line ext</u> → diff. varieties -. new colours, flavours
e.g. Kit Kat →   chunky,
                 low carb
                 mini
                 ice-cream

Adv     low risk way to intro new prods
Dis      brand lose meaning
           at expense of other items

<u>Brand ext</u> → differ. Products – new or modified prods.
e.g. Victorinox (Swiss army knife)  cutlery
                                     pens
                                     watches

Adv     helps est. new prods
Dis      confuses brand image
           failure → harm main brand
           brand dilution

<u>Multibrands</u> → range of prods. – ↗ brands in same cat.
e.g.        Unilever →  Persil
                        Omo
                        Surf

Adv     estab. diff. features
           ↗ shelf space
           finer segmentation
Dis      small market share
           too widely spread
           ↘ corporate brand

<u>New Brands</u> – creates new brand name → ↗ luxury/up-market
e.g.        Toyota → Lexus

Adv     move into new market ↗
Dis      spread resources too thinly

## Diagrams

As well as summarising the content of a text, a diagram of the information shows how the main ideas are related and reflects the organisation of the information. You can use tables, flow charts, tree diagrams, diagrams or mind-maps (Buzan, 1974). You can also include circles, arrows, lines, boxes, etc.

In both ways, list or diagram, you can use headings, underlining, colours and white space to make the relationships clear. Generally there is no best layout – it depends on what you like and your purpose. Some ways of taking notes are more appropriate for some topics. A description of a process suits a flow chart and a classification is shown clearly using a tree diagram. Advantages and disadvantages work well in a table. It is important to show how the ideas are connected and how the information is organised.

## Example

Notes from the same text in table format are shown as follows:

Develop brands (Kotler, Armstrong, Wong & Saunders, 2008, pp.530-533)

4 ways: line extension, brand extension, multibrands, new brands:

| | e.g. | Adv | Dis |
|---|---|---|---|
| Line ext → diff. varieties -. new colours, flavours | Kit Kat → <br>• chunky, <br>• low carb <br>• mini <br>• ice-cream | • low risk way to intro new prods | • brand lose meaning <br>• at expense of other items |
| Brand ext → differ. Products – new or modified prods. | Victorinox (Swiss army knife) <br>• cutlery <br>• pens <br>• watches | • helps est. new prods | • confuses brand image <br>• failure → harm main brand <br>• brand dilution |
| Multibrands → range of prods. – ↗ brands in same cat. | Unilever → <br>• Persil <br>• Omo <br>• Surf | • estab. diff. features <br>• shelf space <br>• finer segmentation | • small market share <br>• too widely spread <br>• ↘ corporate brand |
| New Brands – creates new brand name → ↗ luxury/up-market | Toyota → <br>• Lexus | • move into new market ↗ | • spread resources too thinly |

## Example

This shows notes from the same text but in a tree diagram.

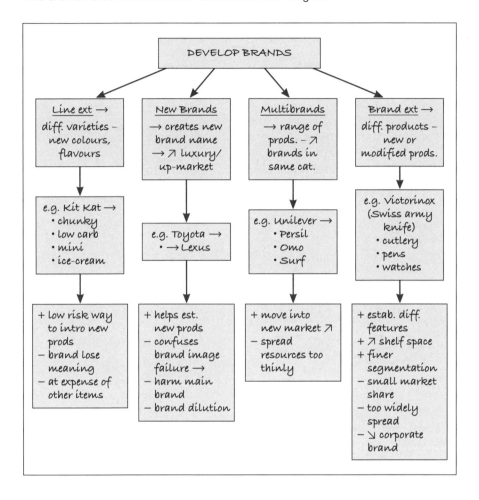

## Example

This shows notes from the same text but in a spidergram.

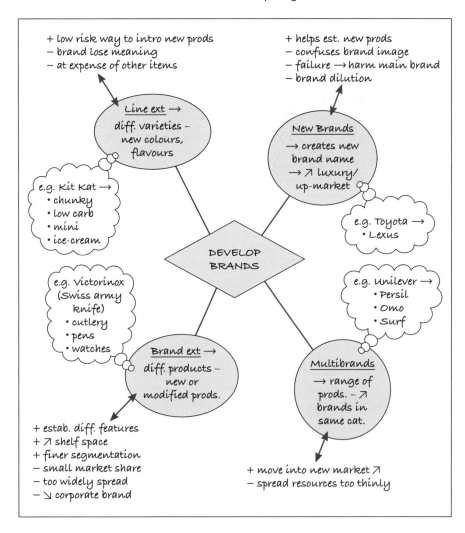

## Activity 5.11 Taking notes

Choose one of the note-taking methods exemplified above and take notes from the following text:

### Background of barristers and solicitors

Lawyers have, in the past, come from a very narrow social background, in terms of sex, race and class; there have also been significant barriers to entrants with disabilities. In recent years the professions have succeeded in opening their doors to a wider range of people, so that they are more representative of the society in which they work.

White, middle class men dominate in most professions, excluding many people who would be highly suited to such careers. A narrow social profile created particular problems for the legal professions in the past. First, it meant that the legal professions have been seen as unapproachable and elitist, which put off some people from using lawyers and thereby benefiting from their legal rights (this issue is examined in chapter 17). Secondly, the English judiciary is drawn from the legal professions and, if their background is narrow, that of the judiciary will be too (this issue is examined in chapter 10). Increasingly, the professions are becoming representative of the society in which they function.

**Women**

The number of women in the professions has increased dramatically since the 1950s. In 1987 women accounted for less than 20 per cent of all solicitors; now 41 per cent of solicitors are women. Today there are more women qualifying for the solicitor profession than men.

For the barrister profession in 2002, equal numbers of men and women qualified to practise and 32 per cent of barristers are women.

The problem now, for women, is less about entry into the professions and more about pay, promotion and working conditions. Female solicitors earn less than male solicitors. Despite the fact that there are more women achieving first and upper second class law degrees than men, in 1998 the Law Society's Annual Statistical Survey found that new female entrants were earning on average 4.4 per cent less than new male entrants. Male assistant solicitors earn £13,000 more than female assistant solicitors. Women who become partners in law firms earn on average £6,000 less than men in the same position.

Fewer women are being promoted to become partners in their law firm. Over 50 per cent of male solicitors are partners in their firm, compared to only 23 per cent of female solicitors. This cannot simply be explained by the fact that the average age of women solicitors is younger: 88 per cent of male solicitors in private practice with 10-19 years of experience were partners, compared with 63 per cent of female solicitors with the same experience. There is a similar problem in the barrister profession. In 2003, 112 men were made Queen's Counsel, but only nine women.

A growing problem exists of women choosing to leave the profession early. This is either because they find it impossible to combine the demands of motherhood with a legal career or because they are frustrated at the 'glass ceiling' which seems to prevent women lawyers from achieving the same success as their male counterparts. Solicitor firms do not tend to have provisions in place for flexible or part-time working for solicitors. Those that do, tend to discourage solicitors from taking advantage of them (Research Study No. 26 of the Law Society Research and Policy Planning Unit (1997)). The Law Society has recognised that in order to retain women and to ensure that the investment in their training is not lost, the profession must consider more flexible work arrangements (including career breaks) to allow women (and men) to continue to work alongside caring responsibilities.

The legal profession also needs to tackle the long hours culture to stem the flow of women lawyers leaving the profession. The macho culture of working long hours forces women, who often have to juggle work and family, out of the legal world.

### Ethnic minorities

Again, the picture is improving. The number of solicitors from ethnic minority groups has increased recently. In 2003, 8 per cent of practising solicitors came from an ethnic minority. This compares with 4 per cent in 1995. In 2003, 17 per cent of trainee solicitors were from a minority ethnic group. There are still, however, very few male Afro-Caribbean solicitors.

As regards the Bar, in 1989, 5 per cent of practising barristers came from an ethnic minority; in 2003 they made up 11 per cent of practising barristers and 20 per cent of pupils. This compares favourably with other professions.

Regrettably, there have in the past been reports in the media of black candidates doing less well in legal examinations than white candidates, particularly at the Bar. It has been suggested that oral examinations may be particularly vulnerable to subjective marking.

The Law Society has recognised that obstacles still exist for ethnic minorities in the solicitor profession. This is because most solicitor firms do not follow proper recruitment procedures, do not have an equal opportunities policy and practice, and the levels of discrimination within society at large are reflected in the perception of solicitors and their clients. Only 23 per cent of black and minority ethnic solicitors are partners in their firms, compared to 39 per cent of white solicitors.

### Class

The biggest obstacle to a career in law now seems to be class background. Law degree students are predominantly middle class, with less than one in five coming from a working class background. A 1989 Law Society Survey found that over a third of solicitors had come from private schools, despite the fact that only 7 per cent of the population attend such schools. In recent years, more lawyers have been educated in the state sector, but this progress could soon be reversed. This is because the lack of funding for legal training has made it very difficult for students without well-off parents to qualify, especially as barristers.

The chair of the Bar Council has warned that Government plans to allow universities to charge top-up fees will stop students from poorer backgrounds pursuing a career in law.

One possible source of change for the future is the number of part-time law degrees and Legal Practice Courses now available to mature students, who tend to come from a much broader range of backgrounds than those who attend university straight from school. Students on part-time courses can support themselves by continuing to work while they study in the evenings and at weekends.

### Disability

Much attention has been paid to the under-representation of working class people, ethnic minorities and women in the legal profession, but disabled people are less often discussed. Skill as a lawyer requires brains, not physical strength or dexterity, yet it seems there are still significant barriers to entry for disabled students, particularly to the Bar. Part of the problem is simply practical: a quarter of court buildings are over 100 years old and were never designed to offer disabled access. Most now have rooms adapted for disabled people, but need notice if they are to be used, which is hardly feasible for junior barristers, who often get cases at very short notice. The other main barrier is effectively the same as that for ethnic minorities, working-class people and women: with fierce competition for places, 'traditional' applicants have the advantage.

Steps are being taken to address the problems of disabled applicants to the Bar. In 1992, the Bar's Disability Panel was established. This offers help to disabled people who are already within the profession or are hoping to enter it, by matching them to people who have overcome or managed to accommodate similar problems. The Inner Temple also gives grants for reading devices, special furniture and other aids, with the aim of creating a 'level playing field' for disabled and able-bodied people.

(Elliott and Quinn: 2008, 171–2)

Make sure you write down where your notes have been taken from. It will save you time when you need to check your facts or write a bibliography. In lecture notes, make sure you write down the name of anyone quoted and the source of the quote. You can then find it if you want to make more detailed use of the information.

**TIP** *Different texts will probably suggest different note-taking styles. Decide which is most suitable for your purpose.*

# SUMMARY

Now that you have completed this chapter, you should have a good idea of the preliminary work you need to do for a piece of academic writing. This chapter has focused on developing effective reading strategies in order for you to manage the large amount of reading you need to do in higher education. It has stressed the importance of making use of all your knowledge and skills to deal with the process of reading. It has also looked at the importance of taking good quality notes and suggested some ways in which you might want to do this.

It is now time to get on to the actual writing.

## References

Buzan, T. (1974) *Use your Head.* London: BBC Publications.

MacLachlan, G. and Reid, I. (1994) *Framing and Interpretation.* Melbourne: Melbourne University Press.

Price, G. and Maier, P. (2007) *Effective Study Skills*. Harlow: Pearson Education.

Details of highlighted references can be found in the Introduction on page xxii.

# 6 ▶ FEATURES OF ACADEMIC WRITING

By joining a course in higher education you have become a member of an academic community. Therefore, when you write academic texts, you are expected to communicate with other members of that community in an acceptable manner. This chapter aims to help you unlock the mystery of academic writing by providing you with guidelines and practical activities.

This chapter will cover:

- the style conventions of an academic text
- developing paragraphs and turning them into organised and cohesive text
- writing plans
- writing drafts.

## USING THIS CHAPTER

# INTRODUCTION

In academic writing you are expected to produce logically-structured ideas with well-argued, substantiated points, taking different opinions into consideration. There are various genres of academic writing, such as essays, reports, lab reports, case studies and dissertations. Regardless of the genre you are writing in, your style of writing should be the same – clear, concise, with appropriately referenced ideas. In higher education one of the main things you will be judged on is the quality of your writing. This chapter considers the various elements required in an academic text from word through to paragraph level. It offers advice on text cohesion and emphasises the need for planning and drafting work.

# ACADEMIC STYLE

If you are not sure about the difference between formal and informal language, try reading widely and critically. Read a popular newspaper article and a friend's letter or email, and then read a page of a book or a journal from your recommended reading list. You will soon begin to see there is a difference in the style of these texts.

## Activity 6.1 Identifying formality

Below are three excerpts.

**(a)** Can you identify the context each one may be found in?
**(b)** Can you recognise the differences between them?

### Excerpt 1

A clear problem in academic writing is that of the assessor or 'assignment setter', as described by Ivanic and Simpson (1992:146). 'This person is posing a challenge and a threat to the student, and positioning him as a writer, and exercising control over him. However stimulating the assignment may be . . . it is also face-threatening because it will be judged.' Students' knowledge that the work they have written will be assessed may oblige them to consider their writing from different perspectives, namely what *they* deem acceptable and what their *tutors* deem acceptable. This is often difficult for students to achieve.

### Excerpt 2

**?4U. Who 8 my pizza? CYAL8R. <3**

(Retrieved 25 June 2008 from http://www.webopedia.com/quick_ref/textmessageabbreviations.asp)

### Excerpt 3

I don't think there is a case for this argument at all. How could anyone imagine putting such a proposal forward when it's so clearly ludicrous? I believe that the more people are aware of this issue, the better off we would all be.

## Activity 6.2 Identifying formal and informal features

1 Find examples of the following features in the excerpts on the preceding page and write them in the appropriate column. (Some squares will remain blank.)

|  | Excerpt 1 is a formal text | Excerpts 2 and 3 are informal texts |
|---|---|---|
| Formal vocabulary |  |  |
| Passive voice |  |  |
| Cautious language |  |  |
| Objective language |  |  |
| Subjective language |  |  |
| Emotive language |  |  |
| Use of questions |  |  |
| Contracted forms |  |  |
| References |  |  |

2 Now look at the content of each column. What differences and similarities do you notice between the features found in each excerpt?

Each of these features of academic writing will now be looked at in more detail. (References are dealt with in Chapter 10.)

# Formal vocabulary

Academic writing uses more formal vocabulary than spoken language. Students often feel that it is difficult to distinguish between formal and less formal language. The following written sentence would be perfectly acceptable for instance:

He tried to show that it was possible to lose weight and eat his favourite food.

Consider the same sentence written more formally:

He attempted to prove that losing weight whilst eating his favourite meals was achievable.

The second example somehow seems more authoritative and is better placed in the academic world rather than in a magazine.

The reason for using formal expressions is not because academic language is pompous, but because it is clearer. Consider the following example:

Roberts (2007) says that lower house prices do not affect you if you are not planning to sell your property.

The use of 'says' seems clear enough but it is not *specific* enough. Does Roberts *think* that is the case, or is he *certain*? Can we tell what his attitude to lower house prices is? Consider how the meaning of the sentence is affected if *says* is replaced by *suggests*, or *stresses*, or even *claims*.

> Roberts (2007) claims that lower house prices do not affect homeowners if they are not planning to sell their property.

See
Chapter 11
The implication with this example is that the reader cannot be sure whether to believe Roberts or not. This nuance in meaning is not there when the word *says* instead of *claims* is used.

## Activity 6.3 From informal to formal

Find more formal words or phrases to replace those underlined below:

1  Research <u>shows</u> ...                                    _____

2  Three problems have been <u>found</u>.                       _____

3  The changes he made were <u>bad</u>.                         _____

4  <u>Lots of</u> people think ...                             _____

5  There were many <u>reasons</u> for this.                    _____

6  Scientists have <u>tried</u> to prove ...                   _____

7  £100,000 was <u>given</u> to charity.                       _____

8  He discussed issues <u>like</u> famine and poverty.         _____

9  She <u>has got to</u> find alternatives.                    _____

10  We do not have <u>enough</u> resources.                    _____

# Multi-word verbs

Multi-word verbs such as 'look up (an entry in an encyclopaedia)' or 'go out of (a building)' are often used in spoken English but are considered too informal for academic writing. Multi-word verbs always have a more formal equivalent; in this case 'consult' and 'leave'.

You need to choose your words carefully to make your meaning as clear as possible. In order to help you find appropriate alternatives, we recommend that you frequently consult a thesaurus.

## Activity 6.4 Finding synonyms

Find suitable synonyms to replace the underlined multi-word verbs below:

1 There are many issues to <u>think about</u>.   _____

2 They <u>carried out</u> an investigation.   _____

3 The situation <u>got worse</u>.   _____

4 The research tried to <u>find out</u> these causes.   _____

5 Many areas were <u>looked into</u>.   _____

6 Interest rates are <u>going up</u>.   _____

7 This has been <u>going on</u> for a while.   _____

8 The information is <u>broken down</u> into sections.   _____

9 He managed to <u>get by</u> on very little food.   _____

10 Five candidates <u>showed up at</u> the interview.   _____

# Use of the passive voice

In your academic studies you will often come across the passive voice, for example:

**The report was written.** (passive: use of 'be' + past participle)

In spoken English a subject such as 'people', 'somebody', 'they', 'we' or 'you' is often used when it is not clear who the person doing the action is. For example, 'they forecast rain for today'. In academic writing, the passive is often preferred: 'rain was forecast for today'.

Compare:

**We interviewed 65 students.** (active)

with

**65 students were interviewed.** (passive)

It is not merely a question of changing your active sentences into passive ones. You will need to consider a number of factors as illustrated below.

If you are a literature student writing about Jane Austen's characterisation in *Pride and Prejudice* you may find that the person you are describing must be stated for the meaning to be clear. Consider:

**Mrs Bennet was looking for a potential suitor for Elizabeth.**

as opposed to:

**A potential suitor for Elizabeth was being sought.**

## 6 Features of academic writing

The second example, which uses the passive, is in this case unclear, as the person doing the seeking is not stated. It would therefore be more appropriate to specify the person rather than use the passive in this case.

If, on the other hand, you are a history student writing about the mummification process, you are more likely to write:

**The body of the dead king was wrapped in linen.**

as opposed to:

**People wrapped the body of the dead king in linen.**

In this case, the second example does not provide the reader with further information by adding the word 'people'. The first example using the passive is more appropriate.

When you are writing you will therefore need to decide whether the action or the result is more important than the person carrying it out. Ask questions such as *Who are "they"?*, and *Are "they" more important in that sentence than the act?* If yes, you may choose to state them using the active voice. If no, you may omit them using the passive voice.

## Activity 6.5 Writing passive sentences

Rewrite the underlined parts of these sentences. Instead of using 'we', 'the researchers', or 'they', write a passive sentence with an appropriate verb form.

Example: <u>We can solve the problem.</u> *The problem can be solved.*

(a) Prices are stable and <u>we have maintained them</u> in this way over generations.

(b) <u>We define tropical forests</u> here as 'evergreen or partly evergreen forests'.

(c) <u>We will confine the discussion</u> to general principles of treatment.

(d) <u>The researchers transcribed many genes and synthesised many proteins.</u>

(e) <u>They replicated these findings.</u>

(a) _____

(b) _____

(c) _____

(d) _____

(e) _____

A further way of avoiding the use of 'they' or 'people' is by introducing the sentence with the impersonal 'it' leading to expressions such as 'it is felt that...' or 'it is thought that...'. Consider the following examples:

**It is felt that the police are doing valuable work.**

**It was thought that the government had shown little regard for public opinion.**

The alternative would have been:

**People feel that the police are doing valuable work.**

Which people? Are they important?

**Everyone thought that the government had shown little regard for public opinion.**

Who is 'everyone' exactly? Is this word needed for the meaning of the sentence to be clear?

In many cases a different construction is also possible such as 'X is felt to ...' or 'X is thought to ...'. For example:

**The police are felt to be doing valuable work.**

**The government was thought to have shown little regard for public opinion.**

The table below indicates some choices to help you construct passive sentences. (Please note that not all combinations are possible.)

| It | is<br>was<br>has/have been<br>may be/could be | felt<br>thought<br>believed<br>claimed | that |
|----|----|----|----|

Or:

| X (the government, the representatives, the producers) | is/are<br>was/were<br>has/have been<br>may be/could be | felt<br>thought<br>believed<br>claimed | to be ...<br>to have done ... |
|----|----|----|----|

Whichever construction you use make sure your meaning is clear.

## Activity 6.6 Constructing passive sentences

Rewrite the following sentences using any of the passive sentence constructions outlined earlier:

1 People consider that this surgeon is a brilliant practitioner.
2 Somebody claims that the drug produced no undesirable side effects.
3 Most people now think that only a small fraction of the nitrous oxide emitted to the atmosphere each year comes from fossil fuel use, primarily coal.
4 Researchers believe that the only problem with daytime sleep is that it is too short.
5 Although the government expects the patient to pay for his treatment, he will be reimbursed via the state medical insurance scheme.

1 _____

2 _____

3 _____

4 _____

5 _____

# Cautious language

See Chapter 11
In any kind of academic writing you do, it is necessary to make decisions about your stance on a particular subject, or the strength of claims you are making. It is unlikely that the evidence you present will be conclusive enough for you to state that something will definitely happen. At the same time, you need to be careful about making sweeping statements which do not consider exceptions. This is why academic writing often calls for a cautious style. There are various ways in which caution can be expressed. This includes using appropriate modal verbs, adverbs, adjectives and other lexical items. Caution will be addressed in more detail in Chapter 11.

# Objective versus subjective language

Written academic language is in general objective rather than personal. It therefore has fewer words that refer to the writer or the reader. This means that the main emphasis should be on the information you want to give and the arguments you want to make, rather than you. People reading your work want to know what you have studied and learned and how this has led you to your various conclusions. The thoughts and beliefs you express should be based on your lectures, reading, discussions and research, and it is important to make this clear in your writing. Compare the following two paragraphs. Which paragraph is the most objective?

---

**Paragraph 1**

Marketers may sometimes face dilemmas when seeking to balance consumer needs and social responsibility. For example, no amount of test results can guarantee product safety in cars if consumers value speed and power more than safety features. Buyers may choose a less expensive chain-saw without a safety guard, although society or a government regulatory agency might deem it irresponsible and unethical for the manufacturer to sell it.

**Paragraph 2**

Marketers have a responsibility to society and they often don't know how to balance that with what customers might need. Why should someone care about the safety features of a car for example, if they like speed and power more? And even though society or the government should not allow shops to sell chain-saws without safety guards, what about if I want a cheaper product which doesn't include the guards?

(Kotler *et al.*, 2008: 77)

---

Generally, in order to write objectively you need to avoid using words like 'I', 'me', and 'you'. If you do not reference an idea, the reader will assume it is yours, so you do not need to make this more explicit by adding 'I think'. It would be more appropriate to use impersonal language such as:

- it is worthwhile to consider . . .
- the data indicates that . . .
- more concrete evidence is needed before . . .
- several possibilities emerge . . .

## Activity 6.7 **Subjective language**

Underline all the examples of subjective language in the following paragraph.

Everybody knows about the threat of global warming to our earth. We all pollute the atmosphere with gases and we all throw away rubbish that could be recycled. As far as I am concerned, these are two aspects that can be improved. I believe that everyone should use more public transport and leave their car at home. I also think that we can all learn to recycle more of our plastic and glass bottles. Even our left-over food can be used as compost.

## Activity 6.8 **Objective style**

Rewrite the paragraph in Activity 6.7 using a more objective and more formal style.

# Emotive language

See
Chapter 9

It follows that using a more objective style in your writing makes the text impersonal. There is therefore little room for emotive language which shows your personal attitude such as unfortunately, luckily, surprisingly, thankfully and other adverbs, unless you are writing reflectively.

# Use of questions

Some student writers use questions to introduce the point they wish to make next.

> **Increasing numbers of students are choosing Business Studies as their university subject. What is the reason for this? Many students believe ...**

You will often find this style in non-academic articles on the Internet though you may also find examples in your coursebooks. Whereas for students this would be an acceptable style for oral presentations, questions should not be used in academic writing. The above example could be rewritten in the following way:

> **Increasing numbers of students are choosing Business Studies as their university subject. The reason for this is that many students believe ...**

## Activity 6.9 Substituting questions

Remove the questions from the following paragraphs and make any necessary adjustments to the texts.

1 What is the symbolic importance of the jury? Jury trial represents judgment by one's peers. The jury is therefore seen as a major control over abuse of state power. **(Elliott and Quinn, 2008: 224)**

2 Suctioning is associated with several complications. What can be done to minimise or decrease these complications? There are several techniques which can be used, such as hyperinflation and hyperoxygenation. **(Kozier et al., 2008: 403)**

3 What is the overall variation of the impedance? As can be seen, for frequency $f_1$, the inductive reactance AB and the capacitive reactance AC are equal in magnitude so that the resultant reactance is zero. Consequently, the impedance is then only the resistance AD of the circuit. **(Hughes, 2008: 300)**

4 What is the financial objective of a business? A business is normally set up with a view to increasing the wealth of its owners. **(McLaney and Atrill, 2008: 25)**

# Contracted forms

See
Chapter 15

Contracted words such as 'don't', 'can't', 'shouldn't' are informal and should not normally be used when writing in an academic context (unless they are quotations which cannot be changed).

# CRITICAL WRITING

As we explained earlier, academic writing involves you expressing ideas, opinions and facts which you have read, heard in lectures and discussed. Remember that the information you consult helps you formulate new ideas and opinions as well as re-inforcing your current knowledge. As you read different texts on your subject, you will be exposed to differing views and these views will help you build your argument in a given academic assignment. Writing critically means making the best use of the material you have consulted which involves careful thought, analysis, comparison and decision-making.

Students who do not write critically tend to regurgitate their lecturers' notes or text-book material with no analysis, overuse quotations without expanding on the ideas further and treat information found in sources as facts to be reproduced. Chapter 8 covers writing critically in more detail – questioning, analysing and comparing the sources. As you progress through your studies, there is an increased expectation that you will write critically.

## Activity 6.10 Identifying features of critical writing

Compare the following extracts from essays.

1 Which extract is a better example of critical writing?
2 What features are more apparent in the better extract?

---

**Extract A**

Martindale (2003) states that Ann Kelley, a neuroscientist at the University of Wisconsin Medical School in Madison claims that she has discovered that rats who overindulge in tasty foods show marked, long-lasting changes in their brain chemistry similar to those caused by extended use of morphine or heroin. When she looked at the brain of rats that received highly palatable food for two weeks, she saw a decrease in gene expression for enkephalin in the nucleus accumbens. 'This says that mere exposure to pleasurable, tasty foods is enough to change gene expression, and that suggests you could be addicted to food.'                                                                    (Martindale, 2003: 43).

---

**Extract B**

The consequences of not moderating the intake of fast food are rather alarming. Experiments on rats carried out at the University of Wisconsin Medical School in Madison indicate that overindulgence in foods high in sugars and fat results in long-lasting changes to the brain chemistry similar to those caused by extended use of morphine or heroin. According to Martindale the results highlight that '... mere exposure to pleasurable, tasty foods is enough to change gene expression, and that suggests you could be addicted to food' (2003: 43). A consequence of eating fast food is therefore a tendency to become

---

addicted to it. As addiction means an abnormal dependency on something (Collins, 1984), there is perhaps cause for concern. It is clearly important that people are made aware of the potential threat of fast food. Coupled with research on young American children and the rise of obesity by more than 42% over the last 25 years (Schlosser, 1998), educating people on the risks associated with fast food from an early age is essential.

You will have noticed that both extracts in Activity 6.10 use sources and reference them appropriately.

You may have also noticed some or all of the following differences between them:

| Points in text | Extract 1 | Extract 2 |
|---|---|---|
| Starting sentence | The main message is lost amidst references to places and people. | It introduces the topic of the paragraph more specifically with writer's own voice coming through. |
| Description of rat experiment | It has been described in too much detail. | The irrelevant detail has been omitted. |
| Use of Martindale reference | The quote is used to make the point rather than to support it. | References are used to support the writer's own point. |
| Synthesis of ideas | Ideas are combined well but irrelevant detail should be omitted and use of sources needs development. | Ideas from two sources are linked well in an attempt to put forward the point about educating people young. |
| Overall | The *start* of a good attempt at critical writing. The information is there but needs to be made clearer with better use of sources and the writer's own voice coming through. | This is a good attempt at critical writing. The writer of extract 2 has begun and ended the paragraph with their own opinion and has used the sources to support their claim. |

A well-written, critical academic text should include the features in Extract 2.

## Activity 6.11 Ensuring you write critically

When writing your own assignment, read through your work carefully using the checklist below as a guide of what not to do. First of all:

- Have you reproduced your lecturer's words or examples?
- Have you copied information from a textbook?
- Have you used too many quotes? (More than three per A4 page, for example.)
- Have you allowed a quote to make your point?

If you have answered yes to any of the above, you will need to look at the following suggestions:

1 You *can* use your lecturer's words or those of an author but you should make sure that:
   - you use your own words (paraphrase) rather than overquote, and, perhaps more importantly,
   - you expand on the idea that the quote provides. (You either discuss it further or link it to another idea, or question it, compare it and provide examples, but you should never let it stand by itself.)
2 Make sure your own voice can be heard through your writing. Look at Chapter 11 for more information on voice.

ter 11

# REFERENCING

Although referencing is covered in more detail in Chapter 10, it is inevitably linked to critical writing as shown in the previous section. When you formulate your arguments based on the sources you have consulted, you need to make sure you are acknowledging the authors of those sources. After all, the ideas came from them. A written text with no references is not an academic one and it will be marked as poor.

A well-written academic text makes use of all the features outlined above and is written in a logical, organised and clear manner. The next part of this chapter helps you achieve this by focusing on the main body of an assignment – the paragraphs in which you express your argument.

# DEVELOPING PARAGRAPHS

Academic texts should be divided into paragraphs. If your text is one continuous piece of writing, it will be very difficult for any reader to follow your argument. More importantly, academic texts need to be divided into paragraphs in a meaningful way.

A paragraph is a group of sentences that develop one theme or idea. The theme of one paragraph should follow logically from the theme of the last paragraph and should lead on to the theme of the next paragraph. The paragraphs have different functions, but all *develop* an idea – that is, they add information, explanation, examples and illustrations to the central theme or idea until the theme is fully developed.

## Topic sentences

You should generally express the main theme of each paragraph by one sentence (the main or topic sentence). This sentence is best placed at the beginning of the paragraph as it will inform the reader of your point early on in the paragraph. The rest of the paragraph should then expand the theme contained in the main sentence, and each idea around the main theme should be supported by further information, evidence and argument. In Chapter 5 you will have seen how you can make use of these topic sentences when reading.

In Extract B of Activity 6.10 you saw the following sentence:

> The consequences of not moderating the intake of fast food are rather alarming.

This first sentence of the paragraph acts as the topic sentence. It expresses the theme that there are disturbing consequences if we eat too much fast food.

## Activity 6.12 Dividing a text into paragraphs

Divide the following text into three paragraphs by adding '//' where you think one paragraph ends and the other begins. Remember that each paragraph should begin with a topic sentence. The idea introduced in that topic sentence is then developed.

Respiration is the act of breathing. External respiration refers to the interchange of oxygen and carbon dioxide between the alveoli of the lungs and the pulmonary blood. Internal respiration, by contrast, takes place throughout the body; it is the interchange of these same gases between the circulating blood and the cells of the body tissues. Inhalation or inspiration refers to the intake of air into the lungs. Exhalation or expiration refers to breathing out or the movement of gases from the lungs to the atmosphere. Ventilation is also used to refer to the movement of air in and out of the lungs. There are basically two types of breathing: costal (thoracic) breathing and diaphragmatic (abdominal) breathing. Costal breathing involves the external intercostal muscles and other accessory muscles, such as the sternocleidomastoid muscles. It can be observed by the movement of the chest upward and outward. By contrast, diaphragmatic breathing involves the contraction and relaxation of the diaphragm, and it is observed by the movement of the abdomen, which occurs as a result of the diaphragm's contraction and downward movement.

(Kozier *et al.*, 2008: 356)

# Supporting sentences

The aim of the supporting sentences (note that there needs to be more than one) is to develop the topic of your paragraph.

If you read the earlier topic sentence by itself:

the consequences of not moderating the intake of fast food are rather alarming

hopefully, your immediate reaction would be, 'What are these consequences?' You would expect the writer now to provide you with answers to:

1 What are these consequences?
2 What makes them alarming?

You would also expect the writer to provide this information with evidence from the sources they have read (with references).

## Activity 6.13 Evaluating supporting sentences

Look back at Extract B of Activity 6.10 and using the two questions above, evaluate to what extent these questions have been answered.

# Creating topic sentences

When writing your topic sentence you need to know what the main theme of your paragraph is. It is important to strike the right balance. You should not write too general a sentence. You should try to focus your idea whilst at the same time you should not give too much detail.

## Activity 6.14 Identifying suitable topic sentences

1 Consider the following examples. In your opinion, and bearing in mind the above criteria, which of the three sentences is the most suitable topic sentence? Why?
   (a) Growing vegetables in your back garden is fun.
   (b) Growing vegetables in your back garden requires time and patience.
   (c) Growing vegetables in your back garden can be very rewarding because you can watch the vegetables grow and then you can pick them and use them in your cooking.

   Answer: _____

2 Now do the same with the following sentences:
   (a) There are three areas to consider when marketing a new product.
   (b) Marketing a new product is difficult.

→

(c) When marketing a new product you need to analyse the market by identifying your target audience and looking at your competitors.

Answer: _____

3 And again with these:
  (a) There seems to be a mismatch between teachers' and students' expectations.
  (b) There seems to be a mismatch between the way teachers and students view academic writing.
  (c) Students seem to rate writing skills relatively low on their learning priority scale as they do not realise the importance of writing in their academic life.

Answer: _____

## Activity 6.15 Matching topic sentences to supporting sentences

Each of the following sentences provides supporting information. Choose a suitable topic sentence from the list below to introduce each of these sentences. The sentences are not dependent on each other and are therefore not intended to be read in a linear way.

1 Firstly, if an island is created by the loss of a land bridge to the mainland, following a sea-level rise, the new 'continental' island might initially be species-rich. (p. 255).
2 Land reclamation suggests that the land can be used again whereas land restoration is about returning the site to its former state. (p. 261).
3 Many regions of the world have experienced major climatic change to which plants and animals have been forced to adjust in order to survive. (p. 250).
4 Islands often provide as near a situation to a scientific laboratory that the biogeographer is likely to encounter. (p. 254).
5 This may be in order to increase the efficiency of its production or to control the spread of pest species. (p. 257).

Choose from the following topic sentences. You will *not* need one of the topic sentences provided:

(a) The study of isolated areas such as islands has provided knowledge and understanding of huge importance.
(b) Many aspects of biogeography have great relevance and impact today.
(c) Several important extensions of land biogeography theory are used in biogeography and elsewhere to explain patterns of distribution.
(d) There is often an economic as well as scientific reason for learning about the preferred 'geography' of a species.
(e) Biogeographical management may involve land restoration or land reclamation.

(f)   Over a lesser but still extended period of time, climatic fluctuations over the past 2 million years have been important determinants of biogeographical change.

Answers: 1 ____, 2 ____, 3 ____, 4 ____, 5 ____

(Holden, J. (ed.) 2008)

## Activity 6.16 Writing topic sentences

Read the following paragraphs and create a suitable topic sentence for each one.

1  (On people's views of nature)

> ................................................... Some feel ruled by it, others feel in harmony with it and still others seek to master it. A long-term trend has been people's growing mastery over nature through technology and the belief that nature is bountiful. More recently, however, people have recognised that nature is finite and fragile – that it can be destroyed or spoiled by human activities.                              **(Kotler *et al.*, 2008: 221)**

2  (On media planners choosing among media types)

> ................................................... They want to choose media that will effectively and efficiently present the advertising message to target customers. Thus, they must consider each medium's impact, message effectiveness and cost. The media habits of target consumers will affect media choice and so will the nature of the product.
>
> **(Kotler *et al.*, 2008: 748)**

3  (On social interactions)

> ...............................................Because of hereditary differences, one child may be more sociable; this child will be the recipient of more interaction. Another child may be abrasive and disagreeable; this child will be treated more coldly. In the case of identical twins, who have no hereditary differences, the amount of interaction with each twin is likely to be similar.                              **(Martin *et al.*, 2008: 657)**

# Developing supporting sentences

To help you develop relevant supporting sentences, it may help if you ask questions of your topic sentence. You could then answer those questions by doing the following:

- Provide an explanation/reasons for the idea in the topic sentence. Why is it so?
- Provide evidence to support the topic sentence.
- Provide examples where appropriate to expand on your claim in the topic sentence.

Look at the following topic sentences and ask questions of them:

(a) Partial dictation may be considered as an alternative.
(b) Plug gages are one of the most common types of fixed gages.
(c) The intensity of the north–south exchange is shown in many, often unexpected, ways.

Now try to answer the questions you formed in Activity 6.17, thus in fact writing supporting sentences. You may of course choose to create your own topic sentences for this activity.

## Concluding sentences

We suggested that you begin each paragraph with a topic sentence to help guide your reader. To assist your reader further, you may also choose to add concluding sentences at the end of the paragraphs. This is particularly useful if your paragraph is long and you have included a number of examples and supporting evidence. It is possible that by the end of the paragraph your reader may have lost the main point you are trying to make. By adding a concluding sentence, you are reiterating your point before moving onto the next paragraph.

Concluding sentences are relatively easy to write. Look at Table 6.1 (signalling words), choose one word or phrase from the 'summary/conclusion' row and rephrase your topic sentence so you are not exactly repeating it. Alternatively you can summarise your paragraph or link with the point in the next paragraph.

Turn the topic sentences you have devised in Activity 6.16 into concluding sentences.

## Connecting ideas within sentences and sentences within paragraphs (signalling)

So far you have practised how to start, develop and end a paragraph. You also need to make clear to the reader how the various parts of your paragraph are connected. The information in the paragraph must flow easily from one sentence to the next. To do this, it is important to structure your information clearly and signal exactly what you want to say by the use of signalling words. Notice that signalling words do not always start a sentence. They may also be found within a sentence as in 'many people attended because of the successful promotion'. Table 6.1 is intended as a guide to which signalling words should be used in which context.

## Table 6.1 Signalling words

| Addition | apart from this, as well as, besides, furthermore, in addition, moreover, nor, not only ... but also, too, what is more |
|---|---|
| Cause and effect | accordingly, as a consequence, as a result, because (of this), consequently, for this reason, hence, in order to, owing to this, so, so that, therefore, this leads to, thus |
| Comparison/ similar ideas | in comparison, in the same way, likewise, similarly |
| Condition | if, in that case, provided that, unless |
| Contradiction | actually, as a matter of fact, in fact |
| Contrast/ opposite ideas | although, but, despite, in spite of, even so, however, in contrast, in spite of this, nevertheless, on the contrary, on the other hand, whereas, yet |
| Emphasis | chiefly, especially, importantly, indeed, in detail, in particular, mainly, notably, particularly |
| Examples | for example, for instance, such as, thus, as follows |
| Explanation/ equivalence | in other words, namely, or rather, this means, to be more precise |
| Generalisation | as a rule, for the most part, generally, in general, normally, on the whole, in most cases, usually |
| Stating the obvious | clearly, naturally, obviously, surely |
| Summary/ conclusion | finally, in brief, in conclusion, in short, in summary, overall, to conclude |
| Support | actually, as a matter of fact, in fact, indeed |
| Time/order | at first, eventually, finally, first(ly), in the first/second place, initially, lastly, later, next, prior to, second(ly) |

Another useful way to show the connection between the ideas in a paragraph is to start the second or subsequent sentence with a phrase such as 'this problem' or 'this situation'. These phrases help provide a connection by summarising the previous sentence.

**Students often struggle to provide adequate links between sentences. This problem can be overcome easily.**

The use of 'this problem' clearly relates to 'struggling to provide adequate links between sentences', which has been replaced by this linking phrase. Using 'this' or 'these' with one such noun is useful in showing the connection between sentences.

Other nouns typically used in this way are shown in Table 6.2.

**Table 6.2 Examples of nouns used as linking devices with 'this' or 'these'**

| account | advice | answer | argument | area | assertion | assumption | claim |
|---------|--------|--------|----------|------|-----------|------------|-------|
| comment | conclusion | criticism | description | difficulty | discussion | distinction | emphasis |
| estimate | example | explanation | finding | idea | improvement | increase | observation |
| proof | proposal | reference | rejection | report | rise | situation | suggestion |
| view | warning | | | | | | |

## Activity 6.20 Identifying signalling expressions

Read the following text and circle all the examples of signalling words and phrases you can find. (There are at least 10 in total.)

Darwin's *The origin of species* published in 1859 was hugely influential in the field of science and in society in general. Indeed it has often been referred to as the 'book that shook the world'. The book outlined how there could be a relatively gradual change in the characteristics of successive generations of a species and that higher plants and animals evolved slowly over time from lower beings. This process occurred as a result of competition within local interacting communities. Darwin's book helped throw the idea that there was a complete difference between humans and the animal world into turmoil as he reinforced the suggestion that humans evolved from lower beings. Prior to this it was believed in the western world, based on biblical works, that humans were created superior to other beings. With the idea that humans could have evolved from lower beings came the undermining of traditional religious opinions. However, although some religious leaders did embrace Darwinism at the time, the theories were very different from those that had come before. These ideas radically shook a society, where, because of the increasing availability of printed books and papers, intellectual knowledge was being transferred in greater quantity than ever before. Darwin's idea therefore influenced most areas of science at the time.

(Holden, 2008: 6)

## Activity 6.21 Using suitable signalling expressions

In the following text on understanding a textbook, at least 10 inappropriate signalling words and phrases have been included. Identify them and either remove them or replace them with a suitable word or phrase using Table 6.1 above to help you.

Research (Slotte and Lonka 1999) on student note-taking methods usually suggests that there are specific ways of reading a textbook which can maximise learning. As a matter of fact, half of the research sample were asked to review their notes during note-taking; the other half were not given any explicit instructions. Besides, analysis of the quality and quantity of notes similarly indicated that reviewing notes during essay writing was associated with good performance on questions that required comprehension of the text and deep, and what is more, detailed knowledge. Moreover, reviewing these notes did not naturally help with drawing original conclusions about the text. In comparison, it was noted that students summarising the text in their own words, apart from this, with their own sub-headings and structure, performed better than those students who took verbatim notes or, in short, took notes in the exact order in which the material appeared in the text. Actually, this finding suggests that deeper understanding (and better performance) comes from having read and understood material in a text and finally expressing it in your own words.

(Martin *et al.*, 2008: 295)

## Connecting paragraphs

As writing an academic text consists of more than one paragraph, you will need to link each paragraph in some way. Table 6.1 on signalling words may also be of use to you when connecting paragraphs together. You will find nevertheless that you often need a longer sentence to help create a link from paragraph to paragraph. The topic sentence can either form part of your linking sentence or it will follow it. Imagine you are outlining the positive and negative issues of a given topic. You may begin one of your 'positive' paragraphs with one of the following:

One of the main advantages of X is ...

One of the positive effects of X is ...

You may then choose to start the next paragraph with one of these phrases:

A further advantage (of X) is ...

X is a further advantage (worth considering)

Another advantage (of X) is ...

X is another advantage ...

When you are ready to change your discussion to the negative issues, you may write one of the following:

Having considered the positive effects of X, negative issues need to be taken into account.

Despite the positive effects outlined above, there are also negative issues to be considered.

The important point here is that paragraphs should not be standing in isolation. Do not expect your reader to make the connection in your ideas, but make those connections explicit. This way, the reader will be led in a logical order through your argument and will be reminded of your current theme or angle.

**107**

## Activity 6.22 Evaluating the importance of links between paragraphs

Compare the following two extracts on the positive and negative issues associated with fast food taken from student work. Which extract signals to the reader what information to expect in each paragraph? Why is this a useful writing tool?

---

### Extract 1

Fast food is also known as convenient food. This is highly processed food that is available on demand. Fast food is important because it has become a significant part of every society today.

Fast food industries improve the society by providing jobs for the unemployed. When new restaurants and fast food outlets are established in an area, new staff, mainly from the locality, is employed. This helps reduce the area's unemployment level.

Many economies have been influenced by fast food companies especially in the agricultural sector of the economy. Most fast food industries do not have their own large farm land to grow the crops needed for production; they depend on both local and international farmers. An increase in the demand for agricultural produce also encourages farmers to expand and grow crops on a larger scale either for exportation or for consumption within their own country.

McDonald's and many other world recognised fast food companies are known for their contribution to society. They award scholarships, sponsor the purchase of new medical facilities and help build health centres. The community programmes organised by these fast food companies include environmental sanitation where items used for production are reduce, reused or recycled to decrease the amount of annual waste produced.

Within the last ten years, there has been an awareness of the dangers of eating fast food. Fatty food is unhealthy. It contains a high amount of unsaturated fat which implies high energy content. This can lead to obesity which can in turn lead to health problems like heart disease, diabetes, and different forms of cancer.

Despite all efforts to keep the environment clean and tidy, it is almost impossible to keep litter off the streets. Take-away packs and unwanted souvenirs from fast food restaurants can often be found littering the streets.

Advertisements are not bad but when children are the target of unhealthy food adverts, then they are bad. Children between the ages of 2–8 are targeted because they can become loyal to the brand ...

---

### Extract 2

Fast food is also known as convenient food. This is highly processed food that is available on demand. Fast food is important because it has become a significant part of every society today.

There are many advantages associated with fast food. Firstly, fast food industries improve the society by providing jobs for the unemployed. When new restaurants and fast food outlets are established in an area, new staff, mainly from the locality, is employed. This helps reduce the area's unemployment level.

A greater advantage and impact of the fast food industry on the world today is that many economies have been influenced by fast food companies especially in the agricultural

---

sector of the economy. Most fast food industries do not have their own large farm land to grow the crops needed for production; they depend on both local and international farmers. An increase in the demand for agricultural produce also encourages farmers to expand and grow crops on a larger scale either for exportation or for consumption within their own country.

The efforts of fast food industries in their contribution to society cannot be overemphasised. They contribute by awarding scholarships, sponsoring the purchase of new medical facilities and helping build health centres. The community programmes organised by these fast food companies include environmental sanitation where items used for production are reduce, reused or recycled to decrease the amount of annual waste produced.

Having considered the advantages of fast food in the world today, some important setbacks will be discussed. Within the last ten years, there has been an awareness of the dangers of eating fast food. Fatty food is unhealthy. It contains a high amount of unsaturated fat which implies high energy content. This can lead to obesity which can in turn lead to health problems like heart disease, diabetes, and different forms of cancer.

A further drawback is that despite all efforts to keep the environment clean and tidy, it is almost impossible to keep litter off the streets. Take-away packs and unwanted souvenirs from fast food restaurants can often be found littering the streets.

The final disadvantage worth considering is advertisements. Advertisements are not bad but when children are the target of unhealthy food adverts, then they are bad. Children between the ages of 2–8 are targeted because they can become loyal to the brand …

## Activity 6.23 Identifying links

Look at Extract 2 in Activity 6.22 and find all the examples used to link paragraphs together.

## Activity 6.24 Adding links between paragraphs

Read the following paragraphs which form part of a text on support staff in classrooms. Add suitable links at the beginning of each paragraph.

Many primary and secondary teachers will find that they have with them a support teacher (ST) or a teaching assistant in the classroom. An ST is a member of staff who may be employed by the local education authority to support the learning of children with specific needs. One common use of a ST is to support children who have English as an additional language. These teachers have got specific expertise and will work on a one-to-one basis or with a group of children to improve their language skills and allow them to engage fully with the school curriculum.

…………………………….. is to help pupils who have specific educational needs like dyslexia. These teachers usually come from a special needs background and will come

→

into mainstream classrooms to support average ability or able pupils who have been identified as having specific learning difficulties.

.................., STs may also be members of staff who have spare contact time and this needs to be used effectively to support those pupils who are identified as needing extra help.

(Davies, 2007: 104)

## Activity 6.25 Checking for paragraph links in your own work

When you next write an assignment ask the following questions as you read through your work:

- Does the start of my paragraph show my reader what it will be about?
- Does my paragraph add to or elaborate on a point made previously and, if so, have I explicitly shown this with an appropriate linking phrase?
- Does my paragraph introduce a completely new point or a different viewpoint to before and if so, have I explicitly shown this with an appropriate linking phrase?
- Have I repeatedly used similar linking phrases? (If yes, try to vary them.)

To sum up, in order to write well-organised, logical, cohesive text, you should:

- identify the area you will concentrate on in each paragraph
- write a topic sentence which will introduce your point
- form a question from your topic sentence which you will then answer by writing supporting sentences
- link the sentences within your paragraph with appropriate signalling language like 'furthermore' or 'in fact'
- write a concluding sentence to remind the reader of your main point (particularly useful in long paragraphs)
- start the next paragraph with an appropriate linking sentence, which may include the topic sentence for that paragraph
- continue in the same way.

# WRITING PLANS

Chapter 2 looked at writing skeletal plans. To reiterate, in order for you to use the above checklist successfully and write well-organised texts, you need to plan your thoughts in advance. It is surprising how many students read a question, particularly in an examination, and immediately begin writing without any thought or planning. Even if you feel extremely confident in your ability to answer the question fully, you should take time to write a plan. Remember the plan is usually only for your own use; you can therefore write it in whatever note form you like. The following guidelines are intended for all assignment writing, including examinations:

- Use the advice on deconstructing the title and overcoming the blank page in Chapter 2 and adapt it to suit you.
- Look at the ideas which you have generated and decide how to group them together in a meaningful and logical way.
- Keep in mind that each idea you have will be expressed in at least one paragraph.
- List your ideas on paper leaving big blanks between each idea on the page (the topic sentence).
- Fill the blanks with examples and points which develop your topic sentence (the supporting sentences).
- Now you have all the points written down, you can begin with your introduction having a clear idea of how your text will develop.

If you have never written plans before, you may like to try these guidelines over the next few assignments. If you have written plans before, you may like to consider whether these hints have provided you with any ideas you have not tried before and you may now like to try.

# WRITING DRAFTS

Writing drafts is a feature of academic writing so unless you are in an examination room where time is limited, try to allow yourself sufficient time to write drafts. Academic writing is a process that takes time and involves a number of additions, revisions and general editing before the final product is ready. If you manage to view academic writing as a way of constructing and developing a product you should feel less fear and anxiety when approaching a given assignment. Just as plans are intended for your personal use, drafts are meant to help you too.

Knowing that you have the flexibility to go back to a text you have written, reread it, rewrite parts of it and move it around before any reader has the chance to look at it should feel quite liberating. So next time you spend ages thinking of a better phrase to express something, write it in a different colour so you can find it easily later and move on. Leave yourself notes on the text in a different font or colour or highlight them and look at them after you have had a break, or indeed on a different day. Start with the conclusion first if you feel you know what you will say! You can always return to it later and adjust it or transform it completely. The point is, it does not really matter if your work does not feel perfect to you yet; it is only a draft.

## Writing drafts for lecturers

Many university lecturers give students the option to hand in drafts. If your course provides you with this opportunity, make sure you use it. The feedback you will

receive will help you see whether you are on the right lines or whether there is a crucial point you have omitted to make. Using this opportunity could mean the difference between a pass and a fail, or a pass and an A grade. If the draft is assessed, make sure you find out what the exact requirements are. Does your lecturer want continuous prose, including an introduction and conclusion, or are bullet points acceptable with the expectation that they will be turned into continuous prose for the final submission? As with any piece of assessed work, make sure you work to the set requirements. Assessment criteria are usually provided with the coursework or in the course handbook.

# SUMMARY

In order for you to thrive in your new academic community, you need to write planned, well-organised, cohesive text in an appropriate style taking care to be objective and cautious with your expressed opinions. You should always endeavour to write critically, analysing and evaluating the ideas you find in sources and ensuring that you reference those sources appropriately. Make sure that you read widely so that you, in turn, produce appropriate academic texts for your academic community.

## References

Details of highlighted references can be found in the Introduction on page xxii.

# WRITING DESCRIPTIVELY

Chapter 7 focuses on descriptive writing. Although at university level descriptive texts will be unlikely to be useful by themselves – you will usually have to analyse and evaluate as well – there may be times when exam questions or assignments simply ask for descriptions. Questions might start with:

- What are ...
- Define ...
- Outline ...
- Describe ....

Descriptive writing includes defining a topic and describing an object, system or process. It also includes categorising and classifying. The chapter will also cover reporting past events, something which you did or something that happened.

This chapter will cover:
- description
  - definition
  - description of objects
  - description of systems
  - description of processes
  - classifying/categorising
  - charts and diagrams
- reporting.

## USING THIS CHAPTER

# INTRODUCTION

Students are asked to write many different kinds of texts. Depending on the subject you are studying, you could be asked to write an essay, a lab report, a case study, a book review, a reflective diary, a poster, a research proposal and so on. These are normally referred to as genres. These different genres, though, can be constructed from a small range of different text types.

If, for example, you are asked to write an essay to answer the following question:

**Evaluate possible solutions to the problem of international brand management.**

You could answer it in the following way:

- You would probably start by defining brand management, saying what it is and giving an example.
- You might then explain why international brand management is a problem in business today, and support your explanation by evidence from your reading.
- After that you would describe some possible solutions to the problem of brand management, again supporting your suggestions with evidence from your reading.
- Next you would evaluate the advantages and disadvantages of each of the possible solutions.
- Finally, you would decide which solution you would prefer and give reasons.

So in order to answer the question you need to be able to write texts that do the following:

- define
- give an example
- explain why
- support your explanation with evidence
- describe a solution
- describe advantages and disadvantages
- evaluate
- choose.

These texts can be categorised into four main types:

1 *Descriptions* – this can include defining a topic, describing an object, system, or a process. It also includes categorising and classifying.
2 *Reports* – this is description of a past activity, something you did or something that happened.
3 *Explanations* – this is why and how something happens or happened. It includes giving reasons and explanations and writing about cause and effect.
4 *Arguments* – this includes giving opinions or holding positions for and against an issue or advantages and disadvantages. It involves giving evidence to support an argument as well as making decisions or recommendations and justifying the action.

While this chapter looks at descriptive texts and reports, Chapter 8 will look at argumentative writing and analytical and evaluative texts.

# DEFINING

In academic writing, it is usually necessary to define your terms. This is especially valuable at the beginning of an assignment or when you are answering an exam question. Many words or phrases have several meanings and in your subject they may be used in very specific ways. It is important to show how you understand the terms that you are using and exactly the sense with which you are using them.

Read the following texts. In the first text 'advertising' is being defined. Notice how the definition is organised and what language is used.

> Advertising is defined as any paid form of non-personal presentation and promotion of ideas, goods or services through mass media such as newspapers, magazines, television or radio by an identified sponsor. **(Kotler *et al*. 2008: 737)**

Here 'mortgage' is defined.

> A mortgage is a form of loan that is secured on an asset, typically land. Financial institutions such as banks, insurance businesses and pension funds are often prepared to lend to businesses on this basis. The mortgage may be over a long period.
> **(McLaney and Atrill, 2008: 578)**

Two typical ways of writing definitions that you might like to use are:

**A mortgage is a form of loan that is secured on an asset.**

or

**A form of loan that is secured on an asset is called a mortgage.**

You will notice that these are written in the form:

**X is a Y that ...**
**A Y that ... is X.**

Other language that you will find useful in writing definitions is:

**X is ...**
**X is called ...**
**X is known as ...**
**X may be defined as ...**
**X is a type of Y that/which ...**
**A type of Y which ... is X.**

## Activity 7.1 Writing definitions

Define the following terms using the phrases suggested above. Use a dictionary if necessary:

- accrued expense
- brand
- contingency fee
- fixed cost
- renewable energy
- retailer
- small claims track.

Make sure that you define rather than just describe or give examples. For example, in the following text, the writer has failed to define and is simply giving an example of what a mentor does.

**The mentor supports and helps you with any school based problems.**

(Davies, 2006: 8)

Sometimes, these definition sentences are followed by more detail. In these cases, the short definitions often form topic sentences and are often followed by more descriptive detail as in the following example:

> Hire purchase is a form of credit that is used to acquire an asset. Under the terms of a hire purchase (HP) agreement a customer pays for an asset by instalments over an agreed period. Normally, the customer will pay an initial deposit (downpayment) and then make instalment payments at regular intervals (perhaps monthly) until the balance outstanding has been paid. The customer will usually take possession of the asset after payment of the initial deposit, although legal ownership of the asset will not be transferred until the final instalment has been paid. **(McLaney and Atrill, 2008: 582)**

**TIP** *Remember definitions of difficult terms in your subject.*

## Activity 7.2 Adding descriptive detail

Add more descriptive detail to this definition of banding.

**Banding is the placing of pupils within a class into ability groupings.**

# DESCRIBING THINGS

In your writing, you will often have to describe something: an object, a system, an organisation or a process.

Read this description of the brain from a psychology textbook. Notice the way that the description is organised and the language that is used. You will see that if you were writing about the brain, you could describe:

- what the brain looks like
- how much it weighs
- how important it is
- what it consists of.

The description is written in the present tense (looks, contains) as it is something that is generally true.

> The brain looks like a lump of porridge and has the consistency of blancmange. This organ, weighing an average 1400g in an adult human, is the most important part of the body. It contains an estimated 10 to 100 billion nerve cells and about as many supporting cells, which take care of important support and 'housekeeping' functions. The brain contains many different types of nerve cell which differ in shape, size and the kinds of chemicals they produce. **(Martin et al., 2007: 120)**

The following text continues describing the brain by describing its function, what it does. You would start by describing the number of functions it has and then give some detail about each function.

> The brain has two roles: controlling the movements of the muscles and regulating the physiological functions of the body. The first role looks outwards towards the environment and the second looks inwards. The outward-looking role includes several functions: perceiving events in the environment, learning about them, making plans, and acting. The inward-looking role requires the brain to measure and regulate internal characteristics such as body temperature, blood pressure and nutrient levels. **(Martin et al., 2007: 146)**

If you are writing a description of an object, you might include, for example:

- physical description
- weight
- size
- colour
- structure
- material
- shape
- properties
- function.

As well as describing simple objects, you may need to describe an organisation or a system. The following description of the European Commission, from a law textbook, gives you an example of how you could do this. Notice that the paragraph describes:

- how the commission is made up
- what its function is.

> The Commission is composed of 27 members, called Commissioners, who are each appointed by the member states for five years. They must be nationals of a member state, and in practice there tend to be two each from the largest states – France, Germany, Italy, Spain and the UK – and one each from the rest. However, the Commissioners do not represent their own countries: they are independent, and their role is to represent the interests of the EU overall. The idea is that the Commission's commitment to furthering EU interests balances the role of the Council, whose members represent national interests.
>
> In addition to its part in making EU legislation, the Commission is responsible for ensuring that member states uphold EU law, and has powers to investigate breaches by member states and, where necessary, bring them before the Court of Justice. It also plays an important role in the relationship of the EU with the rest of the world, negotiating trade agreements and the accession of new members, and draws up the annual draft budget for the EU. It is assisted in all these functions by an administrative staff, which has a similar role to that of the civil service in the UK. **(Elliott and Quinn, 2008: 76–7)**

So when you are describing objects, systems or organisations, you might want to describe physical characteristics, such as:

**Position**

| A is | opposite<br>on the right of<br>diagonally above<br>vertically below | B. |
| --- | --- | --- |
| | between<br>equidistant from | B and C. |

*For example:*

The pivot is vertically above the base.

**Structure**

| X | is | connected<br>attached | to | Y | by | Z. |
| --- | --- | --- | --- | --- | --- | --- |
| | consists | | of | | | |
| | contains<br>includes | | | Y and Z. | | |

*For example:*

The brain contains many different types of nerve cell.

**Size and weight**

| X | is | 6 cm | long.<br>high.<br>wide.<br>in length.<br>in height. |
| --- | --- | --- | --- |

*For example:*

The voltmeter is 4 cm wide and 12 cm long.

| X | weighs<br>has a weight of | 10 kg. |
| --- | --- | --- |

*For example:*

The adult brain weighs approximately 1400 grams.

**Shape**

| X | is | square<br>semi-circular<br>hexagonal<br>elliptical | in shape. |
|---|----|----|----|

*For example:*

**The brain is roughly elliptical in shape.**

You might also want to describe the function of something or its purpose.

**Function**

| The<br>A<br>One | function<br>purpose<br>aim<br>objective<br>role | of the | thermometer<br>tripod<br>brain | is to | measure the temperature.<br>hold the beaker. |
|---|---|---|---|---|---|

## Activity 7.3 **Writing descriptions**

Describe the tooth shown in Figure 7.1. Try to use some of the language presented above.

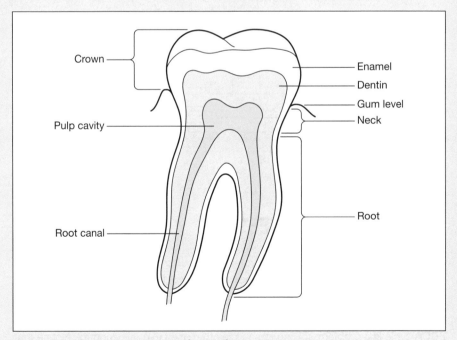

**Figure 7.1 The anatomic parts of a tooth**
(Kozier *et al.*, 2008: 276)

## Activity 7.4 Describing how something works

Describe the operation of the wind turbine shown in Figure 7.2.

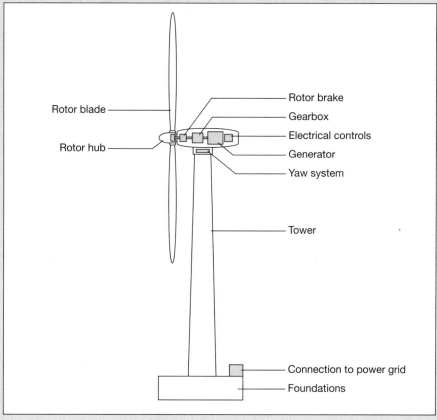

Rotor brake

Rotor blade

Gearbox

Electrical controls

Rotor hub

Generator

Yaw system

Tower

Connection to power grid

Foundations

**Figure 7.2 A wind turbine**
(Hughes, 2008: 812)

# DESCRIBING PROCESSES

As well as describing objects and systems, it is often necessary to describe processes: how things are done or made. These could be products or laws, for example.

Here is a description of the PDCA (Plan Do Check Act) problem-solving cycle. The PDCA cycle is a problem-solving technique often used in quality control. Notice that as the text is about the cycle and how it works, when you write about processes in this way the passive form of the verb (are resolved, is consolidated) is used. This is because in this type of writing, the focus is usually on the process rather than on the people doing the work. In this case, the present tense is used as the procedure is still commonly made use of.

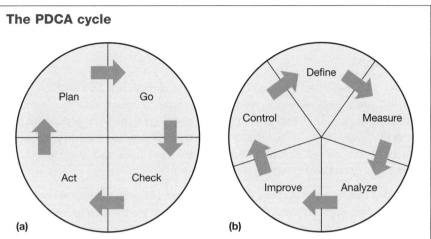

**The PDCA cycle**

(a)

(b)

Figure 7.3 (a) the plan-do-check-act or 'Deming' improvement cycle, and (b) the define-measure-analyse-improve-control or DMAIC Six Sigma improvement cycle

The PDCA cycle model is shown in Figure [7.3]. It starts with the P (for plan) stage, which involves an examination of the current method or the problem area being studied. This involves collecting and analyzing data so as to formulate a plan of action which is intended to improve performance. Once a plan for improvement has been agreed, the next step is the D (for do) stage. This is the implementation stage during which the plan is tried out in the operation. This stage may itself involve a mini-PDCA cycle as the problems of implementation are resolved. Next comes the C (for check) stage where the new implemented solution is evaluated to see whether it has resulted in the expected performance improvement. Finally, at least for this cycle, comes the A (for act) stage. During this stage the change is consolidated or standardised if it has been successful. Alternatively, if the change has not been successful, the lessons learned from the 'trial' are formalised before the cycle starts again. (Slack *et al.*, 2007: 597–8)

The cycle consists of four clear stages, which are explicitly referred to with the following phrases:

It starts with . . .
The next step . . .
Next . . .
Finally . . .

The stages are also connected with linking words or phrases, which you can make use of, such as:

Once a plan for improvement has been agreed, . . .
This is the implementation stage during which . . .
During this stage, . . . .

Make sure that you keep the time sequence clear with words such as:

**firstly**
**next**
**subsequently.**

# Instructions

Make sure you describe how a process works rather than just give instructions. As a student, you will often need to read and understand instructions – for example in a laboratory manual or an assignment briefing sheet – but you will probably not need to write them very often. So make sure you distinguish between them in your writing. Instructions are telling someone how to do something and descriptions are describing how something happens or happened.

Instructions can be given in many ways. A numbered list with the imperative form of the verb is one common way. Continuous text using the passive form of the verb with *should* is also common. Look at the following example of one method of giving instructions. Notice the highlighted language items:

---

**Cleaning**

The following steps should be followed when cleaning objects in a hospital.

1 Rinse the article with cold water to remove organic material. Hot water coagulates the protein of organic material and tends to make it adhere. Examples of organic material are blood and pus.
2 Wash the article in hot water and soap. The emulsifying action of soap reduces surface tension and facilitates the removal of substances. Washing dislodges the emulsified substances.
3 Use an abrasive, such as a stiff-bristled brush, to clean equipment with grooves and corners. Friction helps dislodge foreign material.
4 Rinse the article well with warm to hot water.
5 Dry the article; it is now considered clean.
6 Clean the brush and sink. These are considered soiled until they are cleaned appropriately, usually with a disinfectant. **(Kozier et al., 2008: 214)**

---

**TIP** *Make sure you describe when you should be describing. Do not just give instructions.*

## Activity 7.5 Describing processes

Rewrite the boxed paragraph above titled 'Cleaning' as a process description.

# Sequence

Sequence, or order, is important in describing processes. The table below shows some common expressions that you can use to indicate sequence. Examples are based on **Kotler et al.** (2008: 51–2).

| | |
|---|---|
| First, | The first step is ... |
| To begin with, | ... begins with ... |
| Initially, | ... commences with ... |
| Beforehand, | Before this, |
| At the same time, | During ... |
| Secondly, Thirdly, etc. | After this, |
| Next, | The next step is to ... |
| Subsequently, | In the following stage, |
| Later, | Following this, |
| Lastly, | ... finishes with ... |
| Finally, | ... concludes with ... |
| In the last stage, | The last step is to ... |

*For example:*

> The company first gains a full understanding of the marketplace. It subsequently designs a customer-driven marketing strategy.

You may also want to explain how something is done:

| |
|---|
| ... slowly/carefully |
| ... with care/precision |
| ... in a careful way/manner |
| ... by researching ... |

*For example:*

> The company first gains a full understanding of the marketplace by researching customer needs and managing marketing information.

or why something is done:

> So as to ...
> So as not to ...
> So that ...
> In order to ...
> In order not to ...

*For example:*

It then designs a customer-driven marketing strategy in order to discover which customers they serve and how they can best be served.

**TIP** *Always check that your sequence of actions is clear.*

## Activity 7.6 Describing an operation

Describe the operation of a car braking system as illustrated in the diagram below.

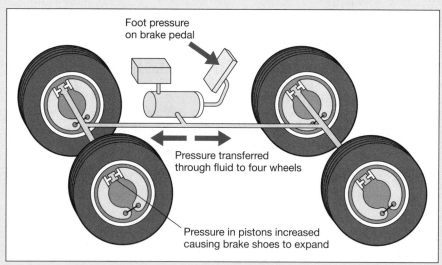

**Figure 7.4 The car braking system**

# INCLUDING CHARTS AND DIAGRAMS

It is often useful when you are describing objects, systems or processes to include reference to tables and charts.

Look at the text below. Notice how Figure 7.5 is explicitly referred to in the written text and also notice the language that is used there. For example, Figure 7.5 shows...

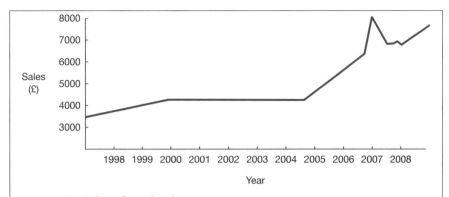

**Figure 7.5 Sales of notebook computers per year**

Figure 7.5 shows sales of notebook computers per month. As can be seen, it covers the years 1998 to 2008 and shows that the sales of notebook computers increased steadily in the first two years, then remained steady from 2000 until 2004. The sales then rose steeply, throughout 2005 and 2006, with a rapid increase at the end of 2007, and reached a peak of 8000 in January 2007. A sharp fall followed in the first half of 2007 but sales levelled off at about 7000 per month in the middle of the year. Sales fluctuated slightly through the second half of 2007, and are now increasing again. The figures strongly indicate that we have recovered from the problems in early 2007 and are on target to improve on our February 2007 peak by the end of 2008.

In such cases, you do not simply add the visual to the text: you usually include some sort of comment or analysis as shown in the text.

Typically, when you are referring to charts and diagrams, you will:

■ make an explicit reference to the diagram or chart
■ draw the reader's attention to the important features and describe them
■ add some kind of comment which will depend on your purpose in including the diagram in your writing.

Here is some language that you might find useful when you are referring to charts and diagrams.

| As can be seen | from | Table 1, | |
|---|---|---|---|
| It can be seen | in | Figure 2, | ... |
| We can see | | Graph 3, | |

*Example:*

As can be seen from Figure 7.5, the sales of notebook computers increased steadily in the first two years.

| From | Table 1 Figure 2 | | it | can | be | seen concluded shown | ... |
|------|------|------|------|------|------|------|------|
| | the | figures chart diagram | | may | | estimated calculated inferred | |

*Example:*

From Figure 7.5, it can be seen that the sales of notebook computers increased steadily in the first two years.

| The graph Figure 1 | shows | ... |
|------|------|------|

*Example:*

Figure 7.5 shows sales of notebook computers per month.

If you want to comment on trends and developments shown in graphs, the following phrases may also be of use:

| | | rise. increase. |
|------|------|------|
| There was a (very) | slight steady dramatic steep | fluctuation. |
| | | decline. reduction. drop. |

| Sales Price Exports, etc. | increased grew rose | slightly. gradually. steadily. markedly. dramatically. sharply. suddenly. |
|------|------|------|
| | declined dropped fell | |

**TIP** *Do not forget to label your diagrams and make sure you refer to them clearly in your own text.*

## Activity 7.7 Describing changes (1)

Describe the changes in inflation between May 1999 and May 2001 as shown in Figure 7.6 below. Make sure you explicitly include a reference to the diagram in your description.

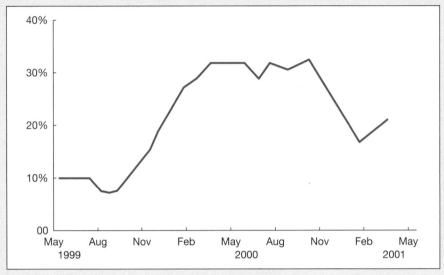

Figure 7.6 **Rate of inflation: May 1999 – May 2001**

# CLASSIFYING/CATEGORISING

When you classify, you arrange things into groups according to certain criteria. For example, if you take the following list:

Physics   Chemistry   Biology   English   History   Art

it is quite clear that all the words are school subjects but some are science subjects and some are arts subjects. As there are only arts subjects and science subjects it is simple to divide the list into two:

| Physics, Chemistry, Biology | AND | English, History, Art |
|---|---|---|

When you are classifying, you need to explain what you are classifying and on what basis you are making your classification – your criterion or criteria. In this case the school subjects are classified according to whether or not they are science subjects or arts subjects.

The following text is classifying the different powers in governments. Notice how the powers are classified into three types, depending on who holds the power. The different powers are then described.

---

**The separation of powers**

One of the fundamental principles underlying our constitution is that of the separation of powers. According to this principle, developed by the eighteenth-century French philosopher Montesquieu, all state power can be divided into three types: executive, legislative and judicial. The executive represents what we would call the Government and its servants, such as the police and civil servants; the legislative power is Parliament; and judicial authority is exercised by the judges. **(Elliott and Quinn, 2008: 2)**

---

In the next example, financial assets are divided into two groups, depending on whether they are short term or long term.

---

**The classification of assets**

Assets may be categorised as being either current or non-current.

. . .

Current assets are basically assets that are held for the short term.

. . .

Non-current assets (also called fixed assets) are simply assets that do not meet the definition of current assets. Generally speaking, they are held for long-term operations.
**(McLaney and Atrill, 2008: 49–50)**

---

**TIP** *Make sure the basis of your classification is always clear, i.e. your criteria are clearly stated.*

The table below show some of the most common language that you can use in texts which have classification as their purpose.

| There are | | types kinds classes | | : current and non-current. . These are current and non-current. |
|---|---|---|---|---|
| | two | categories | of assets | |
| The | | sorts varieties | | are current and non-current. |

You can then follow this sentence with a description of the different groups.

## Activity 7.8 Indentifying classification

Read the following text and identify what is being classified and what the division is based on.

> Coastal landforms have often been classified to provide useful ways to help assess the different forcing factors and controls such as sea-level history, geology, climate, waves and tides that lead to the great variety of coastal land forms we encounter (Bird, 2000). Most early classification schemes were based on the realisation that coastal landforms are largely the product of sea-level variations. Such classifications distinguish between submerged and emerged coasts. Typical submerged coasts are drowned river and glacial valleys, often referred to as rias and fjords, respectively. Coastal plains are characteristic of emerged coasts. Another type of classification distinguishes between primary and secondary coasts. Primary coasts have a configuration resulting mainly from non-marine processes and include drowned river valleys and deltaic coasts. Secondary coasts, on the other hand, are coasts that have a configuration resulting mainly from marine processes or marine organisms. Examples of such coasts are barrier coasts, coral reefs and mangrove coasts.
>
> (Holden, 2008: 481–2)

## Activity 7.9 Describing changes (2)

Look at the following table of changes that are made in the law. Using this information, write a paragraph describing the different kinds of change and give an example of each type.

| Changes in law | | |
| --- | --- | --- |
| Causes of change | Law needs to respond to changes in society | Necessary to keep law in working order |
| Examples of change | Political, social and economic changes, technological advancements and changing moral beliefs $\rightarrow$ changes in the law | Complicated legal systems must be kept in a neat and tidy condition, on a regular basis, essential repairs undertaken as necessary |

# REPORTING

In any writing you do, you might also have to report on how something came into being or how something was done. Read the following text, from a law textbook, and notice how the text is organised and the language that is used. You will notice that the text starts with a one-sentence introduction to put the narrative in context.

It then provides a chronological (time-order) history of the formation of the European Union. It finishes with a prediction about the future.

Before discussing the role of the EU in European law, the text provides a short history of the EU.

> The European Union (EU) currently comprises 27 western European countries. The original members – France, West Germany, Belgium, Luxembourg, Italy and The Netherlands – laid the foundations in 1951, when they created the European Coal and Steel Community (ECSC). Six years later, they signed the Treaty of Rome, creating the European Economic Community (EEC) and the European Atomic Energy Community (Euratom). The original six were joined by the UK, Ireland and Denmark in 1973, Greece in 1981 and Spain and Portugal in 1986 and, in the same year, the member countries signed the Single European Act, which developed free movement of goods and people within the Community (the single market), and greater political unity. Finland, Austria and Sweden joined in 1995. Following the Nice summit in 2004, the EU increased its membership from 15 to 27 in 2004, with most of the new members coming from eastern Europe.
>
> In 1993 the Maastricht Treaty renamed the European Economic Community the European Community and the European Economic Treaty was renamed the European Treaty. It also created the European Union (EU), which is likely to become the most important body in Europe and so will be the label that we will refer to in this book.
>
> **(Elliott and Quinn, 2008: 74)**

When you write such a report you will normally organise your text chronologically and use the past tense (laid, created, signed, ...). When you are writing about past events in this way, it is necessary to be explicit about the order in which things happened. To make the order clear, you should mention dates and times, and also use various links and connections.

Here are some phrases you can use to refer to time:

**In 1981, ...**
**During the 20th century, ...**
**Yesterday, ...**
**Twenty five years ago, ...**

And here are some phrases you can use to make your sequence clear:

| Before this, ... | When ..., ... | X years later, ... |
|---|---|---|
| For the previous X years, ... | As soon as ..., ... | After ... |
| Prior to this, ... | For the following X years, ... | Following this, ... |
| Previously, ... | While ..., ... | Subsequently, ... |
| X years previously, ... | During this period, ... | Soon/Shortly/Immediately |
| | Throughout this period ... | afterwards, ... |

As with describing processes, make sure you distinguish between giving instructions – that is, telling someone how to do something – and reporting – that is, describing what you did or how something happened.

## Activity 7.10 Distinguishing between instructions and descriptions

Read the following instructions that explain how to clean an object in hospital: you have seen these before. Rewrite them as a report – that is as something that you did – using the passive voice and keeping your sequence clear.

---

**Cleaning**

The following steps should be followed when cleaning objects in a hospital.

1 Rinse the article with cold water to remove organic material. Hot water coagulates the protein of organic material and tends to make it adhere. Examples of organic material are blood and pus.
2 Wash the article in hot water and soap. The emulsifying action of soap reduces surface tension and facilitates the removal of substances. Washing dislodges the emulsified substances.
3 Use an abrasive, such as a stiff-bristled brush, to clean equipment with grooves and corners. Friction helps dislodge foreign material.
4 Rinse the article well with warm to hot water.
5 Dry the article; it is now considered clean.
6 Clean the brush and sink. These are considered soiled until they are cleaned appropriately, usually with a disinfectant.                                  (Kozier et al., 2008: 214)

---

The methods section of an experimental report (Gillett and Weetman, 2006) typically uses the passive voice (were taught, were selected, were excluded) as in the example below.

---

**Method**

Two groups of students in Higher Education on a one-year Pre-Masters English for Academic Purposes course, each comprising 50 students were taught academic writing by different methods and compared. In each group there were 50 students from five different academic departments – computer science, business, engineering, life sciences and law – and four different countries – China, Japan, Korea and Thailand. The subjects were selected from the second semester of the University of Hertfordshire Pre-Masters Programme in the 2007-2008 academic year.

The subjects were selected from the 250 students on the Pre-Masters Programme on the basis of performance at a satisfactory level in the Semester A examination. Students who had performed below the minimum level on the semester A examination were excluded. This criterion was employed to ensure competent understanding of the tasks and adequate motivation.

One group – Group A – studied English writing in the traditional way in a class with a teacher. This class met for 2 hours each week in a classroom for 12 weeks and was supplemented with written homework assignments given by the teacher each week. The second group – Group B – met together in a class with a teacher for one hour per week for 12 weeks and were assigned a homework task of spending one hour per week doing exercises from a website

131

> Both groups A and B were given the same written examination at the end of the semester. The students took the examination under standard university examination conditions as part of their end of semester examination. The tests were marked using the following categories: task achievement, communicative quality, organisation, ideas, content and relevance and grammar and vocabulary, by two experienced writing examiners and moderated in the standard way to ensure reliability. In this way it was possible to see the relationship between the students' main academic subjects, and the improvement in their writing ability depending on the teaching method.

**TIP** *Always make sure your sequence is clear and that you are reporting, not giving instructions.*

## Activity 7.11 Reporting an experiment

Read the following instructions for carrying out two short experiments in Physics. Assume now that you have carried out the experiments. Convert the instructions into a report. Make sure you clearly distinguish between these instructions and your report.

**Experiment 1**
1 Take a thin flexible steel rod.
2 Bend the rod to feel how tough and springy it is.
3 Hold the rod in a Bunsen burner flame.
4 Heat the rod until the end is bright red and dip it very quickly into cold water.
5 Try to bend the rod as you did before.
6 Record your results.

**Experiment 2**
1 Take a second rod and bend it to see how tough and springy it is.
2 Heat it until it is red hot.
3 Keep the rod in the heat for about 15 seconds after it has turned red.
4 Remove it from the heat very slowly and allow it to cool gradually.
5 Try to bend the rod when it has cooled sufficiently.
6 Record your results.

# SUMMARY

In this chapter, we have looked at some of the text types that form the building blocks of longer student texts. These descriptive texts will be needed by most students in their writing, although they will probably not be enough in themselves.

We have divided the chapter into two main sections: descriptive writing and reporting. Description consists of defining and describing objects, systems and processes. This was followed by classifying and categorising and finally reporting. In Chapter 8, we will follow this up by looking at the kind of critical writing that is expected in higher education.

## References

Gillett, A.J. and Weetman, C. (2006) 'Investigation of the use of a VLE group discussion facility by East Asian postgraduate students.' *The East Asian Learner* 2 (2). Available at http://www.brookes.ac.uk/schools/education/eal

Details of highlighted references can be found in the Introduction on page xxii.

# 8 ▶ WRITING CRITICALLY

Chapter 8 focuses on writing critically. Building on what you have learned in Chapter 7, it starts with texts that explain and justify then moves on to texts that analyse and evaluate, that is texts that use the process of argument. When you write critically, you need to justify and give evidence for your ideas, suggest what other points of view there are and evaluate them.

Most exam questions and assignments will expect some level of criticality. However, exam questions and assignments that explicitly ask for analysis and evaluation might start with phrases like:

- Analyse ...
- Criticise ...
- Evaluate ...
- Discuss ...

- Compare and contrast ...
- Why ...?
- Examine ...
- Can ...?

This chapter will cover:

- providing reasons and explanations
- arguing a point of view
- evaluating a point of view
- comparing and contrasting
- providing support by giving examples or providing evidence
- drawing conclusions.

## USING THIS CHAPTER

# INTRODUCTION

Chapter 7 focused on descriptive writing and gave examples of writing that define, describe, report and classify or categorise. This process of description is essential. However, it is not enough for work in higher education. Nash (1990: 10) clearly points out:

> The student who gives only the facts, with no assessment or interpretation, gets poor marks; the student who floats on clouds of subjectivity without ever touching hard propositional ground probably gets no marks at all.

In other words, you will need to write more critically. If you do not, you will be accused of being too descriptive, not engaging with the subject or being uncritical. All these will lose you marks.

Description may answer questions regarding what or how, but you also need to go beyond that: you need to justify and give evidence for your claims, suggest what other points of view there are and evaluate them. This is what being critical means in this context. It does not mean finding fault with everything and being wholly negative – in fact, in some subjects you will rarely be negative. When you write critically, you will compare and contrast arguments and ideas; you will find advantages and disadvantages of solutions to problems; you will find explanations for actions and processes and provide evidence and support for your points of view.

In Chapter 7, we looked at the following essay title:

**Evaluate possible solutions to the problem of international brand management**

and suggested that you could answer it in several ways that involved a variety of text types (see pp. 114). In Chapter 7, we looked at some of these texts, and in this chapter we will look at the remainder.

## Writing critically

Writing critically involves analysing and evaluating your own and others' work and presenting a point of view which you can support (see Table 8.1).

## Arguing and discussing

In academic writing, arguing and discussing is often part of a larger piece of writing. It may be an exam question with an instruction such as 'discuss' or it may be part of the discussion section of a longer report. Engineers may not have to write essays, but they will certainly need to discuss the results of any practical work they have been involved in. In arguing and discussing, you are expected to consider different points of view and discuss the positive and negative aspects of each case. On the basis of your discussion, you can then choose one point of view and persuade your readers that you are correct. This means giving your opinions (positive and negative) on the work of others and your own opinions based on what you have learned or found.

## Table 8.1 Writing critically

| Analysis | Evaluation | Presenting your point of view |
|---|---|---|
| Examines and breaks information into parts: | Makes judgements about the value of information, ideas or materials for a given purpose in a given context: | Involves giving your opinion: |
| ■ it identifies causes and effects<br>■ it draws conclusions<br>■ it finds evidence and examples to support generalisations<br>■ it makes connections, comparisons and contrasts<br>■ it distinguishes between facts and inferences<br>■ it tries to provide reasons | ■ it investigates to what extent something is true<br>■ it investigates importance<br>■ it interprets and justifies | ■ it provides reasoned evidence to support your point of view<br>■ it deals with other people's point of view |
| e.g.<br>■ How is . . . related to . . .?<br>■ Can you show a connection between . . . and . . .?<br>■ Why . . .?<br>■ How would you prove/disprove . . .? | e.g.<br>■ Do you agree with the actions/outcomes . . .?<br>■ How important is . . .? | e.g.<br>■ What is your opinion of . . .?<br>■ Provide a solution to . . . |

As always, all your opinions must be supported: you should produce your evidence and explain why this evidence supports your point of view. It is important that when you present your point of view, you distinguish between your point of view, your evidence and your reasons for believing what you do. You need to be clear about how the evidence you have provided leads to the claim you are making (Toulmin, 1958).

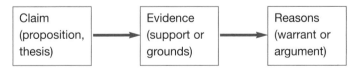

137

There are two main methods of presenting an argument, and in general the one you choose will depend on exactly how you need to present your argument and the preferences of your subject.

## 1 The inductive or balanced approach

In this case you present both sides of an argument, without necessarily committing yourself to any opinions, which should always be based on evidence, until the final sentences.

At its simplest your plan will be as follows:

- Introduce the argument to the reader (e.g. why it is particularly relevant).
- Reasons against the argument (state the position, the evidence and the reasons).
- Reasons in favour of the argument (state the position, the evidence and the reasons).
- After summarising the two sides, state your own point of view, and explain why you think as you do.

## 2 The deductive or persuasive approach

This second type of argumentative text involves stating your own point of view immediately, and trying to convince the reader by reasoned argument that you are right. The form of the text will be, in outline, as follows:

- Introduce the topic briefly in general terms, and then state your own point of view.
- Explain what you plan to prove.
- Reasons against the argument.
- Dispose briefly of the main objections to your case, providing evidence and your reasons.
- Reasons for your argument (the arguments to support your own view, with evidence, reasons and examples).
- Conclusion – restates your claim and explains why it is important.

**TIP** *If you are unsure which kind of argument you need to make, ask your lecturer.*

# PROVIDING REASONS AND EXPLANATIONS

Being critical includes making connections between the ideas of your subject and trying to explain why things happen as they do. You need to give reasons and provide explanations.

Take the following situation:

**Pollution is increasing.**

You might want to ask why this is happening and want the reason or explanation for this. One reason is that:

**People are burning more fossil fuels.**

So:

**Pollution is increasing** – is the situation.

**People are burning more fossil fuels** – is the reason or explanation.

Read the following text and observe the explanatory relationships.

> There are several factors to be taken into account when studying why some plants become weak or die. One reason is lack of water. Dryness in the soil causes the leaves to wilt, and may give rise to the death of the plant. On the other hand, too much water may result in the leaves drooping, or becoming yellow. While sunshine is necessary for plants, if it is too strong, the soil may be baked and the roots killed. However, if there is no light, the leaves will become pale and the stems thin. Consequently the plant may die.

The text is about why plants become weak or die. The text attempts to explain why this occurs. It suggests reasons to do with water (too little or too much) and sunshine (too little or too much). The following explanatory relationships exist:

- Lack of water $\rightarrow$ dryness in the soil $\rightarrow$ leaves to wilt $\rightarrow$ death of plant.
- Too much water $\rightarrow$ leaves droop or become yellow $\rightarrow$ death of the plant.
- Too strong sun $\rightarrow$ baked soil $\rightarrow$ roots killed.
- Lack of light $\rightarrow$ pale leaves and thin stems $\rightarrow$ death of the plant.

You might also have noticed that the text starts with an introductory sentence, explaining the situation. It then clearly offers several explanations for the situation.

## Activity 8.1 Identifying explanations

Identify the situation and the explanations in the following text.

> Most road traffic accidents occur between four and six o'clock in the morning, with a second, slightly smaller peak occurring in the middle of the afternoon (Home and Reyner 1999). Most researchers attribute this finding to sleeplessness and/or fatigue. A lack of sleep seems to exacerbate driving performance as does a feeling of fatigue and the ingestion of carbohydrates (London et al., 2004).　　　　　　　　　**(Martin *et al.*, 2007: 385)**

## Activity 8.2 Writing explanations

Use the following information to explain why star dunes attain the greatest height.

| Reason | Situation |
|---|---|
| Star dunes develop in the depositional centres of sand seas, where net sediment accumulation and sand-transporting wind directional variability is greatest. | Of the main dune types identified in Figure 12.11, star dunes usually attain the greatest size. |

## Activity 8.3 Explaining why

Use the following notes to explain why new products fail.

- Good idea but overestimate market – no demand – e.g. electronic books.
- Poor design – technological drawbacks – readers read e-books in range of situations and positions.
- No better than other product.
- Incorrectly positioned.
- Development costs high.
- Competitors fight back hard.

There are many different ways in which you can express these explanatory relationships, for example using introductory sentences:

There are several reasons why . . .

. . . for several reasons.

The first reason why . . . is . . .

First of all, . . .

The second reason why . . . is . . .

Secondly, . . .

The most important . . .

In addition, . . .

Furthermore, . . .

What is more, . . .

Besides, . . .

Another reason is . . . .

You can also emphasise the reason or explanation as follows:

| Pollution is increasing | because<br>owing to the fact that | people are burning more fossil fuels. |
|---|---|---|

| Pollution is increasing. | This is because<br>One reason for this is that | people are burning more fossil fuels. |
|---|---|---|

| The<br>One | reason for<br>cause of | the increase in pollution | is that<br>could be that | people are burning more fossil fuels. |
|---|---|---|---|---|

| An increase in pollution | is<br>may be | one consequence of<br>caused by<br>due to | people burning more fossil fuels. |
|---|---|---|---|
| | results from<br>arises from | | |

Finally, you can emphasise the present situation as follows:

| As<br>Because<br>Since | people are burning more fossil fuels, | pollution is increasing. |
|---|---|---|

| People are burning more fossil fuels. | Therefore,<br>Consequently,<br>For this reason,<br>As a result, | pollution is increasing. |
|---|---|---|

| People are burning more fossil fuels, | as a result of which<br>with the result that | pollution is increasing. |
|---|---|---|

| One<br>The | effect of<br>result of<br>consequence of | people burning more fossil fuels | is that | pollution is increasing. |
|---|---|---|---|---|
| | | | is to | increase pollution. |

| People are burning more fossil fuels, | (so)<br>(thus)<br>(thereby) | resulting in<br>producing<br>causing<br>bringing about | an increase in pollution. |
|---|---|---|---|

# ARGUING A POINT OF VIEW

An argument is a statement of your claim (your point of view) supported by your evidence along with the reasons why you believe that your evidence supports your claim. Your statement will most likely be debatable in that you will believe in it but other people may disagree. The objective of your argument is to show your reader that you are correct.

The statement of your claim will usually be a general declaration of fact but in academic writing it is often stated cautiously.

See Chapter 6

Look at the first sentence in the following text.

> There are certain aspects of language processing that may not decline with age and may actually improve. One of the greatest gains is seen in vocabulary (Bayley and Oden, 1955; Jones, 1959). However, older individuals have difficulty in retrieving or accessing these words and exhibit a greater number of tip-of-the-tongue responses than do young individuals during retrieval (Bowles and Poon, 1985). **(Martin, *et al*., 2007: 491)**

It is a clear statement of the claim being made by the writer – that language processing does not decline with age but improves. It is expressed cautiously in 'certain aspects', 'may not', 'may actually'. The remainder of the paragraph gives more information and provides examples and support for the claim.

## Activity 8.4 **Indentifying arguments**

Read the following text and identify the claim being made.

> There seems to be a clear, obvious and important link between intelligence and nutrition. Malnutrition can impair brain function (Brown and Pollitt, 1996) and IQ in the long term; iodine deficiency during pregnancy can lead to retardation and cretinism. In the late 1980s and early 1990s, a series of studies reported significant differences in non-verbal IQ between schoolchildren who received vitamin and mineral supplements (VMS) and those who received a placebo (Benton, 1992; Haller, 1995; Eysenck and Schoenthaler, 1997). Those who received the supplements scored significantly better.
>
> In non-verbal IQ between schoolchildren who received vitamin and mineral supplements (VMS) and those who received a placebo (Benton, 1992; Haller, 1995; Eysenck and Schoenthaler, 1997), those who received the supplements scored significantly better.
>
> (Martin, *et al*., 2007: 486)

See Chapters 6 and 11

Note that, although the sentence is your – the writer's – point of view it is not correct to say 'I think' in this case. This is because if no other source is mentioned, it will be assumed that the point of view is yours. The statement of your point of view will probably be quite general and cautious; your points of view may be qualified and generalisations may be made. You may also have different degrees of certainty about your claims.

# Generalisations

Usually the claims you make will be quite general. They will apply to a wide range of situations and contexts, not just your own. Generalisations are often written in the present tense ('there is') as in the example below.

**There seems to be a clear, obvious and important link between intelligence and nutrition.**

Plural nouns are often used for broad generalisations (e.g. 'schoolchildren who received vitamin and mineral supplements').

You can be specific about the degree of generalisation that you are making by the use of modal verbs, adjectives and adverbs such as the following:

| Degree of generalisation | Quantity | Frequency | Certainty | Verbs |
|---|---|---|---|---|
| 100% | all/every/each most a majority (of) many/much<br><br>some a number (of) several<br><br>a minority (of) a few/a little | always<br><br>usual(ly) normal(ly) general(ly) as a rule on the whole often frequent(ly) sometimes occasional(ly) | certain(ly) definite(ly) undoubtedly clearly presumably probably/ probable likely<br><br>conceivably possibly/ possible perhaps maybe | will is/are must have to<br><br>should ought to<br><br>can could may might |
| 0% | few/little<br><br><br><br>no/none/not any | rare(ly) seldom hardly ever scarcely ever never | uncertain unlikely | could not will not cannot is/are not |

You can also modify the strength of your claim that something is true by using phrases such as those given below:

| It | is | fairly<br>very quite<br>rather<br>quite | certain<br>likely<br>probable<br>possible<br>unlikely | that ... |
|---|---|---|---|---|
| | seems appears | | | |

Sometimes, you may want to qualify your generalisations in the following way:

| In | the (vast) majority<br>a large number | of | |
| | most<br>some<br>a few | | cases, ... |

# Cautious language

As pointed out already in Chapter 6, you need to be careful about the strength of your claims. Notice the cautious language used in the claim made in the first sentence of the following text.

> Of the main dune types identified in Figure 12.11, star dunes usually attain the greatest size. This is because they develop in the depositional centres of sand seas, where net sediment accumulation and sand-transporting wind directional variability is greatest.
>
> (Holden, 2008: 458)

However, in the next example the writer is quite confident about what he believes.

> Most road traffic accidents occur between four and six o'clock in the morning, with a second, slightly smaller peak occurring in the middle of the afternoon (Home and Reyner 1999). Most researchers attribute this finding to sleeplessness and/or fatigue. A lack of sleep seems to exacerbate driving performance as does a feeling of fatigue and the ingestion of carbohydrates (London *et al.*, 2004). (Martin *et al.*, 2007: 385)

**TIP** *Academic writing is always cautious to some extent.*

## Activity 8.5 Identifying degrees of caution

Identify the degree of caution or generality in the claims made in the following sentences.

> Pupils are normally keen to see how teachers perform and will want to settle so that they can weigh them up. (Davies, 2006: 130)
>
> The elderly may also have difficulty in comprehending and initiating grammatically complex sentences (Kemper, 1992). (Martin *et al.*, 2007: 491)
>
> Oceans are very important in controlling the climate of the Earth. (Holden, 2008: 59)
>
> The main practical difference between these is that a public company can offer its shares for sale to the general public, but a private company is restricted from doing so.
> (McLaney and Atrill, 2008: 119)

## Activity 8.6 Writing cautiously

Rewrite the following texts to make them more cautious. Add a word in the gap.

Numerically, there are _____ more private limited companies in the UK than there are public ones.                                            **(McLaney and Atrill, 2008: 119)**

Such developments and their effects become _____ important for social work, within the values and ethics which qualified and registered social workers now have to adhere to, as set out in the General Social Care Council's Code of Practice (2002).
**(Wilson *et al.*, 2008: 514)**

_____ one of the most salient perceptual features of infant development is the gradual shift in preference from simple stimuli to patterned ones.     **(Martin *et al.*, 2007: 532)**

The marketing information system _____ serves the company's marketing and other managers.                                                    **(Kotler *et al.*, 2008: 326)**

# EVALUATING A POINT OF VIEW

As well as stating your own point of view, you will probably need to comment on and evaluate ideas that you have learned and read about, as well as the work of others. As always, all your opinions must be supported – you should produce your evidence and explain why this evidence supports your point of view.

When evaluating a point of view or a conclusion, you may want to:

- present the point of view
- comment on it positively or negatively.

Look at the following texts which present other people's points of view. Notice the kind of language you can use to introduce these viewpoints:

So, some people have argued that the right of people suspected of committing a crime to remain silent when questioned, without this being taken as evidence of guilt, was part of our constitution; nevertheless, that right was essentially abolished by the Criminal Justice and Public Order Act 1994.                               **(Elliott and Quinn, 2008: 5)**

Those in favour of our unwritten constitution argue that it is the product of centuries of gradual development, forming part of our cultural heritage which it would be wrong to destroy.                                                           **(Elliott and Quinn, 2008: 6)**

They also point out that the lack of any special procedural requirements for changing it allows flexibility, so that the constitution develops along with the changing needs of society.                                                            **(Elliott and Quinn, 2008: 5)**

> According to Smith and Jones (2006), commercial lawyers would be most likely to survive, since they have a specialist knowledge that solicitors cannot provide.
>
> (Elliott and Quinn, 2008: 184–6)

Other language that you might want to use to introduce other people's arguments is as follows:

| | maintain(s) argue(s) believe(s) claim(s) point(s) out seem(s) to believe | | |
|---|---|---|---|
| Some people X In a study of Y, X | | that | ... |
| It is the view of X It can be argued It might be said | | | |
| According to X | | | |

## Activity 8.7 Identifying points of view

Identify other people's points of view in the texts below. Indicate the phrases used to show this.

> There has been much discussion over recent years as to whether the professions will eventually fuse. (Elliott and Quinn, 2008: 185)
>
> Others have suggested that common law barristers have a better chance of surviving competition from solicitors. They cater for the needs of ordinary high street solicitors, who generally have a wide-ranging practice, and spend much of their time seeing clients and gathering case information. (Elliott and Quinn, 2008: 185)
>
> Alternatively, it has been suggested that the Bar might survive, but in a much reduced form, and there is much debate about which areas would suffer most.
> (Elliott and Quinn, 2008: 185)
>
> Some studies, however, have shown that it is not necessarily distraction that is responsible for reducing pain but rather the emotional quality of the distractor. Positive stimuli, such as humour and laughter, are known to reduce pain perception (Cogan *et al.*, 1987; Rotton and Shats, 1996) but increasing the attention required to complete cognitive tasks (distraction without emotion) does not (McCaul and Malott, 1984). (Martin *et al.*, 2007: 376)

Look at the following texts which present comments on other people's points of view. These comments can be either positive or negative. Both the examples here are negative. This is shown by the linking word 'however' and the evaluative word 'little'.

> This leaves little opportunity to swot up on the finer details of every area of law with which clients need help so, where specialist legal analysis is needed, they refer the client to a barrister with experience in the relevant area. **(Elliott and Quinn, 2008: 185)**
>
> Some studies, however, have shown that it is not necessarily distraction that is responsible for reducing pain but rather the emotional quality of the distractor. Positive stimuli, such as humour and laughter, are known to reduce pain perception (Cogan *et al.*, 1987; Rotton and Shats, 1996) but increasing the attention required to complete cognitive tasks (distraction without emotion) does not (McCaul and Malott, 1984). **(Martin *et al.*, 2007: 376)**

Here are some examples of the kind of language you could use to show your positive or negative evaluation of other people's ideas.

## Positive evaluation

| X is certainly correct<br>X may be right<br>X is accurate | when he | says | that ... |
|---|---|---|---|
| | in saying | | |

| One advantage of<br>Another point in favour of<br>One other advantage of<br>One of the main arguments in favour of | X | is | ... |
|---|---|---|---|

## Negative evaluation

| They<br>X<br>This | is/are<br>may be<br>seem(s) to be<br>would seem to be | somewhat<br>rather | mistaken.<br>wrong.<br>rigid.<br>inadequate.<br>deficient. |
|---|---|---|---|
| X's | approach methods | | | |

| One of the main arguments | against | X is that | ... |
|---|---|---|---|

| One (main) disadvantage of<br>Another point against<br>A further argument against<br>One other disadvantage of | X | is | ... |
|---|---|---|---|
| One objection to this argument | | | |

Identify the evaluative phrases in the following texts:

> Mental health problems are intensely personal experiences for both the person who is directly affected, but also for those close to them. However, the causes of mental health difficulties are not just personal but also social and political, or as is sometimes said, 'psycho-social'.
> **(Wilson *et al.*, 2008: 566)**

> The main disadvantage of these early classifications is that the emphasis on geological inheritance and sea-level history leaves only limited concern for the hydrodynamic processes. The morphology of depositional coastal environments (those consisting of mud, sand and gravel, rather than eroding rocky shores) responds to the relative dominance of river, wave and tidal factors (Boyd *et al.*, 1992).
> **(Holden, 2008: 480)**

# Advantages and disadvantages

One important way to evaluate a proposal or an idea is to look at its advantages and disadvantages. The following text discusses the advantages and disadvantages of tidal barrages as an alternative form of energy production.

> Like other means of generating power tidal barrages have their advantages and disadvantages. The tides are very predictable, unlike the wind, so even though generation is intermittent the output can readily be scheduled along with other generating capacity. Barrages give flood protection and also benefits for transport, since a dam provides a new estuary crossing. While construction technology is well understood, the capital costs are very high, and such barrages are not without their environmental difficulties either. They change an estuary ecosystem and silt can accumulate behind the dam. The cost and environmental problems make it unlikely that a new tidal barrage will be built, even though several attractive sites worldwide, including the Severn Estuary in the UK, have been studied because of their large tidal range and trapped area.
> **(Hughes, 2008: 824)**

Notice how the text is organised:

- introduction – explains the situation
- advantages – tides are predictable, barrages give flood protection, dams provide benefits for transport
- disadvantages – high costs, changes the ecosystem
- evaluation – too expensive therefore unlikely to be used.

## Activity 8.9 **Identifying advantages and disadvantages**

Identify the advantages and disadvantages in the following text:

---

**Advantages and disadvantages of wave power**

The environmental impact is low. There is little visual impact and, since only a fraction of the overall wave energy is extracted, the impact on coastlines is minimal. Chemical pollution is also minimal. Wave energy devices present no problems for marine life, but may present some hazard to shipping. Economies can be achieved by installing them in groups which can be connected to a single submarine cable bringing power ashore. Installation, maintenance and operating costs are then spread over a much larger total generating capacity.

However, a number of difficulties await. Peak power is generally only available far from land, in locations remote from population centres. As waves come close to the shore they give up energy due to friction between the water and the seabed. The typical wave frequency (about 0.1 Hz) is difficult to couple to a generator frequency of 50 or 60 Hz. The capital costs of the structures required to withstand the harsh climatic conditions at sea are high. (Hughes, 2008: 818)

---

## Activity 8.10 **Describing disadvantages**

In the following text, you can read about the advantages and disadvantages of using wind power. The first paragraph is given. Use the notes provided to write the second paragraph.

---

**Advantages and disadvantages of wind generation**

Wind generation does not involve the production of carbon dioxide or oxides of sulphur and nitrogen. In August 2007, the British Wind Energy Association (BWEA) reported that some 2200 MW of wind generation were currently operational in the UK with:

| | |
|---|---|
| Equivalent carbon dioxide reductions (p.a.) | 4 952 366 tonnes (about 1 kg $CO_2$/kW h) |
| Sulphur dioxide reductions (p.a.) | 57 586 tonnes |
| NOx reductions (p.a.) | 17 276 tonnes |

In addition, there is no radioactivity, no nuclear waste storage and no consumption of water supplies. (Hughes, 2008: 814)

Disadvantages:
- *Visual problems – depend on size, colour, design etc. of turbine and position*
- *Electricity distribution – need long cables*
- *Acoustic disturbance possible, but modern designs → quieter than cars*
- *Access*
- *Impact on wildlife*

---

## Activity 8.11 Writing about advantages and disadvantages

The notes in the following table show the advantages and disadvantages of franchising from the point of view of the franchisor. Use the information given to write a short text.

| Advantages | | Disadvantages | |
|---|---|---|---|
| Financial | • Franchisee's finance → rapid growth in market penetration<br>• No problem with: capital assets and working capital<br>• No risk if fail: risks borne by franchisee | Handling franchisee – relationship. | May be difficult, ineffective, remote. |
| Managerial | • Franchisee is legal owner ∴ fails or succeeds<br>• Franchisee's management skills used, e.g. promotion, resource control, motivate staff. | Formation of small franchise groups. | Could challenge power of franchisor. |
| Others | • Develop economies of scale in purchasing, branding etc.<br>• Can divorce design and planning from delivery and operations. | | |

(Brassington and Pettitt, 2006: 1086–7)

# COMPARING AND CONTRASTING

When you are writing, you need to do much more than just give information: you should always be trying to do something with your writing. One common function in academic writing is comparing and contrasting, writing about similarities and differences. There are many ways of expressing comparison and contrast in English.

First, you need to decide which features of the items or ideas you want to compare and then organise the comparison.

## Example

Look at the following table and read the text below. Pay attention to the comparisons and contrasts. Notice that three of the computers in the text are compared: the Gloucester Axis 1.33 SK, the Aran R850 P4 and the Elite 1.7 GT Pro. They are compared with respect to price, processor speed and size of hard disk, in that order.

| | Price | Processor Speed | Screen Size | Hard Disk | RAM |
|---|---|---|---|---|---|
| Gloucester Axis 1.33 SK | £1,174 | 1.33 GHz | 17" | 40 GB | 256 MB |
| Aran R850 P4 | £2,467 | 1.7 GHz | 19" | 40 GB | 256 MB |
| Elite 1.7GT Pro | £1,938 | 1.7 GHz | 19" | 57 GB | 256 MB |
| WebSurfer Pro | £1,174 | 1.2 GHz | 17" | 38.1 GB | 128 MB |

> Three personal computers, the Gloucester Axis 1.33 SK, the Aran R850 P4 and the Elite 1.7 GT Pro, were compared with respect to the following factors: price, processor speed and size of hard disk. The Gloucester Axis, which costs £1,174, is by far the cheapest of the three, the Aran and the Elite costing £2,467 and £1,938 respectively. The Gloucester Axis has the same hard disk size as the Aran, 40 MB, whereas the Elite is the largest at 57 GB. Regarding the processor speed, the Aran and the Elite are similar – the processor speed, at 1.7 GHz, being 0.37 GHz faster than the Gloucester Axis.

You could organise the text differently, by taking the computers in order and discussing all the features of each one before moving on to the next.

The following text compares public and private companies. Notice that it starts by stating what it is comparing. It then gives details of the differences.

> **Public and private companies**
>
> When a company is registered with the Registrar of Companies, it must be registered either as a public or as a private company. The main practical difference between these is that a public company can offer its shares for sale to the general public, but a private company is restricted from doing so. A public limited company must signal its status to all interested parties by having the words 'public limited company', or its abbreviation 'plc' in its name. For a private limited company, the word 'limited' or 'Ltd' must appear as part of its name.
>
> Private limited companies tend to be smaller businesses where the ownership is divided among relatively few shareholders who are usually fairly close to one another – for example, a family company. Numerically, there are vastly more private limited companies in the UK than there are public ones. Of the 2.1 million UK limited companies now in existence, only 11,500 (representing 0.5 per cent of the total) are public limited companies.
>
> **(McLaney and Atrill, 2008: 119)**

## 8 Writing critically

The information in the text can be summarised in the following table.

| Public or private | |
| --- | --- |
| Public offers shares to general public | Private does not |
| Public signals its status with plc | Private signals its status with Ltd |
| Public – owned by general public | Private – small business, ownership divided between few |
| Public – only 0.5% | Private – 99.5% |

**TIP** *Similarities and differences are usually a matter of opinion.*

The comparisons and contrasts can be explicitly signalled in the following way:

| | | |
| --- | --- | --- |
| The Gloucester Axis | is like the WebSurfer<br>and the WebSurfer are similar<br>is similar to the WebSurfer<br>is the same as the WebSurfer<br>resembles the WebSurfer | with respect to price.<br>as regards price.<br>as far as price is concerned.<br>regarding price.<br>in that the price is the same.<br>in terms of price.<br>in price. |

| |
| --- |
| Both the Gloucester Axis and the WebSurfer cost £1,174.<br>The Gloucester Axis is as expensive as the WebSurfer.<br>The Gloucester Axis costs the same as the WebSurfer.<br>The Gloucester Axis is the same price as the WebSurfer. |

| | |
| --- | --- |
| The Elite has a large screen. | Similarly, it has a high capacity hard disk.<br>Likewise, it has a high capacity hard disk.<br>Correspondingly, it has a high capacity hard disk.<br>It has a high capacity hard disk, too.<br>It also has a high capacity hard disk. |

Similarly for the differences:

| | | |
| --- | --- | --- |
| The Gloucester Axis | differs from the Aran<br>is unlike the Aran<br>and the Aran differ<br>is different from the Aran<br>contrasts with the Aran | with respect to price.<br>as far as price is concerned.<br>regarding price.<br>in terms of price.<br>in price. |

| |
| --- |
| The Gloucester Axis costs £1,174, whereas the Aran costs £2,467.<br>The Gloucester Axis costs £1,174, while the Aran costs £2,467.<br>The Gloucester Axis costs £1,174, in contrast to the Aran, which costs £2,467.<br>The Aran is more expensive than the Gloucester Axis.<br>The Gloucester Axis is not as expensive as the Aran. |

| The Aran is expensive to buy. | On the other hand, it is very fast and has a large screen.<br>In contrast, it is very fast and has a large screen.<br>Conversely, it is very fast and has a large screen.<br>However, it is very fast and has a large screen. |
| --- | --- |

| Although the Aran is expensive to buy,<br>Despite the high price of the Aran, | it is very fast and has a large screen. |
| --- | --- |

## Activity 8.12 Comparing

Identify what is being compared in the following text:

In the late 1980s and early 1990s, a series of studies reported significant differences in non-verbal IQ between schoolchildren who received vitamin and mineral supplements (VMS) and those who received a placebo (Benton, 1992; Haller, 1995; Eysenck and Schoenthaler, 1997). **(Martin et al., 2007: 486)**

Notice the explicit comparison words which you can make use of in the following:

However, older individuals have difficulty in retrieving or accessing these words and exhibit a greater number of tip-of-the-tongue responses than do young individuals during retrieval (Bowles and Poon, 1985). **(Martin et al., 2007: 491)**

## Activity 8.13 Contrasting

Identify the words which indicate the contrast in the following text:

There is a wealth of research to demonstrate that disabled children are more vulnerable to abuse and neglect than their non-disabled peers (Kelly, 1992; Miller, 2003). In addition to this, research also demonstrates that disabled children are not protected from harm to the same extent as their non-disabled peers. **(Wilson et al., 2008: 566)**

Sometimes the comparison is not explicitly signalled, although it is clear that the similarity exists. In the following text, both Tesco and Dell are given as examples of external partners that can benefit in a similar way from a company's marketing information system.

The marketing information system primarily serves the company's marketing and other managers. However, it may also provide information to external partners. For example Tesco gives key suppliers access to information on customer buying patterns and inventory levels, and Dell creates tailored Premium Pages for large customers, giving them access to product design, order status and product support and service information.
**(Kotler et al., 2008: 326)**

## Activity 8.14 Discussing differences

Using the information in the table below, discuss the attainment of students from different socio-economic classes. Show some of the similarities and differences.

Table 8.1 GCSE attainment[1]: by parents' socio-economic classification (DfES, 2002)

| England and Wales – all figures are percentages | | | | | | |
|---|---|---|---|---|---|---|
| | 5 or more GCSE grades A*–C | 1–4 GCSE grades A*–C[2] | 5 or more GCSE grades D–G | 1–4 GCSE grades D–G | None reported | All |
| Higher professional | 77 | 13 | 6 | – | 3 | 100 |
| Lower professional | 64 | 21 | 11 | 2 | 2 | 100 |
| Intermediate | 52 | 25 | 17 | 2 | 4 | 100 |
| Lower supervisory | 35 | 30 | 27 | 4 | 4 | 100 |
| Routine | 32 | 32 | 25 | 5 | 6 | 100 |
| Other | 32 | 29 | 26 | 4 | 9 | 100 |

[1]For pupils in Year 11. Includes equivalent GNVQ qualifications achieved in Year 11.
[2]Consists of those with 1–4 GCSE grades A*–C and any number of other grades.

Source: DfES (2002) Youth cohort study. www.statistics.gov.uk/statbase/ as cited in **Davies (2006: 38)**.

# PROVIDING SUPPORT

Most of the claims that you make in your discussions will be quite general. This is as it should be: one purpose of studying in higher eduction is to learn how to generalise from specific examples. You need to be able to draw general conclusions that will be valuable in problem-solving in the future.

In academic writing it is therefore common to make generalisations. It is necessary, though, to support these generalisations with examples, details or evidence.

## Examples

Look at the following examples involving generalisations. Notice how the generalisation is supported by details or examples. In the first example, the claim 'gender is only the fifth most important determinant of a child's academic ability' is supported by statistics provided by the government (DfES).

> Table [8.1] supports the view that parental socio-economic status is the most important determinant of a child's academic success.

> (Davies, 2006:38)

In the next example, the claim 'The issue of language has been hugely important in thinking about ways to address the discrimination and oppression of disabled people' has been supported by a quotation from Neil Thompson, as well as first-hand evidence from disabled people.

---

**What's in a name?**

The issue of language has been hugely important in thinking about ways to address the discrimination and oppression of disabled people. Neil Thompson, a social work academic, writer and former practitioner states, 'The language we use either reinforces discrimination through constructing it as normal or contributes in some small way at least to undermining the continuance of a discriminatory discourse' (2007: 39). The debate on language is ongoing, for example, in changing terms used to describe people who are in receipt of welfare services from 'clients' to 'service users' or 'customers' and more recently in the move to discuss 'safeguarding' children rather than 'child protection'. In terms of disability, using 'person first' terminology has been one cause for debate. Some disabled adults endorse person first terminology (e.g. people with disabilities) stating that the person comes before the disability (Datillo and Smith, 1990; Kailes, 1985; Millington and Leierer, 1996). Others argue that a person's disability is part of their identity in much the same way as their ethnicity or gender is.                                           (Wilson *et al.*, 2008: 540)

---

## Activity 8.15 **Identifying evidence**

Identify the evidence provided which supports the claim that oceans are important in controlling the climate of the earth.

---

Oceans are very important in controlling the climate of the Earth. The surface of the ocean gains heat by radiation from the Sun, particularly in lower latitudes, and by conduction and convection from warm air flowing over the waves. Heat is lost by evaporation, by reradiation to space and by conduction to cold air above (Barry and Chorley, 2003). Measurements made over the Earth's surface show that more heat is gained than lost at the low latitudes, while more heat is lost than gained at the high latitudes. Because water has a very high specific heat, it acts as a major store of the energy of the Sun. The movement of ocean currents from the low latitudes to the high latitudes is very important in transferring energy to the colder regions and thus maintaining the Earth's temperatures in the present range, which is basically conducive to life as we know it. When ocean circulation changes occur, such as during El Nino events, then they can have a dramatic effect on the climate of the Earth. El Nino is the situation where unusually the entire central Pacific from Australia to Peru is covered with a relatively thin layer of warm water. As a result of this change, weather patterns alter not only adjacent to the current, such as rainfall and floods in the Atacama Desert and snowfall in Mexico City, but also over much of the world.

(Holden, 2008: 59)

---

## Supporting with examples

Claims can be supported by examples. Look at the way examples are used in the following texts.

Rivers vary greatly in appearance with changes both from source to mouth and between individual rivers. It is this morphological diversity that is the fascination for many people. In the case of Europe, contrast the quietly flowing small chalk-fed streams shaded by overhanging willows of southern England with the turbulent milky-coloured torrents draining glacial regions of the Alps.

The size, shape and location of a river can also be transformed overnight by a single large flood, by depositing sediment in some areas and reactivating other reaches by erosion. Few people in the United Kingdom will, for example, have escaped seeing the horrifying images of the destructive forces of the flood that hit the small Cornish village of Boscastle, England in the summer of 2004.                    (Holden, 2008: 381)

It was once thought that distraction was enough to help people take their mind off pain. Some studies, however, have shown that it is not necessarily distraction that is responsible for reducing pain but rather the emotional quality of the distractor. Positive stimuli, such as humour and laughter, are known to reduce pain perception (Cogan *et al.*, 1987; Rotton and Shats, 1996) but increasing the attention required to complete cognitive tasks (distraction without emotion) does not (McCaul and Malott, 1984).          **(Martin *et al.*, 2007: 376)**

## Activity 8.16 Identifying examples

Identify the explicit example signal in the following texts.

River maintenance is needed where human use of rivers does not allow natural fluvial processes to be fully maintained or where the channel dynamics are in conflict with human use. For example, river flow regulation by dams can cause sedimentation and siltation of gravels below tributary junctions due to the reduced frequency and magnitude of Roods. This, in turn, can have adverse impacts on aquatic organisms such as salmon, which require uncovered gravels to spawn.                    **(Holden, 2008: 406)**

Where there is a plentiful supply of material, and the process which moves it can only move a limited amount for a short distance, the rate of transport is limited by the transporting capacity of the process, which is defined as the maximum amount of material which the process can carry (Kirkby, 1971). A transport process like this, such as rainsplash, is described as transport limited.                    **(Holden, 2008: 302)**

**TIP** *Always make sure you support your points.*

Some of the words and phrases that you can use to indicate that you are supporting your point of view are as follows:

| This … | is | shown exemplified illustrated | by | … |
|---|---|---|---|---|

| For example, For instance, | … |
|---|---|

| This is shown by the following examples, The following are examples of this: The following is a case in point: | . . . |
|---|---|

| . . . | institutions | such as | the family | . . . |
|---|---|---|---|---|

## Activity 8.17 Adding support

Add support to the following text by using the information given in italics below. Rewrite the text incorporating the extra information by use of a signalling phrase.

> The marketing information system primarily serves the company's marketing and other managers. However, it may also provide information to external partners, such as suppliers, resellers or marketing services agencies. **(Kotler et al., 2008: 326)**
>
> *Tesco gives key suppliers access to information on customer buying patterns and inventory levels, and Dell creates tailored Premium Pages for large customers, giving them access to product design, order status and product support and service information.*

# Providing evidence to support your claims

As well as examples, you can use research findings, other people's work, your knowledge or other people's words to support your claims.

## Using research findings

> Even at an early age girls are out-performing boys in English:
>
> ■ at age 7, 85% of girls gained a level 2+ while only 72% of boys achieved this
> ■ some 30% of girls attained a level 3 and only 20% of boys, and by the end of primary schooling girls are on average half a level ahead of boys in English
> ■ national statistics show that this gap continues and widens until GCSE, where the gap in performance in English is one of the highest. **(Davies, 2006: 36–7)**

## Using other people's work

> There is a wealth of research to demonstrate that disabled children are more vulnerable to abuse and neglect than their non-disabled peers (Kelly, 1992; Miller, 2003). In addition to this, research also demonstrates that disabled children are not protected from harm to the same extent as their non-disabled peers (Edwards and Richardson, 2003; Marchant and Page, 2003; Cooke, 2000). **(Wilson et al., 2008: 556)**

## Using your knowledge

> The law affects every aspect of our lives; it governs our conduct from the cradle to the grave and its influence even extends from before our birth to after our death. We live in a society which has developed a complex body of rules to control the activities of its members. There are laws which govern working conditions (e.g. by laying down minimum standards of health and safety), laws which regulate leisure pursuits (e.g. by banning alcohol on coaches and trains travelling to football matches), and laws which control personal relationships (e.g. by prohibiting marriage between close relatives).
>
> **(Keenan and Riches, 2007: 3)**

## Using other people's words

See
Chapter 10

> The issue of language has been hugely important in thinking about ways to address the discrimination and oppression of disabled people. Neil Thompson, a social work academic, writer and former practitioner states, 'The language we use either reinforces discrimination through constructing it as normal or contributes in some small way at least to undermining the continuance of a discriminatory discourse' (2007: 39).
>
> **(Wilson et al., 2008: 540)**

## Activity 8.18 Supporting arguments

Use the information in the following extract to support the argument that we should invest in more hydroelectricity. Write a short paragraph.

> Hydroelectricity is a renewable resource, unlike conventional fossil fuel and nuclear generating plant, and has no fuel cost. There are no flue-gas emissions and no nuclear waste. Hydroelectric plants have a predictable output since they can generate power when needed to match electricity demand. Labour costs associated with operating such plant are low as the plant is usually automated. Hydroelectric plants have long economic lives, with some plants now in service having been built 50 to 100 years ago. Reservoirs for hydroelectric schemes often provide opportunities for leisure and tourism, such as fishing and sailing. Large dams can also control floods, which might otherwise have adversely affected the downstream environment. **(Hughes, 2008: 810)**

# DRAWING CONCLUSIONS

After presenting your point of view, evaluating the possible choices, all well-supported with evidence, you need to come to a conclusion. The central function of the conclusion is to confirm that the main purpose of the text has been achieved.

This concluding section should:

- recall the issues raised in the introduction – remind the reader of your task
- draw together the points made in the main body of the piece of writing,
- come to a clear conclusion.

In an exam or other kind of assessment, the conclusion should make it absolutely clear that the question has been addressed and answered fully.

Read the following example of the conclusion from a text on computer assisted language learning and teaching. The study investigated the use of the World Wide Web for teaching writing in a UK university. You will see that sentence 1 provides background information to the problem that the research hoped to solve. Sentence 2 clearly states the problem. Sentence 3 gives the purpose of the study. Sentence 4 summarises the conclusion from the results. Sentence 5 draws it all together by making suggestions for the future.

---

**Conclusion**

[1]During the past 10 years, the use of computers in education has increased dramatically and a wide range of educational computer programmes are now widely available for individual and classroom use. [2]However, there has been very little research reported on the effectiveness of such use. [3]The purpose of the present study was therefore to ascertain the effectiveness of using computer-assisted instruction as compared to traditional classroom instruction in an EAP writing class. [4]The findings clearly suggest that the inclusion of web-based materials in EAP writing courses for post-graduate students from East-Asia on an English language preparation course is effective. [5]Further research is needed, however, before the use of such materials can be recommended for all students in all subject areas at all levels.

(Gillett and Weetman, 2006)

---

## Activity 8.19 Writing conclusions

Read the following notes on a research project on the usefulness of a virtual learning environment (VLE) conducted recently. Write the conclusion.

---

Internat Postgrads find discussion difficult

Can we help using VLE?

Tried to use discussion facility of VLE

Problem – no teacher present – will students take it seriously?

Studied it for two years

Asked students what they thought

Looked at what they were producing

Found students take it seriously if they know why

Ss need help

---

In all cases, your conclusion will be cautious, it will probably be qualified and generalisations may be made. You may also have different degrees of certainty about the claims you are making.

**TIP** *Make sure your conclusions follow from your data.*

You need, though, to signal your conclusion explicitly in some way. Some words and phrases that you can use to do that are given below:

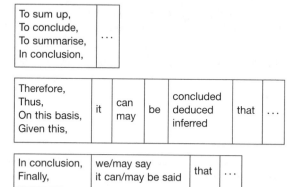

## Recommendations

Many conclusions, especially after reports, finish with recommendations or suggestions for further work. For example:

> Further research is needed, however, before the use of such materials can be recommended for all students in all subject areas at all levels.

> However these solutions will only be temporary and the only long-term solution definitely seems to be conservation and pollution control.

As with all parts of your conclusion, your recommendations may be cautious.

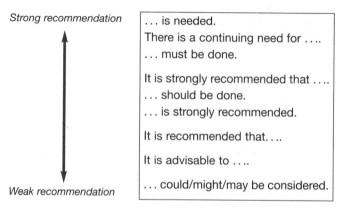

# SUMMARY

Chapter 8 has focused on a difficult area for many students, writing critically. It started with texts that explain and justify then moved on to texts that analyse and evaluate. That is, it tried to help with the process of argument. This is because we believe that these higher-level thinking and writing skills are essential for success in higher education.

Chapter 8 therefore builds on Chapter 7 to help you to write critically. It includes how to justify and give evidence for your ideas, suggests what other points of view there are and shows how to evaluate them.

## References

Gillett, A. J. and Weetman, C. (2006) 'Investigation of the use of a VLE group discussion facility by East Asian postgraduate students', *The East Asian Learner*, 2(2). Available at http://www.brookes.ac.uk/schools/education/eal/

Nash, W. (1990) 'The stuff these people write', in W. Nash (ed.), *The Writing Scholar*, pp. 8–30. London: Sage.

Toulmin, S. (1958) *The Uses of Argument*. Cambridge: Cambridge University Press.

Details of highlighted references can be found in the Introduction on page xxii.

# 9 ▶ PERSONAL AND REFLECTIVE WRITING

This chapter looks at a personal kind of writing that is beginning to feature more prominently in higher education and which comes under the general term of 'reflection' or 'reflective writing'. It looks at the type of language that is used and suggests some frameworks to help you develop this way of writing.

The chapter will cover:

■ the nature of reflective writing
■ its uses in higher education
■ sample frameworks to help prompt reflection.

## USING THIS CHAPTER

# INTRODUCTION

Reflection is valuable when you take the long view of education and think about *why* rather than *what* you are studying. Its power lies in being able to help you develop your understanding of the way you learn, the subjects you are studying and to define your longer-term goals. It can help promote critical thinking and problem-solving skills, both of which are key to academic success. But it has further uses that relate to life skills: it is an essential part of personal development and prepares you for the world of work, encouraging you to develop the habit of analysing your actions or events and considering the consequences. The ability to reflect upon practice is a vital professional skill.

A further thing to be said for reflective writing is that it is one way of freeing you up from the unwritten rule that you cannot use 'I' when you are writing in an academic context. That rule is of course a good one, because it signals the importance of moving away from taking a subjective approach to adopting an objective, analytical and impartial way of writing.

Here is an example of one student's experience of reflective writing.

---

**Clinical anecdote**

Aida, a third-year student nurse:

*'I always thought throughout my nurse education in the first and second year that reflection and reflective practice was a waste of time. I often used to think why keep a reflective journal and diary? Now that I look back to the entries I made in my first and second year I can see how my skills and understanding have developed as a nurse. If anyone were to ask me as they start their nurse education, is it worth keeping a reflective diary and looking at their practice after a shift, I would say definitely. I can see my development fully now and how theory applies to practice.'* (Kozier *et al.*, 2008: 140)

---

# LEVELS OF REFLECTION

You might have kept a diary in the past, or you may keep one still – perhaps in the form of a blog or a reflective journal. The value of any of these forms is that they:

- record events
- help you make sense of things
- build up an understanding of events over time
- allow you to write freely.

However, in order to be useful in academic writing and study, a diary needs to do more than this. It needs to track how a person learns from experience, to enable them to reflect upon experience and develop their awareness of the way they learn, so helping them to place it in a wider context. Good quality reflection needs to demonstrate depth and not just present the surface when describing events. This is of course a quality that is important in all academic writing.

# Moving up through the levels

Hatton and Smith (1995) attribute many of our current ideas about reflection to John Dewey (writing in the first half of the twentieth century), who saw the link between reflection and problem-solving, a key skill in academic study. Hatton and Smith carried out research on reflection in teacher education and developed a framework to describe reflective writing which moves from pure description to the writer conducting a dialogue with the self and finally standing back from events to put them in a broader context. They define the framework, with its four stages, as follows:

1 descriptive writing (a straightforward account of events)
2 descriptive reflection (an account with reasons, justifications and explanations for events)
3 dialogic reflection (the writer begins to stand back from the account and analyse it)
4 critical reflection (the writer puts their account into a broader perspective).

## Examples of reflection

Look at these examples that all describe the same situation.

> 1 Last week was the start of the new term. I have lectures on Mondays, Tuesdays and Thursdays until the end of the semester. That gives me a lot of free time, which is great. It also means I can carry on with my part-time job.
>
> 2 Last week was the start of the new term. I have lectures on Mondays, Tuesdays and Thursdays until the end of the semester. That gives me a lot of free time, which is great. It also means I can carry on with my part-time job but I will have to be very organised in the way I manage my time.
>
> 3 Last week was the start of the new term. I have lectures on Mondays, Tuesdays and Thursdays until the end of the semester. That gives me a lot of free time, which is great. It also means I can carry on with my part-time job but I will have to be very organised in the way I manage my time. I don't want to end up in the same situation as last year, when I was constantly running to stand still and always handing in work at the last minute. It really put me under pressure and made me realise the value of planning ahead.

In Example 1, the writer simply describes a situation (starting a new term, their timetable). In Example 2, they mention part-time work and the need to be organised. In Example 3, they are exploring the impact of something and resolving to do better. They are moving through the first three of the four stages of reflection mentioned earlier.

# THE LANGUAGE OF REFLECTION

As we said in the introduction to this chapter, there is a freedom in writing reflectively that you do not normally receive in academic writing. 'I' is allowed, along with contractions, exclamation marks, stray thoughts and unfinished sentences. In the examples given above the writer uses 'I', talks about their feelings ('great', 'put me under pressure') and uses far more casual language than you would normally see in academic writing where 'don't' is unacceptable and 'running to stand still' would be seen as inappropriate. In previous chapters we have warned you against using emotive language and emphasised the importance of cautious language in academic writing. While you can allow yourself to write in a way that may come more naturally to you, make sure you do not just put down random thoughts that you cannot make any sense of later on.

## The need for structure

Reflective writing in an academic context must still be thorough and systematic and aim for depth of understanding and analysis. As a writer you will have more control over the subject matter, but you need to make sure that you follow certain academic standards to produce good quality reflective writing. This means you must try to:

- support the points you make with examples drawn from your experience
- explore the implications and consequences of your actions
- consider different perspectives on the events you write about.

◄
See
Chapters 7
and 8 That way you will demonstrate your ability to analyse, evaluate and synthesise – and so show that you are able to use the higher order of intellectual skills expected in academic study.

Even though there are no real rules for *what* to write, you do need to think about *how* to express your thoughts. Hatton and Smith's research (1995) found that the following kind of language helped writers develop their skill at reflecting:

'This was quite possibly due to ... Alternatively, ...'

'The problem here, I believe, was the fact that...'

'On the one hand, ... yet on the other ...'

'In thinking back, ... On reflection ...'

If you think about these words you will see that the writer(s) are considering:

- reasons for an event
- alternative solutions
- different points of view
- problems that were caused.

In addition, they are demonstrating the ability to analyse and evaluate.

---

### Activity 9.1 Phrases to encourage reflection

Think of other phrases that you could use to develop your skills of reflection:

_____

_____

_____

_____

# JUDGING THE QUALITY OF REFLECTIVE WRITING

One of the problem areas in reflective writing is how and whether to assess it. Since it is a very personal way of writing standard methods of assessment are less suitable. However it *is* possible to look for certain characteristics and to try to develop them in your own writing. Examples of these characteristics are that the writing:

- considers time-frames
- is aware of uncertainties and the relative nature of things
- speculates on the consequences of actions
- thinks about change
- focuses on one or two events that it then explores in depth
- relates events to personal development.

Here are three examples for you to compare. Each account is of the same event (the writer's experience of group work).

---

**Example A**

Last week was the group presentation for our project. It went fairly well, we passed. Some of the group had really not pulled their weight; they never turned up to meetings or replied to their emails. I remember our lecturer covered group work at the beginning of the term, when she handed out the assignment. We did a questionnaire and I came out as the sort that always gets things done in the end, which is more than you can say for some of the others in my group. Still, maybe the next time I have to do group work I'll be luckier.

**Example B**

Last week I took part in a group presentation about the project we have been doing all this term. It went fairly well, we passed and were given some really useful feedback. Some of the group had not contributed much over the term, they rarely turned up to meetings or replied to emails. That meant that we hardly ever had everyone there at the same time so

---

it was very difficult to agree the different jobs that had to be done, who should do them and in what order.

I remember our lecturer covered group work at the beginning of the term, when she handed out the assignment. We talked about what makes an effective team, the stages you have to go through, team roles and team types. We completed a questionnaire and I was classified as the sort that always gets things done in the end. I was pleased about that, I think that is one of the types you really need in a team and I like to think of myself as cooperative and hardworking, which is more than you can say for some of the others in my group. Still, maybe the next time I have to do group work I'll be luckier or I might insist we draw up some ground rules before the first meeting.

### Example C

Last week I took part in a group presentation about the project we have been doing all this term. It went fairly well, we passed and were given some really useful feedback. It said that we spoke well, kept to time and used very effective computer visuals. However it marked us down on evidence of working as a team. Some of the group had not contributed much over the term, they rarely turned up to meetings or replied to emails. That meant that we hardly ever had everyone there at the same time so it was very difficult to agree the different jobs that had to be done, who should do them and in what order. It meant that some of us had to do far more than our fair share. Looking back on it now, we should have tried to do something about it earlier.

I remember our lecturer covered group work at the beginning of the term, when she handed out the assignment. We talked about what makes an effective team, the stages you have to go through, team roles and team types. We discussed how you can build up a team and how you can ruin a team, that was very helpful. We completed a questionnaire and I was classified as the sort that always gets things done in the end. I was pleased about that, I think that is one of the types you really need in a team (as well as in any future employment) and I like to think of myself as cooperative and hardworking, which is more than you can say for some of the others in my group. Still, maybe the next time I have to do group work I'll be luckier or I might insist we draw up some ground rules before the first meeting. I mustn't pretend I was perfect though – I did skip a few meetings without warning anyone. I'll certainly make sure I don't behave like that again, it shows a lack of respect. On balance, I would say this was a useful exercise to go through, but the problem with it was that we were not all fully committed as a team.

The areas that have been highlighted show examples of some of the characteristics of reflective writing mentioned above. Account B has more reflection than A, and C has more reflection than B.

> It is not sufficient simply to have an experience in order to learn. Without reflecting upon this experience it may quickly be forgotten, or its learning potential lost. It is from the feelings and thoughts emerging from this reflection that generalisations or concepts can be generated. And it is generalisations that allow new situations to be tackled effectively.
>
> (Gibbs, 1988: 9)

## Activity 9.2 Questions that call for reflective writing

Look at these questions from a psychology textbook. Which ones lend themselves to a reflective approach in the writing? Why?

---

**Learning in practice**

1 Why should deep learning lead to better academic success?
2 Why should personality mediate academic success?
3 How do you learn? Examine how you approach your course reading or revision – do you think that your approach is the best one? Has your approach changed as the course has progressed?
4 Is it better to study in a group or on your own?
5 To what extent does your learning benefit from your confidence in your abilities?

(Martin *et al.*, 2007: 298)

---

# REFLECTION ON YOUR STUDIES

There are a number of areas where you may be asked to write reflectively during your studies that can help you gain insight into your learning.

## Preparation

You might write about:

- how you chose a topic for an essay
- how you planned your essay
- how you prepared for a seminar.

## Performance

You could reflect on:

- how you took notes
- how you performed in a recent examination
- how you conducted an experiment
- what experiences you gained from some part-time or voluntary work.

## Problem-solving

You could discuss and analyse:

- how you contributed to some group work
- how you solved a particular maths problem
- how you understood a complex theory.

# PERSONAL DEVELOPMENT

Since you are focusing on yourself in reflective writing it is important to be aware of and assess your skills and abilities. This section has a series of exercises and ideas to help you think clearly about your skills and abilities, and suggests areas to consider when you are writing about yourself. The table below has divided studying into six main categories to help you think about what kind of skills are needed in higher education. You could use it to think about your levels of ability in each category.

## Study skills: six areas

| Communication | Data handling |
|---|---|
| Speaking | Collecting data |
| Listening | Analysing data |
| Reading | Understanding statistics |
| Writing | Using spreadsheets |
| Giving a presentation | |
| **Research/study** | **Individual** |
| Organising your work | Time management |
| Using ideas | Action planning |
| Making notes | Understanding your strengths and weaknesses |
| Analysing | Managing your learning |
| Problem-solving | Focusing on the task |
| Questioning what you learn | |
| **Teamwork** | **Information handling** |
| Listening to other people's ideas or opinions | Using the internet |
| Taking the lead | Evaluating information |
| Working with others | Remembering facts |
| Negotiating | IT skills |

# SWOT analysis

A SWOT analysis (Strengths, Weaknesses, Opportunities, Threats) is a tool that is often used in business but can be used in other ways, for example to help you think about your learning. Here we are suggesting you use it to think about your abilities as a student and the environment you are studying in.

## SWOT analysis

| Strengths | Weaknesses |
|---|---|
| Things you are good at, skills you already have e.g. *quick reader* | Things you need to improve on, skills you do not have e.g. *poor time management* |
| **Opportunities** | **Threats** |
| e.g. *career opportunities in your subject area* | e.g. *things that get in the way of those career opportunities* |

## Activity 9.3 SWOT analysis (individual)

Carry out a SWOT analysis on yourself and your current situation as a student.

| Strengths | Weaknesses |
|---|---|
| | |
| **Opportunities** | **Threats** |
| | |

## Activity 9.4 SWOT analysis (one of your subjects)

Now try it in relation to one of the subjects you are studying. Think about your strengths and weaknesses in the subject then consider advantages and disadvantages of studying the subject.

| Strengths | Weaknesses |
|---|---|
| | |
| **Opportunities** | **Threats** |
| | |

## Activity 9.5 Placing your skills in a wider context

Now that you have done a SWOT analysis you can use the following table to help you think about some of those skills in a wider context. Mark your assessment on a scale of 1–5 (1 is low, 5 is high).

| Skills | Your ability | Importance for studies | Importance for life outside | Plan to improve |
|---|---|---|---|---|
| Communication | | | | |
| Managing your workload | | | | |
| Team-working | | | | |
| Prioritising | | | | |
| Problem-solving | | | | |

Put an asterisk in the final column against any that you think you should focus on in particular. Make notes elsewhere on how you can do this.

# The way you learn

Here are further areas that you could use for your reflection:

## Study habits

- what time of day you prefer to study (e.g. late at night, first thing in the morning)
- whether you need to work in complete silence or prefer background noise
- whether you prefer to work on your own or in a group
- your concentration span.

## Assignments

- how well you plan your time
- how good you are at managing deadlines
- whether you leave things to the last minute
- whether you prefer exams to coursework or vice versa.

## In class

- how easy you find it to speak out in a group
- how good you are at giving a presentation
- whether you ask questions if you do not understand
- whether you join in class discussions or prefer to stay quiet.

### Learning strategies

- what use you make of any feedback you get
- whether you enjoy problem-solving exercises
- ways you like to make notes (pictures, diagrams, mind-maps, etc.)
- how you use information technology in your learning.

# LEARNING JOURNALS

Sometimes it is easier to use a template to help you write reflectively. One of the most common is called a learning journal, of the type shown earlier. A learning journal (also known as a learning log, learning diary, reflective log or journal) is something that describes processes as well as outcomes or products. It is written over a period of time, often to accompany the main areas of study (e.g. a single module). It considers the wider implications of events and attempts to place them in context. It can help you to clarify and develop ideas and help resolve problems. Used effectively it can promote problem-solving and critical thinking, just as in many science disciplines where a log book is kept during an experiment or throughout a field study.

There is no set structure to a learning journal: what is important is that the writer uses it to complete a cycle of development modelled on the learning cycle defined by Kolb (1984) in order to learn from their experience.

## The learning cycle

The process of learning from experience is often referred to as the learning cycle and shown as a diagram, adapted from the stages that Kolb first defined. The stages of the process are:

1 describe an event
2 review it
3 reach conclusions
4 plan for the next time.

Figure 9.1 on page 174 gives an example. Read in a clockwise direction, starting at the top.

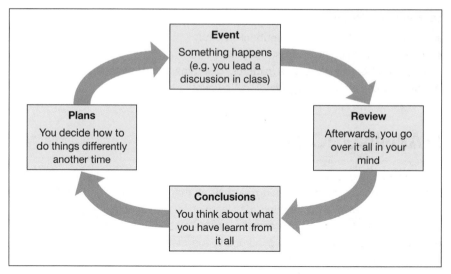

Figure 9.1 **A reflective learning cycle**

## Activity 9.6 **Using the learning cycle**

Choose from one of the following and describe it using the four steps of Kolb's learning cycle. Make your own decision whether to write by hand or to type it, as well as how much to write.

- a recent lecture
- an interview for a job
- a holiday with friends
- a recent assignment.

## Things to write about

As a student, your reflection will normally be about your studies. The kind of language you need to use to make sure it remains within an academic framework can be presented as follows:

◀
See
Chapters 7
and 8

### Description, explanation

- what you did and why
- what other people did and why
- how you felt about what others did.

### Analysis

- what was good and bad about what you did and why
- what you liked about what you did
- why you felt like that
- what you found easy or difficult and why.

## Evaluation

- the impact of what you did
- how useful your contribution to an exercise was
- how much you have achieved in your learning.

## Application

- how you have used what you have been taught in class
- what you are going to do differently in this type of situation next time
- what steps you are going to take on the basis of what you have learned
- what you are going to do next.

# Templates for reflective writing

The following templates give you some frameworks to help you order your thoughts. They may also give you ideas to develop your own templates. Remember that there are no set rules for reflective writing – it is the depth of analysis that counts, rather than a set structure.

## Activity 9.7 Three examples of a template to record your thoughts

### 1 Thinking about a lecture or tutorial

| What was the lecture/tutorial about this week? |
| --- |
| Did you have any problems with following it? |
| What connections can you make between this lecture/tutorial and the ones before? |
| How will the lecture/tutorial be useful for your studies as a whole? |

→

## 2 Thinking about an assignment

| |
|---|
| Did you find this assignment easy to do? |
| How useful do you think it was? |
| What do you think you learnt from doing it? |
| How would you do things differently another time? |

## 3 Reflecting on a work placement

| |
|---|
| What were your responsibilities during the placement? |
| How well do you think you carried them out? |
| What connections can you make between the work placement and your studies? |
| How has the work placement helped your future career prospects? |

# SUMMARY

This chapter has shown you how reflection can be a valuable part of academic study and shown you some examples of reflective writing. It has shown you areas to use when writing about yourself and your development as a student. It has suggested templates you can use to structure your answers.

## References

Gibbs, G. (1988) *Learning by Doing: A Guide to Teaching and Learning Methods*. London: Further Education Unit.

Hatton, N. and Smith, D. (1995) 'Reflection in Teacher Education', *Teaching and Teacher Education*, 11(1), pp. 33–49.

Kolb, D. A. (1984) *Experiential Learning: Experience as the Source of Learning and Development*. New York: Prentice Hall.

Details of highlighted references can be found in the Introduction on page xxii.

# WORKING WITH OTHER PEOPLE'S IDEAS AND VOICES

This chapter will cover using other people's ideas to support the points that you make or the arguments that you raise in your assignments. It will address the reasons for and methods of citing, referencing and quoting authors as well as looking at strategies for avoiding plagiarism.

This chapter will cover:

■ how to include sources in your work through
   - summary
   - paraphrase
   - synthesis
   - referencing
■ how to avoid plagiarism.

## USING THIS CHAPTER

# INTRODUCTION

One of the most important aspects of academic writing is making use of the ideas of other people, but when you are writing you need to be careful to use that information appropriately. This is a difficult area because, as a student, when you are doing assignments, you need to use what you have read or been taught in your lectures but you also need to show that you have understood what you have read and that you can use other people's ideas and findings in your own way. Early on in your life as a student, you need to find the right balance between insufficient use of other people's ideas and overuse of their words.

There are several reasons why you should be including other authors' words, mainly:

- *To show that you have read and understood specific texts*. You need to show that you have read around the subject, not just confined your reading to one textbook or set of lecture notes. This is to ensure that you are aware of the major areas of thought in your specific subject.
- *To support the points you are making by referring to other people's work*. This will strengthen your argument. The main way to do this is to cite authors that agree with the points you are making. You can, however, cite authors who do not agree with your points, as long as you explain why you think they are wrong. Do not make a statement that will cause your reader to ask, 'Who says?' or 'How do you know?'

See
Chapter 14

# INCLUDING SOURCES IN YOUR WORK

Much of what you write will come from other people's ideas – from the textbooks you read, the lectures and the seminars you attend, and your discussions with other students. This is what academic study is all about. Remember to be selective in your choice of sources. Getting information from a newspaper and a few lecture handouts will never be enough. You need to make sure that the texts you access are appropriate. Here is a list of suggestions:

- a peer-reviewed journal
- a text on your reading list
- a credible website
- an information database
- a text recommended by your lecturer.

The ideas and people that you refer to need to be made explicit by a system of referencing: if you use another person's ideas or words, you must say where you have taken them from; if you do not, you risk being accused of plagiarism. This section will cover citation, summarising, paraphrasing, synthesising and writing a list of references as ways of including sources.

# Citation

There are two ways in which you can refer to, or cite, another person's work: (1) by direct quotation or (2) by reporting (through summary or paraphrase). These will now be looked at in turn.

## 1 Direct quotation

Occasionally, you may want to quote the precise words of another author in your work. For example:

> A further way of showing that a school is fully inclusive as suggested by Davies is when 'schools will monitor the progress of boys and girls and where there is an attainment gap will put in intervention strategies to improve performance'.

(Davies, 2006: 155)

If you choose to quote, keep the quotation as brief as possible and quote only when it is necessary. As a guide, try to use no more than three short quotes per page. You must always have a good reason for using a quote – and feeling unable to change the words of the original is never a good reason. The emphasis should be on working with other people's ideas, not reproducing their words. Your piece of work should be a synthesis of information from sources, expressed in your own words, not a collection of quotations.

*Reasons for using quotations*:
- if you want to use another person's exact words because the language used in the quotation says what you want to say particularly well
- when you need to support your points by
  - quoting evidence
  - giving examples/illustrating
  - adding the weight of authority.

*Reasons for **not** using quotations*:
- the information is well-known in your subject area
- the quote disagrees with your argument, unless you can prove it is wrong
- you cannot understand the meaning of the original source
- you are not able to summarise the original
- in order to *make* your points for you (use quotes to *support* your points)
- if the quotation repeats (rather than expands on) the point you have just made.

If you decide to use a quotation, you must be very careful to make it clear that the words or ideas that you are using are taken from another writer.

There are usually three items of information needed to acknowledge a quote within your assignment: author or authors' surname(s) only, year of publication and page number from which the quote was taken. The position of this information can vary as illustrated below:

> Brassington and Pettitt (2006: 312) state that: 'The danger is, of course, that by trying to avoid challenging anyone linguistically, imagination is lost and the Eurobrand becomes the Eurobland.'

According to Brassington and Pettitt (2006), 'The danger is, of course, that by trying to avoid challenging anyone linguistically, imagination is lost and the Eurobrand becomes the Eurobland' (p. 312).

According to Brassington and Pettitt, 'The danger is, of course, that by trying to avoid challenging anyone linguistically, imagination is lost and the Eurobrand becomes the Eurobland' (2006: 312).

'The danger is, of course, that by trying to avoid challenging anyone linguistically, imagination is lost and the Eurobrand becomes the Eurobland' (Brassington and Pettitt, 2006: 312).

In all cases, on your reference list at the end of the essay you should write:

References
Brassington, F. and Pettitt, S. (2006) *Principles of Marketing* (4th edn). Harlow: Pearson Education.

You may have noticed that when the authors are not in brackets, expressions such as 'according to' or 'X and Y state that ...' are used to introduce the quotation. Quote marks (either '...' or "...") are also used around the quoted text. Below are some useful expressions you can use in order to introduce quotes. 'X' stands for the author:

As X stated/states, '...'.

As X wrote/writes, '...'.

As X commented/comments, '...'.

As X observed/observes, '...'.

As X pointed/points out, '...'.

This example is given by X: '...'.

According to X, '...'.

X claims that, '...'.

X found that, '...'.

The opinion of X is that, '...'.

➡ See Chapter 11 There are many other expressions which are linked to finding your own voice when writing academic texts. These will be explored further in Chapter 11.

To reiterate, when you are using a direct quotation of a single phrase or sentence, quotation marks should be used around the words, which must be quoted exactly as they are in the original. Remember to include the author, year of publication and page number of the quote.

There will be times when you may wish to omit some of the author's original words that are not relevant to your writing, or you may wish to insert material (additions or explanations) into a quotation.

### Omitting words

In this case, use three dots (. . .) to indicate where you have omitted words. If you omit any of the author's original words, make sure you do not change the meaning and the sentence remains grammatically correct.

> 'The danger is ... that by trying to avoid challenging anyone linguistically, imagination is lost and the Eurobrand becomes the Eurobland' (Brassington and Pettitt, 2006: 312).

### Inserting words

If you need to insert words into a quotation (usually to clarify meaning), use square brackets [. . .] around your inserted text.

> 'This [academic writing] is then further developed in their undergraduate study' (Martala, 2006: 40).

### Quoted text within a quote

There may be times where the material quoted already contains a quotation. In this case, use double quotation marks for the original quotation ("..." ).

> Cai (2008: 7) stated 'different persuasion theories operate well in certain contexts and are then combined in an "integrative framework" '.

Note that you may choose to adopt the convention of using double quotation marks for quotations and then use single quotation marks for the original quotation. This book, for example, uses single quotation marks and then double ones within them, as shown immediately above.

### Long quotations

If the direct quotation is long – more than two or three lines – it should be indented as a separate paragraph with no quotation marks.

> According to Keenan and Riches (2007: 114):

> The Enterprise Act 2002 is designed to promote enterprise by minimising the effects of business failure. In this connection the Act differentiates between 'culpable' bankrupts who set out to run a business in a way that would mislead the public and other businesses and the 'non-culpable' bankrupt who for reasons beyond his or her control and despite best efforts has suffered business failure.

In all cases, on your reference list at the end of the essay you should state the full details as in the example below:

References
Keenan, D. and Riches, S. (2007) Business Law (8th edn). Harlow: Pearson Education.

## Activity 10.1 Finding and correcting referencing errors

Find and correct the mistakes in the following quoted texts. There may be more than one mistake per exercise. You will need to use the reference list at the end of the activity to help you.

1 School readiness is a term that refers to a child's ability to go to school ready to learn, having already gained... skills that will prepare them for class learning beforehand. (Davies, 2006: 47).
2 'Biogeography is an important area of science and informs global environmental policy as well as local land management practice'. (Hilary S.C. Thomas 2008, p. 241).
3 According to McLaney and Atrill, 'the relevant/marginal cost approach deduces the minimum price for which the business can offer the product for sale'.
4 In practice, airlines are major users of a relevant/marginal costing approach. McLaney.
5 'Damage to the **amygdala**, a cluster of neurons located deep in the temporal lobe, affects emotional behaviour...' (Martin, G.N., Carlson, N.R. and Buskist, W. Psychology. 3rd edn. London: Pearson Education. p. 157).

**References:**

Davies, S. (2006) *The Essential Guide to Teaching*. Harlow: Pearson Education.

McLaney, E. and Atrill, P. (2008) *Accounting. An Introduction* (4th edn). Harlow: Pearson Education. (Extracts are from page 420.)

Martin, G. N., Carlson, N.R. and Buskist, W. (2007) *Psychology* (3rd edn). Harlow: Pearson Education.

Thomas, H. S. C. (2008) 'Biogeographical concepts'. In J. Holden (ed.) *Physical Geography and the Environment* (2nd edn). pp. 153–92. Harlow: Pearson Education.

## Activity 10.2 The mechanics of quoting

Assume you used the following quotations in your essay and so need to cite them appropriately. Use the information below to do this.

1 This quote can be found on page 197 of a book called 'Psychology'. The book was written by three authors: Dr G. Neil Martin, Dr Neil R. Carlson and Dr William Buskist. This third edition was published in 2007 by Pearson Education, in London. 'One of the key features of the visual system is that it is organised hierarchically at the neural level'.
2 The following quote is from a book written by Philip Kotler, Gary Armstrong, Veronica Wong and John Saunders. The title of the book is Principles of Marketing and this quote, which can be found on page 475, is from the fifth European edition published in 2008. The publishers are Pearson Education and the publishing place is Harlow. 'Market leaders can expand the market by developing new users, new uses and more usage of its products.'
3 'Since 1999 LEAs have had specific duties to combat bullying. Schools *must* have anti-bullying policies and LEAs must ensure that their schools comply with their duties.' This quote was taken from a book written by Susan Davies and published in Harlow in 2006. The title of the book is 'The essential guide to teaching'. The publishers are Pearson Education. The quote was taken from page 269.

*Multi-authored works*

Where several authors have written a book or journal article then it is a widely used convention to cite the main author and then use *et al*. (short for the Latin term *et alii* meaning 'and others') rather than listing them all. Usually more than two or three authors listed are treated in this way. So, in point 2 of Activity 10.2 you would write: Kotler *et al*.

## 2 Reporting

This simply means reporting the other writer's ideas *in your own words* and the best method to use is summary. There are two main ways of showing that you have used another writer's ideas – integral or non-integral – depending on whether or not the name of the cited author occurs within the cited sentence or in brackets.

*Integral (author as part of sentence)*

According to Davies (2006) it is essential that pupils learn how to evaluate their strengths and weaknesses.

The importance of pupils learning how to evaluate their strengths and weaknesses was stressed by Davies (2006).

*Non-integral (author in brackets)*

Evidence from classroom learning (Davies, 2006) suggests that it is essential for pupils to learn how to evaluate their strengths and weaknesses.

It is important that pupils learn how to evaluate their strengths and weaknesses (Davies, 2006).

At the end of the essay, the reference list will state:

Davies, S. (2006) *The Essential Guide to Teaching*. Harlow: Pearson Education.

# SUMMARISING

When you read texts for pleasure you are not usually expected to summarise them. However, in order to have sufficient material for you to work with when writing your assignments, you need to read a variety of texts and select information which is relevant to your work. Once you have identified suitable material, you need to make a number of adjustments before you can incorporate it into your assignment. A summary, which is basically a shortened version of a text, is one such adjustment. A summary should contain your chosen main points from the original text in a condensed manner. It should be written in your own words and the source must be acknowledged.

Notice how you can retell a text with which you are familiar. This could be a novel, magazine or newspaper article. What would you need to do if you were reading it out loud to a friend? You would probably find that you were reading the sentences word for word. If you put the text aside for half a day or so and then try to retell the content of the text without looking at it, you will notice that you cannot remember the text word for word, unless you have a photographic memory of course. Hopefully, you can remember the main points or sequence of the text and you can retell it *in your own* words. Which of these two ways of telling the story is more like a summary?

## Activity 10.3 Summarising unfamiliar text

Try reading a text whose subject you are not familiar with. How easy did you find relating the original in your own words without referring back to the text?

## Activity 10.4 Noticing features in summarised text

Read the original text and the summary which follows and note down the differences between the two texts in the table below.

**Original version**

There are a number of ways of expressing the total amount of water in the oceans. Seawater covers 361 million square kilometres ($361 \times 10^6$ km$^2$) which represents 71% of the surface of the globe. The total volume of water is enormous: 1.37 thousand million cubic kilometres ($1.37 \times 10^9$ km$^3$). Most of this water is contained in the three great oceans of the world: the Pacific, Atlantic and Indian Oceans.          (Holden, 2008: 57)

**Summary**

The surface of the earth comprises 71% seawater, most of which can be found in the Indian, Pacific and Atlantic Oceans.

| Features you identify | Original version | Summarised version |
|---|---|---|
| Length of text | | Shorter than the original |
| | | |

## Points to help you summarise

1 Make sure you understand the original text.

2 Think about your purpose in using this text. What is your purpose in writing your summary?

- Are you summarising to support your points? or
- Are you summarising so you can criticise the work before you introduce your main points?

3 Select the relevant information. This depends on your purpose.

4 Find the important ideas (words and phrases) and mark them in some way or list them elsewhere.
- Distinguish between main and subsidiary information.
- Delete most details and examples, unimportant information, anecdotes, examples, illustrations, data, etc.

5 Find synonyms or alternative phrases for those words (a thesaurus would help). You do not need to change specialised vocabulary.

6 Change the structure of the text. This includes:
- changing adjectives to adverbs and nouns to verbs
- breaking up long sentences and combining short sentences
- identifying the relationships between words and ideas and expressing them in a different way. (Be careful you do not change the meaning.)

7 Once you have completed the above steps, you can begin to rewrite the main ideas in complete sentences combining your notes into a piece of continuous writing. Use conjunctions and adverbs such as 'therefore', 'however', 'although', 'since', to show the connections between the ideas.

8 Check your work.

**TIP** *Make sure:*
- *your purpose is clear*
- *you have not copied any text (unless you are quoting)*
- *you do not misinterpret the original*
- *the length of your text is shorter*
- *the style of writing is your own*
- *you acknowledge other people's work.*

## Activity 10.5 Evaluating summarised text

Read the following extract and the two summaries that follow it. Which text is a better summary and why? Remember to take into account the summarising points above.

> Fossil fuel continues to be the main source of energy. Moreover, the developing world, which consists of about five sixths of humankind, will increase its population and its fossil fuel burning for many years after the rich countries have stabilised and decreased their dependency on fossil fuels. Some poor countries have neither fossil fuels nor any other supply of energy, and so cannot develop. Even fuel-wood is in short supply.

→

Nuclear power was developed enthusiastically by many countries in the 1950s, and 29 countries were running 437 nuclear power plants by 1998. Early optimism about development of an energy economy from nuclear fission faded following nuclear accidents and leakages such as Chernobyl in the USSR (now in the Russia Federation) in 1986. Many environmentalists believe that the risks that are inherent in nuclear fission are quite unacceptable. Power from nuclear fission is very expensive, once the costs of handling radioactive waste and decommissioning old power stations are taken into account. Despite all this, many governments are in favour of continuing and even expanding their nuclear power programmes, and for many it is the only practical way to reduce carbon emissions.                                                    (Holden, 2008: 612–13)

**Summary 1**

Currently, fossil fuel remains the main energy source and whereas rich countries will be in a position to turn to alternative forms of fuel in the future, developing countries will become more dependent on it. Alternative forms such as nuclear power seemed a likely alternative in the 1950s but its development in the 40 years that followed had some disastrous results. Although environmentalists view it as risky and expensive, certain governments are continuing to pursue nuclear power programmes and for many there are no other practical alternatives of reducing carbon emissions.                                         (Holden, 2008)

**Summary 2**

Fossil fuel remains the main energy source. Rich countries will reduce their reliance on fossil fuel in the future, whereas developing countries which make up about five sixths of humankind will become more dependent on it. Some poor countries will not develop due to a lack of energy supplies as even fuel-wood is decreasing.

Nuclear power was exploited by many countries in the 1950s, and 29 countries were running 437 nuclear power plants by 1998. However nuclear accidents and leakages such as Chernobyl in the USSR in 1986 have led to a decrease in its development. This is further supported by environmentalists' views that the risks are too high in addition to the high cost of developing power from nuclear fission. In spite of the negative evidence, many governments are continuing and in certain cases expanding their nuclear power programmes. For many governments nuclear power is the only practical way to reduce carbon emissions.                                                                (Holden, 2008)

## Activity 10.6 Summarising short texts

Using the information provided in this chapter, summarise the following short text. Use the summarising tips on page 187 to check your work.

Home detention curfews were introduced by the Crime and Disorder Act 1998. Prisoners sentenced to between three months' and four years' imprisonment can be released early (usually 60 days early) on a licence that includes a curfew condition. This requires the released prisoners to remain at a certain address at set times, during which period they will be subjected to electronic monitoring. Most curfews are set for 12 hours between 7 pm and

7 am. The person can be recalled to prison if there is a failure to comply with the conditions of the curfew condition or in order to protect the public from serious harm. Private contractors fit the tag to a person's ankle, install monitoring equipment which plugs into the telephone system in their home and connects with a central computer system, and notify breaches of curfew to the Prison Service. (143 words)          **(Elliott and Quinn, 2008: 413)**

## Activity 10.7 Summarising longer texts

Using the information provided in this chapter on summarising, summarise the following text. Use the summarising tips on page 187 to check your work.

Micturition, voiding and urination all refer to the process of emptying the urinary bladder. Urine collects in the bladder until pressure stimulates special sensory nerve endings in the bladder wall called stretch receptors. This occurs when the adult bladder contains 250–450 ml of urine. In children, a considerably smaller volume, 50–200 ml, stimulates these nerves.

The stretch receptors transmit impulses to the spinal cord, specifically to the voiding reflex centre located at the level of the second to fourth sacral vertebrae, causing the internal sphincter to relax and stimulating the urge to void. If the time and place are appropriate for urination, the conscious portion of the brain relaxes the external urethral sphincter muscle and urination takes place. If the time and place are inappropriate, the micturition reflex usually subsides until the bladder becomes more filled and the reflex is stimulated again.

Voluntary control of urination is possible only if the nerves supplying the bladder and urethra, the neural tracts of the cord and brain, and the motor area of the cerebrum are all intact. The individual must be able to sense that the bladder is full. Injury to any of these parts of the nervous system – for example, by a cerebral haemorrhage or spinal cord injury above the level of the sacral region – results in intermittent involuntary emptying of the bladder. Older adults whose cognition is impaired may not be aware of the need to urinate or able to respond to this urge by seeking toilet facilities. (248 words)          **(Kozier *et al.*, 2008: 489)**

## Activity 10.8 Using your own texts

Taking into account the suggestions above, use your own reading material and summarise texts relevant to your assignments. Use the summarising tips on page 187 to check your work.

# PARAPHRASING

There may be times when you are writing when a summary of ideas is just not appropriate or relevant. You may wish to maintain a closer link with the original but you do not want to quote word for word. Paraphrasing is one solution. It is best to limit paraphrasing to short chunks of text. You need to change the words and the structure of the original but keep the meaning the same. Do remember that even when you paraphrase someone's work you must acknowledge it.

Notice the changes which have been made in the paraphrase extract of the following example:

### Example
*Original*

> The mere physical proximity of one person to another is a potent facilitator of attraction (Martin *et al.*, 2007: 757).

*Paraphrase*

> Attraction between two people is greatly influenced by their physical closeness (Martin *et al.*, 2007).

| Original | Paraphrase |
|---|---|
| Physical proximity | Physical closeness |
| Of one person to another | Between two people |
| X is a potent facilitator of Y | Y is greatly influenced by X |
| 'Physical proximity' is the subject of the sentence | 'Attraction' is the subject of the sentence |

Paraphrasing the words of the original is not a particularly difficult task provided you understand the original text. Remember to use a thesaurus to help you find alternative vocabulary.

## Points to help you paraphrase

1 Make sure you understand the original text.
2 Find the important ideas (words and phrases) and mark them in some way or list them elsewhere.
3 Find synonyms or alternative phrases for those words (a thesaurus would help). You do not need to change specialised vocabulary.
4 Change the structure of the text. This includes:
   - changing adjectives to adverbs and nouns to verbs
   - breaking up long sentences and combining short sentences

- identifying the relationships between words and ideas and expressing them in a different way. (Be careful you do not change the meaning.)

5  Once you have completed the above steps, you can begin to rewrite the main ideas in complete sentences combining your notes into a piece of continuous writing.

6  Check your work.

**TIP** *Make sure:*
- *you have not copied any text*
- *the meaning is the same as the original*
- *the style of writing is your own*
- *your paraphrase is the same length as the original*
- *you acknowledge other people's work through appropriate referencing.*

Remember that when paraphrasing you are actually trying to avoid overquoting in your work. Paraphrasing is the alternative to direct quoting. You will probably therefore only need to paraphrase short texts. When dealing with long paragraphs or indeed pages or chapters, summarising the main ideas in the text would be more appropriate.

Here are some additional expressions you can use to refer to someone's work that you are paraphrasing. They are equally useful for summarising text.

The work of X indicates that ...

The work of X reveals that ...

The work of X shows that ...

Reference to X reveals that ...

In an article by X, ...

As X has indicated ...

A study by X shows that ...

X has expressed a similar view.

X has drawn attention to the fact that ...

X reports that ...

X notes that ...

X concludes that ...

X argues that ...

X discovered that ...

Research by X suggests that ...

Once again, please refer to Chapter 11 with reference to how these expressions can be included to help you find your voice in your written work.

pter 11

## Activity 10.9 Evaluating paraphrased text

Read the following short text and the two examples of paraphrase which follow it. Which example is a better paraphrase and why? Remember to take into account the paraphrasing tips above.

**Anorexia nervosa** is an eating disorder characterised by a severe decrease in eating. The literal meaning of the word 'anorexia' suggests a loss of appetite, but people with this disorder generally do not lose their appetite. **(Martin *et al*., 2007: 606)**

**Paraphrase 1**

An extreme reduction in food consumed by a person may indicate they have the eating disorder anorexia nervosa. Although the term 'anorexia' literally means losing your appetite, this is generally not the case with sufferers. **(Martin *et al*., 2007)**

**Paraphrase 2**

Anorexia nervosa is an eating disorder indicated by an extreme reduction in eating. 'Anorexia' literally means a loss of appetite, but people with this disorder do not generally lose their hunger. **(Martin *et al*., 2007)**

## Activity 10.10 Paraphrasing text

Using the information provided in this chapter on paraphrasing, paraphrase the following texts. Use the paraphrasing tips on page 191 to check your work.

**Text 1**

One study found worse outcomes among children adopted from an at-risk register than among those fostered or returned home. The explanation for this finding is not clear. Possibly the adoptive parents chosen were less thoroughly assessed than would have been the case if they had been offered more 'popular' children for whom the competition would have been greater. **(Wilson *et al*., 2008: 502)**

**Text 2**

The shift toward segmented marketing and the explosive developments in information and communications technology have had a dramatic impact on marketing communications. Just as mass marketing once gave rise to a new generation of mass-media communications, the shift towards targeted marketing and the changing communications environment are giving birth to a new marketing communications model. **(Kotler *et al*., 2008: 693)**

Taking into account the suggestions above, use your own reading material and paraphrase short texts relevant to your assignments. Once again, use the paraphrasing tips on page 191 to check your work.

# SYNTHESISING

When reading for assignments, you are advised to read widely. Do not try to base your entire piece of work on one or two articles or books. You need to ensure that you have ample material to incorporate into your work. The previous two areas you have worked on are summarising and paraphrasing, which should help you cut down on superfluous quotes. They will also be useful in this third strategy – synthesising. A synthesis is a combination, usually a shortened version, of several texts made into one. Once you have selected relevant parts of your sources to work with, you can use your paraphrase and summary skills to write the information in your own words. The information from all sources has to fit together into one continuous text and the sources must be acknowledged and appropriately referenced.

All of the points provided in the earlier tips for summarising and paraphrasing are relevant when you synthesise with the addition of the tip below, which you should add to the summarising tips.

**TIP** *Organise the information you have from summarising the different texts. You could give all similar ideas in different texts the same number or colour to help you group them together. You may find the information on planning and developing paragraphs in Chapter 6 useful at this stage.*

ter 6

Please note that synthesising material is insufficient in itself. In order for synthesis to become an academically well-written piece of work, you will need to refer to other chapters in this book.

Activity 10.12 **Synthesising your own texts**

Taking into account the suggestions above, use your own reading material and synthesise texts relevant to your assignments. Use the summarising and synthesising tips on pages 187 and 191 to check your work.

# WRITING A LIST OF REFERENCES

In addition to the references within the text, you need to provide a list of materials that you have used or referred to, at the end of all pieces of academic writing. This usually has a heading: *References*. Make sure you cross-check all the references within your text against the reference list at the end. The purpose of this reference list is to supply the information needed to allow a reader to find a source. The authors appear in alphabetical order in the reference list.

Some of the referencing methods used in the academic world are:

- the Vancouver system
- the MLA
- the APA style
- the Harvard system.

There is no definitive version of the Harvard system, however, and most universities use their own varieties.

## Example

This is an example of the Harvard system style. Each reference written in this style is ordered as follows depending on the source. (Note that all the commas and full stops form an important part of the referencing system.)

### Textbook

> Martin, G. N., Carlson, N. R. and Buskist, W. (2007) *Psychology* (3rd edn.). Harlow: Pearson Education.

Note the following:

- surname of author and author's initial (this information is repeated for each of the co-authors)
- year of publication in brackets
- title of book in italics
- edition number in brackets if applicable (e.g. 3rd edn)
- publishing location
- publisher's name.

### A text from an edited collection

> Thomas, H. S. C. (2008). 'Biogeographical concepts'. In J. Holden, (Ed.), *Physical Geography and the Environment* (2nd edn), pp. 39–64. Harlow: Pearson Education.

Note the following:

- surname of author of chapter and author's initial (this information is repeated for each of the co-authors)
- year of publication in brackets
- title of chapter in quotation marks

- initial and surname of editor of book followed by (ed.)
- title of book in italics
- edition number in brackets (if applicable)
- page numbers of chapter
- publishing location
- publisher's name.

## Journal article

> Woodward-Kron, R. (2002) 'Critical analysis versus description? Examining the relationship in successful student writing'. *Journal of English for Academic Purposes, 1,* 121–143.

Note the following:

- surname of author of chapter and author's initial (this information is repeated for each of the co-authors)
- year of publication in brackets
- title of article in quotation marks
- title of journal in italics
- volume number in italics
- page numbers of article.

## Newspaper article

> Curtis, P. (2008). 'University entrants hit record high.' *The Guardian,* 22 August, p. 4.

Note the following:

- surname of author and author's initial
- year of publication in brackets
- title of article in quotation marks
- name of newspaper in italics
- day and month of article
- page number of article.

## Website article

> Harnack, A. and Kleppinger, E. (2003) *Online! A reference guide to using internet sources.* Retrieved, August 22, 2008 from http://www.bedfordstmartins.com/online/cite6.html#1

Note the following:

- surname of author and author's initial (if available) (this information is repeated for each of the co-authors)
- year of publication in brackets
- title of complete work in italics
- other relevant information (volume number, page numbers, etc., if available)
- full date article was accessed
- URL.

*Encyclopedia or dictionary*

> *Longman dictionary of contemporary English* (1978) London: Longman

Note the following:

- title of publication
- date
- publishing location
- publisher.

It is important to check which system is used by your department but also by individual lecturers. Handbooks supplied by your subject leaders usually provide a referencing guide.

## Activity 10.13 Finding and correcting errors on reference list

Find and correct the mistakes in the following five references. There may be more than one mistake in each reference.

Thompson. (2001) *Interaction in Academic Writing: Learning to Argue with the Reader*. Applied Linguistics, 22, 58–78.
Davies, S. (2006) *The essential guide to teaching*. Harlow.
Jeffries, S. (2008, 21 August) The ice age. The Guardian, pp 4–6.
Brassington, F. and Pettitt, S. *Principles of marketing* (4th edn.) Harlow: Pearson Education.
Holden J (ed.) (2008) Physical Geography and the Environment. 2nd edn. Pearson Education.

## Activity 10.14 Find the overall error

Looking at the five references above as a whole and ignoring the numbering, what is the overall error?

## Activity 10.15 The mechanics of referencing

Write a reference list using the style shown in the example above for the following three quotes:

> 1 This quote can be found on page 197 of a book called 'Psychology'. The book was written by 3 authors: Dr G. Neil Martin, Dr Neil R. Carlson and Dr William Buskist. This third edition was published in 2007 by Pearson Education, in London. 'One of the key features of the visual system is that it is organised hierarchically at the neural level.'

**2** The following quote is from a book written by Philip Kotler, Gary Armstrong, Veronica Wong and John Saunders. The title of the book is Principles of Marketing and this quote, which can be found on page 475, is from the fifth European edition published in 2008. The publishers are Pearson Education and the publishing place is Harlow. 'Market leaders can expand the market by developing new users, new uses and more usage of its products.'

**3** 'Since 1999 LEAs have had specific duties to combat bullying. Schools *must* have anti-bullying policies and LEAs must ensure that their schools comply with their duties.' This quote was taken from a book written by Susan Davies and published in Harlow in 2006. The title of the book is 'The essential guide to teaching'. The publishers are Pearson Education. The quote was taken from page 269.

# WHAT IS PLAGIARISM AND HOW CAN IT BE AVOIDED?

Plagiarism is using the ideas or words of another person without acknowledgement. Plagiarism can happen either deliberately or non-deliberately, and for many reasons. Reasons for deliberate plagiarism may be because you do not have the time or the energy to do the work yourself or you think your lecturer will not care or notice; or, perhaps, because you are not able to do the work yourself. The end result is a copied piece of work, either from a fellow student or from printed matter or the internet. In the academic world, plagiarism equals theft; it is therefore against university regulations and regarded as a very serious offence.

Whatever the reason for deliberate plagiarism is, if you do not do the work yourself, you are unlikely to learn from it. It is therefore a waste of your time. There are many ways your lecturer can check whether or not you have plagiarised and it is not worth the risk of being caught and excluded from your course of study.

Accidental plagiarism occurs when you unintentionally, through carelessness or lack of skill, use another person's words without acknowledging them. This can happen for several reasons:

- You may not know the correct systems for indicating that you are using another person's words or ideas.
- When you take notes from a book or journal, you copy out some sections and do not make this clear in your notes. Later when you reread the notes, you forget that they are not your words or ideas.
- You may feel your written work is not good enough so you borrow your friend's notes, not realising that some of the words are copied.

It will always be assumed that the words or ideas are your own if you do not say otherwise through appropriate citation. When the words or ideas you are using are taken from another writer, you must make this clear through citation and referencing.

If you do not, this is plagiarism. The aim of this acknowledgement is to supply the information needed to allow a user to find a source.

# How to avoid plagiarism

You need to acknowledge the source of an idea unless it is common knowledge within your subject area and this is sometimes difficult to determine. In general, if your lecturers, in lectures or handouts, do not acknowledge the source then you can assume that it is common knowledge within your subject.

See Chapters 7 to 11
You usually cite by reporting the work of others in your own words. As this chapter has shown, you can summarise the main points of the original, paraphrase short texts or synthesise when you use information from several sources. Do not forget that the central line of argument, the main voice, should be your own. This means that you will need to comment on or evaluate any other works that you use. If you do not, you will be accused of being too descriptive, of not being critical or analytical enough, or of not producing a clear argument.

## Activity 10.16 Identifying acceptable referencing methods

When using authors' ideas or words in your work, which of the following would you consider acceptable? Mark each box with a '✓' for acceptable and a '✗' for unacceptable.

| | ✓ ✗ |
|---|---|
| **1** Replacing some of the author's words in your text with synonyms, but maintaining the overall structure and the vocabulary of the original. | |
| **2** Collecting some short fixed phrases from a number of different texts and putting them together with some of your own words. | |
| **3** Paraphrasing a paragraph: rewriting ideas in the paragraph but changing the language, organisation and detail, and adding your own examples as well as acknowledging the source. | |
| **4** Copying out an article from a journal or textbook and submitting it as a piece of your own coursework. | |
| **5** Cutting and pasting a paragraph: using the sentences of the original but putting one or two in a different order and leaving one or two out. | |
| **6** Copying a sentence or paragraph directly from the original text with no changes. | |
| **7** Quoting a paragraph by placing it in quotation marks and acknowledging the source. | |
| **8** Using another author's organisation and way of arguing. | |

# SUMMARY

As part of your academic work you will need to read extensively and write assignments which incorporate the ideas of authors in your field. This indicates that you are increasing your knowledge by reading material which is relevant. You then need to show that you are not merely regurgitating what you read or hear in your lectures but you are thinking about it critically. Moreover, you need to build on the skill of combining and evaluating all the information that you need in order to answer a set question. Finally, part of the academic writing requirement is that you reference the authors that you use both within your written assignments and on the last page as a list. Appropriate referencing can increase your marks; lack of referencing can dramatically decrease them.

## References

Martala, M. (2006) 'Tracking Pre-Sessional Students' Writing Abilities at the University of Hertfordshire'. In A. Gillett and L. Wray (eds), *Assessing the Effectiveness of EAP Programmes,* pp. 40–55. London: BALEAP.

Details of highlighted references can be found in the Introduction on page xxii.

# 11 ▶ FINDING YOUR OWN VOICE

This chapter will look at the place of the writer in a piece of academic writing. Its aim is to help students establish when it is appropriate to express their own point of view and opinion. It will also suggest ways of ensuring that they keep their own voice clear, whilst incorporating the meanings and ideas of others.

This chapter will cover:

■ understanding voices
■ expressing your own voice to:
  – show confidence
  – show relationships
  – show the strength of your claim
  – evaluate statements.

## USING THIS CHAPTER

# INTRODUCTION

← See Chapters 4 and 10

Much of the writing that you do will be in response to an assignment title or question. In order to answer this, you need to gather the facts and evidence from a variety of sources, as you saw in Chapter 10. This will probably just help you to pass, but in order to do better and to develop your knowledge you need to combine these facts and ideas in your own way, using your own words. Your own words allow you to put your stamp on the assignment and this is what we call your 'voice'.

If you do badly in an assignment it may be because you have not answered the question. You may not have had the correct information to do so, or it may be the case that, even though you know and have given all the information necessary, you have not applied this knowledge in your own way to the title. What the lecturer wants you to do is to show you can make use of the knowledge and facts that you have learned to respond appropriately to the assignment title.

So as well as getting the information right, you need to make sure that your voice is identified and clear throughout. You need to give *your* answer to the question, to answer the question in your own voice.

# UNDERSTANDING DIFFERENT VOICES

You will find that in any academic text you read, there are ideas present from different people – different sources – including the author of the text.

## Activity 11.1 Recognising voices

Read the following text and try to identify the different ideas contained in it. When you have identified the ideas, try to decide where they come from.

> People make allowances for the age of the child with whom they are talking. Mothers talk differently to 2-year-olds compared with 10-year-olds (Snow, 1972a). Even 4-year-old children talk differently to 2-year-olds compared with how they talk to adults or other 4-year-olds (Shatz and Gelman, 1973). It seems unlikely that these differentiated speech patterns are innately determined. Snow (1972a) compared the speech patterns of a mother talking to a child with her speech patterns when she only pretended to be talking to a child. The woman's speech when the child was absent was simpler than it would have been if addressed to an adult, but when the child was present, it was simpler still. Clearly, then, feedback from children is important.                    (Martin *et al.*, 2007: 420)

We think you will find that there are ideas present in the above text from different people: there are different voices.

| Text | Voice |
|---|---|
| People make allowances for the age of the child with whom they are talking. | Voice of text writer. |
| Mothers talk differently to 2-year-olds compared with 10-year-olds (Snow, 1972a). | Voice of Snow. |
| Even 4-year-old children talk differently to 2-year-olds compared with how they talk to adults or other 4-year-olds (Shatz and Gelman, 1973). | Voice of Shatz and Gelman. |
| It seems unlikely that these differentiated speech patterns are innately determined. | Voice of text writer. |
| Snow (1972a) compared the speech patterns of a mother talking to a child with her speech patterns when she only pretended to be talking to a child. | Voice of Snow. |
| The woman's speech when the child was absent was simpler than it would have been if addressed to an adult, but when the child was present, it was simpler still. | Voice of text writer. |
| Clearly, then, feedback from children is important. | Voice of text writer. |

The first sentence presents the voice of the writers – Martin *et al*. In the following sentences, though, as well as Martin *et al*.'s voice, there is also the voice of a researcher called Snow as well as that of writers called Shatz and Gelman. Martin *et al*. make the point that people speak differently when they are speaking to small children. Snow gives an example of how mothers speak differently depending on the age of the child they are talking to. Shatz and Gelman give evidence that children speak differently to younger children. The writers (Martin *et al*.) use this information to make their point – that people speak differently to children.

The following text is similar except the information is presented in another way. In the third sentence, as well as having Marchant and Page's ideas indirectly through a summary, there are also their actual words, their direct voice. Towards the end of the paragraph, we also have Morris's voice, indirectly through a summary.

The definition of communication used by social workers needs to be wide and open. Marchant and Page (2003) point out that, sadly, the biggest barrier to communicating with disabled children continues to be the attitudes and behaviour of professionals and the failure to follow guidance. They state, 'We see it as vital that communication is understood as more than the use of speech and language and that all professionals' working definition of communication includes the wide range of ways [disabled] children make their wishes and feelings known' (Marchant and Page 2003: 60). Morris (2002) points out that as the majority of people use spoken language to communicate, disabled children who use other means of communication often find their way is undervalued and unrecognised. This can apply equally to disabled adults. (Wilson *et al*., 2008: 324)

## Activity 11.2 Identifying voices (1)

Complete the table below, showing the different voices that are used in the text above.

| Text | Voice |
|---|---|
| The definition of communication used by social workers needs to be wide and open. | |
| Marchant and Page (2003) point out that, sadly, the biggest barrier to communicating with disabled children continues to be the attitudes and behaviour of professionals and the failure to follow guidance. | |
| They state, 'We see it as vital that communication is understood as more than the use of speech and language and that all professionals' working definition of communication includes the wide range of ways [disabled] children make their wishes and feelings known' (Marchant and Page 2003: 60). | |
| Morris (2002) points out that as the majority of people use spoken language to communicate, disabled children who use other means of communication often find their way is undervalued and unrecognised. | |
| This can apply equally to disabled adults. | |

So it is possible to identify three different kinds of voice: the author's voice as well as other people's voices, both directly through a quotation and indirectly as a summary. Chapter 10 included summaries of other people's ideas (indirect voice) and quotations from other people (direct voices). In this chapter you will look at your own voice. It is important that in any writing you do your voice is easily identified and clear throughout. Otherwise, in an assessment, you may be accused of not answering the question.

See
Chapter 14

**TIP** *Whenever you are reading, make sure that you are aware of the different voices present.*

In your written work, your voice needs to be used to structure your work, to introduce new points and present and support your arguments. Other voices may be used to provide specific information. These other voices must be acknowledged to indicate where they are from. Any voices that are not acknowledged as being from another author are assumed to be yours.

See
Chapter 10

## Activity 11.3 Identifying voices (2)

Now try to identify the voices in the following text.

> Infants also exert control over what their carers talk about. The topic of conversation usually involves what the infant is playing with or is guided by what the infant is gazing at (Bohannon, 1993). This practice means that infants hear speech that concerns what they are already paying attention to, which undoubtedly facilitates learning. In fact, Tomasello and Farrar (1986) found that infants of mothers who talked mostly about the objects of their infants' gazes uttered their first words earlier than other infants and also developed larger vocabularies early in life. (Martin *et al.*, 2007: 420)

# EXPRESSING YOUR VOICE

In academic writing, it is always necessary to make your position clear. This is often called your voice or your claim. Any voices that are not acknowledged as being from another author are assumed to be yours, and there is a danger that this voice may not be expressed very strongly. However, there are many things you can do to make your voice clearer, more obvious and more explicit. You can also make it more or less powerful. In any kind of academic writing you do, it is necessary to make decisions about your stance on a particular subject, or the strength of the claim you are making. It is unlikely that the evidence you present will be conclusive enough for you to state that something is definitely true. At the same time, you need to be careful of making sweeping statements which do not consider exceptions. This is why academic writing often calls for a cautious style, and there are various ways in which caution can be expressed.

It is not enough to simply describe a situation or recall the facts; you need to take a stance or position yourself in relation to the situation or the facts. In the following sentence:

> **Previous studies have indicated that the intensity of physiotherapy provision may affect some patient outcomes including reduced mortality following a stroke.**

the words 'indicate', 'may' and 'some' show the writer's position towards the facts. Instead of 'indicated', the words 'shown', 'proved' or 'suggested' could have been used. The word 'may' might have been replaced by 'could', 'will' or nothing. 'Some' was chosen, where 'many', 'few' or 'most' were also possible. These are choices that you – as a writer – have to make. And every choice you make will influence your voice.

The rest of this chapter will provide you with some other words and phrases that you can use to show your position. If you change them, you will see that they have a different effect on what you are trying to say. If you have a choice, then you are changing your voice by changing the words.

Your voice can:

- show confidence
- show relationships
- show the strength of your claim.

# Showing confidence

You can show your degree of confidence in your claim by:

- showing caution in your claim though the use of hedges such as 'probable', 'might', 'may', 'possibly'
- showing confidence in your claim by using boosters such as 'definite', 'will', 'must', 'obviously', 'clearly'.

The sentences below is quite confident.

**It is clear that schools need to introduce sport at a young age.**

Although your evidence may strongly support this argument, in academic writing the sentence may be expressed more cautiously with the use of a modal verb such as 'may':

**It is clear that schools may need to introduce sport at a young age.**

You can use various verbs, adjectives or adverbs to show your degree of confidence as shown below:

| Modal verbs | e.g. **will, may, might, could** |
|---|---|
| Apart from neuroanatomical differences, there may be differences in the amount of, or sensitivity to, hormones. (Martin *et al.*, 2007: 472) | |
| **Modal adverbs** | e.g. **certainly, definitely, probably, perhaps** |
| Abstract words are definitely first understood as adjectives. (Martin *et al.*, 2007: 415) The origin of language probably lies in the motor system of our brain. (Martin *et al.*, 2007: 450) Production has perhaps the greatest potential to clash with marketing. (Brassington and Pettitt, 2006: 26) | |
| **Modal adjectives** | e.g. **certain, definite** |
| The oligopoly creates a certain amount of interdependence between the key players, each of which is large enough for its actions to have a big impact on the market and on the behaviour of its competitors. (Brassington and Pettitt, 2006: 79) | |
| **Signalling phrases** | e.g. **it may be possible..., it could be..., there is a chance that ..., in general** |
| As students are funding more of their studies there is a strong likelihood that they will be heavily in debt at the end of their degree. ... and it may be that the novel can be understood purely as entertainment ... | |

## Activity 11.4 Showing confidence

Identify the words and phrases in the following sentences that show the writer's stance with regard to showing confidence.

> The behaviour of ocean waves can be estimated using linear wave theory.
> (Holden, 2008: 474)
>
> This certainly occurs in large-scale, worldwide industrial markets, such as chemicals, oil and pharmaceuticals.                    (Brassington and Pettitt, 2006: 76)
>
> It is accompanied by much more definite and often more valuable criticism of earlier schemes.

**TIP** *Whenever you are writing, make sure that you are clear about how confident you are in your claims.*

## Showing relationships

You can show your stance towards the relationships in the text and its organisation. In this way you can explicitly show the reader how you think the sections of your text are related.

Compare

A short period of counselling will often help clarify whether such a referral is necessary. Patients with long-standing depression may be helped by cognitive therapy.

with

A short period of counselling will often help clarify whether such a referral is necessary. Similarly, patients with long-standing depression may be helped by cognitive therapy.

or

A short period of counselling will often help clarify whether such a referral is necessary. However, patients with long-standing depression may be helped by cognitive therapy.

Here are some more examples of phrases you can use to show explicitly how the sections in your text are related:

■ 'for example' – you think the following is an example and you are using it to support your argument.

> Few people in the United Kingdom will, for example, have escaped seeing the horrifying images of the destructive forces of the flood that hit the small Cornish village of Boscastle, England in the summer of 2004. **(Holden, 2008: 381)**

■ 'furthermore', 'similarly', 'moreover' – you want to show that you think there is another piece of evidence, or more of the same, to provide more support.

> Through fieldwork, laboratory investigation and numerical modelling geographers are able to understand a wide variety of environmental processes and how these processes interact.... Furthermore, because of the history of physical geography, geographers have had experience of bringing together large-scale approaches with small-scale approaches, linking case-studies with general context. **(Holden, 2008: 23)**
>
> Lightweight plastics and glass, recycled and recyclable materials, and cans that incorporate a device to give canned beer the character and quality of draught are examples of packaging innovations that have helped to make products more appealing, enhance their image or keep their cost down. Additionally, developments in areas such as lamination and printing techniques have increased the attractiveness and quality of packaging, again helping to enhance the product image. **(Brassington and Pettitt, 2006: 68)**

■ 'in contrast', 'however' – you want to show something different is coming or you are providing a contrast, and you want to signal it.

> There are certain aspects of language processing that may not decline with age and may actually improve. One of the greatest gains is seen in vocabulary. However, older individuals have difficulty in retrieving or accessing these words and exhibit a greater number of tip-of-the-tongue responses than do young individuals during retrieval.
> **(Martin et al., 2007: 491)**
>
> Written constitutions can be changed, but usually only by means of a special procedure, more difficult than that for changing ordinary law. In contrast, our unwritten constitution can be altered by an ordinary piece of legislation. **(Elliott and Quinn, 2008: 5)**

■ 'therefore', 'thus' – you want to show that you think that one idea is a consequence of a previous item.

> Written constitutions can be changed, but usually only by means of a special procedure, more difficult than that for changing ordinary law. Thus, it might be necessary to hold a referendum on the proposed change, or gain a larger than usual majority in Parliament, or both. **(Elliott and Quinn, 2008: 5–6)**

## Activity 11.5 Making relationships clear

Identify the words and phrases in the following sentences that show the writer's stance with regard to showing relationships.

> Ultimately, competitive edge is the name of the game.
> (Brassington and Pettitt, 2006: 34)
>
> The evidence discussed so far indicates that cognitive ability, especially certain types of memory, declines with age.... They suggest that the decline reported is due to psychology not ageing per se. Similarly, Salthouse (1992, 1993; Craik and Salthouse, 2000) has argued that the elderly perform more poorly at cognitive tasks because they become slower at performing them.
> (Martin *et al*., 2007: 491)

**TIP** *Whenever you are writing, make sure that you are clear about how parts of your text are related.*

# Showing the strength of your claim

You can show your attitude to the viewpoints, sources or the evidence that you have presented. The word that you choose in these two examples will alter the strength of the claim you are making about the relationship.

Compare

Research suggests that we possess at least four forms of memory.
(Martin *et al*., 2007: 304)

with

Research proves that we possess at least four forms of memory.
(Martin *et al*., 2007: 304)

Or

Nowadays the urinary symptoms are of a lower order.

with

Nowadays the urinary symptoms appear to be of a lower order.

As you can see, you can choose to use another word or phrase instead of the highlighted word, depending on how strongly you want to make your point. Remember always to support your points with evidence.

You could choose one of the following expressions:

| | | |
|---|---|---|
| X | indicates<br>suggests<br>proves | that ... |

For example:

**The evidence discussed so far indicates that cognitive ability, especially certain types of memory, declines with age.** (Martin *et al.*, 2007: 491)

In the following sentences, you have similar choices and you can choose one of the following phrases.

| | | |
|---|---|---|
| X | seems<br>appears<br>is believed<br>is thought<br>is presumed<br>is assumed<br>is known | to ... |

For example:

**The reported figures for incidence of disease are thought to represent 1 per cent of the true numbers.**

Alternatively, when you are explicitly reporting the work of others, you have a choice of reporting verb:

| | | |
|---|---|---|
| X | believes<br>suggests<br>found<br>argued<br>discovered<br>shows<br>confirmed<br>proved | that ... |

For example:

**Within the food sector, Bolton (1989) found that whereas coffee brands and convenience foods are very price elastic, certain types of fresh fruit and vegetables are price inelastic.** (Brassington and Pettitt, 2006: 448)

**Harré (2002) suggested that there were 12 uses of an experiment.**
(Holden, 2008: 14)

**In fact Lane (2001) argued that one of the ways science moves forward is by trying to solve disagreements between one set of findings and another set of findings that have been produced by a different method.** (Holden, 2008: 14)

In all cases, try changing the phrase and see what effect it has.

## Activity 11.6 Identifying the strength of claims

Identify the words and phrases in the following sentences that show the strength of the writer's claim.

> In other words, materialism still seems to play a big part in influencing perceptions and attitudes towards others. **(Brassington and Pettitt, 2006: 61)**
>
> A study by Dittmar and Pepper (1994) showed that adolescents, regardless of their own social background, generally formed better impressions of people who own rather than lack expensive possessions. **(Brassington and Pettitt, 2006: 61)**

**TIP** *Whenever you are writing, make sure that you are clear about the strength of your claims.*

# EVALUATING STATEMENTS

You can evaluate your statements and show your attitude in either a positive or a negative way, depending on how true you want your claim to be.

Compare:

**Poor driving conditions lead to accidents.**

with

**Poor driving conditions frequently lead to accidents.**

Or

**Malnutrition causes death.**

with

**Malnutrition is a frequent cause of death.**

You can modify your claims using the following words and phrases:

| Adjectives | e.g. **important, misguided, wrong, inaccurate, incorrect, remarkable, surprising** |
|---|---|
| The major cognitive impairment in Alzheimer's disease is memory loss. | **(Martin *et al.*, 2007: 495)** |
| Intelligence testing has a long and controversial history. | **(Martin *et al.*, 2007: 474)** |
| The needs of the environmental manager are simple. | **(Holden, 2008: 687)** |
| Many definitions of the environment are somewhat limited. | **(Holden, 2008: 680)** |
| Infiltration is the process of water entry into the surface of a soil and it plays a key role in surface runoff. | **(Holden, 2008: 361)** |

| Adverbs | e.g. **accurately, unsatisfactorily, unfortunately, hopefully** |
|---|---|
| Such drugs often have been inappropriately prescribed and also have been used in the overdose. | |

| Nouns | e.g. **difficulty, problem, crisis, shortcoming, assumption** |
|---|---|
| The main shortcoming of these early classifications is that the emphasis on geological inheritance and sea-level history leaves only limited concern for the hydrodynamic process. **(Holden, 2008: 482)** | |
| There are two problems with this approach. **(Holden, 2008: 9)** | |
| But what is important about these disagreements is the shared assumption that it was good for Scotland. | |

| Frequency adjectives | e.g. **probable, possible, frequent** |
|---|---|
| Malnutrition is a frequent cause of death. | |

| Frequency adverbs | e.g. **probably, possibly, frequently** |
|---|---|
| Poor driving conditions frequently lead to accidents. | |

## Activity 11.7 Identifying evaluative statements

Identify the words and phrases in the following sentences that show how the writer evaluates statements.

Often a 'tsunami' is referred to as a 'tidal wave'. However, this term is inappropriate because tides and tsunami differ from each other in many respects. **(Holden, 2008: 481)**

The practice has grown up in recent years of referring, however inaccurately, to a mistress as a 'common law wife'.

There is also the danger that R & D and engineering may become focused on the product for the product's sake. **(Brassington and Pettitt, 2006: 26)**

Services often depend on people to perform them, creating and delivering the product as the customer waits. **(Brassington and Pettitt, 2006: 31)**

The difficulty lay in the fact it was characterised as classless and free of exploitation.

**TIP** *Whenever you are writing, make sure that you evaluate the statements you make.*

# EXAMPLE OF A WRITER'S VOICE

Look at the following example from the field of Psychology and notice how the lexical items outlined in this chapter are combined to show the writer's voice.

> There are certain aspects of language processing that may not decline with age and may actually improve. One of the greatest gains is seen in vocabulary (Bayley and Oden, 1955; Jones, 1959). However, older individuals have difficulty in retrieving or accessing these words and exhibit a greater number of tip-of-the-tongue responses than do young individuals during retrieval (Bowles and Poon, 1985). According to LaRue (1992), the types of linguistic error made by elderly participants include: circumlocutions (giving inaccurate multi-word responses), nominalisations (describing functions not objects), perceptual errors (misidentifying stimuli) and semantic association errors (naming an object/feature associated with a target object). The elderly may also have difficulty in comprehending and initiating grammatically complex sentences (Kemper, 1992). **(Martin *et al.*, 2007: 491)**

The following highlighted words show the author's voice:

| Phrase | Comment |
|---|---|
| There are certain aspects of language processing | 'Certain' indicates that the writer believes that it is not all aspects of language processing. |
| that may not decline with age and | By using 'may', the writer is allowing for other possibilities to exist. |
| may actually improve. | Again, by using 'may', the writer is allowing for other possibilities to exist. 'Actually' is showing the strength of the writer's claim. The first sentence could say 'Language processing does not decline with age; it improves.' The writer, however, chose to be more cautious. |
| One of | There may be more. |
| the greatest gains is seen in vocabulary (Bayley and Oden, 1955; Jones, 1959). | 'Is' is quite confident. The writer does not use 'may' or 'can'. 'Greatest' evaluates the writer's statement. The second sentence could have been: 'The greatest gain may be seen in vocabulary.' The writer, though, chose to be more confident. |
| However, older individuals have difficulty in retrieving or accessing these words and exhibit a greater number of tip-of-the-tongue responses than do young individuals during retrieval (Bowles and Poon, 1985). | 'However' shows that the writer is presenting a change of direction. The writer has decided to be explicit about the differences in older individuals. A word like 'furthermore' or 'similarly' would have expressed a different view. |

→

| Phrase | Comment |
|---|---|
| According to LaRue (1992), | The writer is attributing this opinion to another writer. |
| the types of linguistic error made by elderly participants include a number of responses ranging from circumlocutions to semantic association errors. | By using 'include' the writer is being cautious by suggesting that there may be other kinds of errors. |
| The elderly may | Again, by using 'may', the writer is allowing for other possibilities to exist. |
| also have difficulty in comprehending and initiating grammatically complex sentences (Kemper, 1992). | With 'also' the writer is being explicit about the number of difficulties. |

## Activity 11.8 Understanding how voices are used

Indentify the words and phrases in the following text that show the writer's voice.

There is a clear, obvious and important link between intelligence and nutrition. Brown and Pollitt (1999) claimed that malnutrition can impair brain function and IQ in the long term; and iodine deficiency during pregnancy may lead to retardation and cretinism. In the late 1980s and early 1990s, a series of studies reported large differences in non-verbal IQ between schoolchildren who received vitamin and mineral supplements (VMS) and those who received a placebo (Benton, 1992; Haller, 1995; Eysenck and Schoenthaler, 1997). Those who received the supplements scored considerably better.

In non-verbal IQ between schoolchildren who received vitamin and mineral supplements (VMS) and those who received a placebo (Benton, 1992; Haller, 1995; Eysenck and Schoenthaler, 1997), those who received the supplements scored significantly better.

(Martin *et al.*, 2007: 486)

# SUMMARY

This chapter has looked at the place of the writer in a piece of academic writing, with a view to helping you establish when it is appropriate to express your own point of view and opinion. It suggests ways of ensuring that you integrate your own meaning into the meaning and ideas of others. Finally, you have looked at ways of using writing to influence or persuade others.

It should now be clear that it is important to make your voice clear throughout your writing and you should have some more specific ideas about how to do this. We cannot stress enough the importance of making your voice clear, obvious and explicit.

# References

Details of highlighted references can be found in the Introduction on page xxii.

# 12 ▶ GENRE AND DISCIPLINE-SPECIFIC WRITING

This chapter will pull together the building blocks of the previous chapters and focus on providing advice on how to use different genres. The thinking behind the need for this chapter is that most genres of writing use a range of text types for their purposes. For example, an engineering report will have some general reporting in the literature review, some narrative in the methodology, some specific reporting in the results and some argument in the discussion and conclusion. A reflective essay, on the other hand, might combine description with speculation about the past and reflection on the future.

This chapter will cover:

- essays
- research proposals
- literature reviews
- reports
- experimental/research reports
- book reviews
- abstracts
- case studies
- reflection.

## USING THIS CHAPTER

# INTRODUCTION

In Chapters 6–8 of this book, we covered elements of a complete text such as style and paragraphs. We then looked at short texts that define, describe, categorise and report. This was followed by texts that argue, compare, analyse, explain, support and evaluate. In Chapter 9, we then covered personal and reflective writing. In this chapter we look at how you can combine what you learned in those chapters to write whole texts.

You may be asked to write different types of text or genres. As a student, you will probably not be asked to write a novel or a textbook, but you may be expected to write an essay, a book review or a report. These different genres have different purposes and are organised in different ways. These ways of organisation are understood and expected by the communities that use the particular genre. They are defined by their purpose, their expected audiences and their structure. They are 'staged, goal oriented social processes' (Martin, 1992: 505).

Some of the typical genres that students may be expected to write are as follows:

- essays – both out of class and in exams
- research proposals – written before an extended piece of work
- reports – business and laboratory
- book reviews and other critiques
- literature reviews – as complete texts or part of a longer piece of writing
- abstracts – as complete texts or part of a longer piece of writing
- case studies – narrowly focused studies
- reflections – as complete texts.

Different subjects or institutions may use the words slightly differently, but they are all very common in higher education.

## Activity 12.1 Identifying genres

Look through your course handbooks. Which of the genres above are you expected to produce?

**TIP** *Check which genre you are supposed to be writing.*

The writing you do may include the following sections:

| | |
|---|---|
| Preliminaries | Title page<br>Abstract<br>Content |
| Main text | Introduction<br>Development<br>Conclusion |
| End matter | References<br>Appendices |

# Preliminaries

Before the main part of your text there should be a title page. If the work is to be assessed, the title page should contain information to enable your lecturer and departmental office to identify exactly what the piece of work is. It should include, for example, your name – or student number – and course, the title of the assignment and any reference numbers that identify the piece of work, the lecturer it is for and so on. Check with your department for specific information as departments may vary in their requirements. As well as the title page, you may also be asked to include an abstract and a table of contents.

# End matter

At the end of the piece of writing, there will almost certainly be a list of references. This should give full information about the materials that you have used in the writing. There may also be one or more appendices which contain raw data and

ter 10 other materials not central to the main work.

# The main text

This chapter will concentrate on the main text, showing you how it can be built up from the shorter texts presented in Chapters 6–9. Some of the larger texts, for example abstract and literature review, can either stand alone as pieces of writing in themselves or can form part of longer texts. We will treat them as separate texts in this chapter.

ter 6 English academic writing is linear: it starts at the beginning and finishes at the end, with every part contributing to the main line of argument, without digression or repetition. As the writer, you are responsible for making your line of argument clear and presenting it in a methodical way so that the reader can follow it easily. The piece of writing will usually consist of several paragraphs and each paragraph will discuss one major point. Every paragraph will continue from the previous paragraph and lead directly to the next. The paragraphs are tied together with an introduction and a conclusion.

As well as the preliminaries and end matter, the main text has three main parts (see Figure 12.1):

**1** An introduction
**2** A development section
**3** A conclusion.

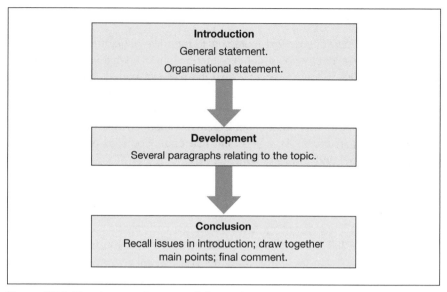

**Figure 12.1 The three main parts of the main text**

## The introduction

The introduction should consist of two main parts:

**1** It should include a few general descriptive statements about the subject to provide a background to your writing and to show the reader that you know why the topic is important. It should try to explain why you are writing. This may mean rewording the question to make it into a problem for you to discuss. It may also include a definition of terms in the context of the piece of writing.

**2** It should also include some indication of how the topic is going to be tackled in order specifically to address the question.

The introduction should introduce the central idea or the main purpose of the writing. If you are writing an assignment or exam, it should clearly persuade the reader that you are addressing the question you have been given. Writing the introduction will also help you keep on track by reminding you what you have to do.

## The development

The development section consists of several paragraphs of ideas and arguments. Each paragraph develops a subdivision of the topic. The paragraphs contain the main ideas and arguments together with illustrations or examples. The paragraphs are linked in order to connect the ideas. The purpose of the piece of writing must be kept clear throughout and the reader must be able to follow its development.

## The conclusion

The conclusion will include your final points. It should:

- summarise the issues raised in the introduction and draw together the points made in the development section
- explain the overall significance of the conclusions. What general points can be drawn from the essay as a whole?

The conclusion should clearly signal to the reader that the piece of writing is finished and leave a clear impression that the purpose of the text has been achieved. In the context of an assignment or exam, it should show that you have answered the question.

# ESSAYS

You will at some time be expected to write an essay. Although the specific format, content and organisation of the essay will differ from subject to subject, what all essays share is their purpose, which is to present a clear argument to your reader. This may be in response to an essay title or question, or it may be part of a longer piece of writing such as the discussion section of a dissertation or report.

In the essay you will be expected to argue your position clearly and support it with evidence. Your own voice will be clear throughout and it will be supported by the voices of other people you have collected from your reading. You will say something using your own ideas, the ideas of the subject and of other people. In other words, you will present ideas you have learned in your own way. As in all academic writing, the ideas and people that you refer to need to be made explicit by a system of referencing.

Essays are normally written as continuous pieces of writing without headings and subheadings. Diagrams and tables are not normally used in essays, neither are bullet points or numbered lists. Words and sentences are used to show the structure. The development section of the essay will depend on its purpose, which should be clearly specified by the title or assignment question. As already stated, the purpose of an essay is to argue a point, to present a position and defend it with evidence.

- Start by introducing the topic.
- Decide what your position is and provide reasons and evidence to support it.
- You will almost certainly need to consider other points of view and evaluate them positively or negatively.
- At this point you may need to give examples and to compare and contrast the different points of view.
- Finish by concluding, making it clear what your position is.

TIP *Essays do not usually have a heading and subheadings, but check with your department.*

See Chapters 7 and 8

# Organisation of the essay

A typical essay will have the stages shown in Figure 12.2.

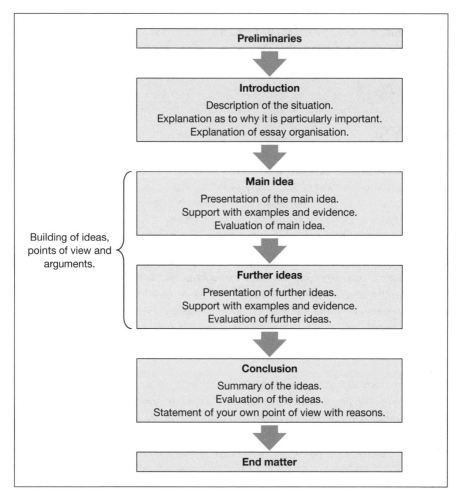

Figure 12.2 **Stages of a typical essay**

## Activity 12.2 **Understanding the structure of essays**

Match the stages in the outline above to the text types described in various sections of this book. For example, 'Description of the situation' is covered in Chapter 7; pp. 117–124 and 'Explanation as to why it is particularly important' is covered in Chapter 8, pp. 138–141.

# RESEARCH PROPOSALS

As an undergraduate, you may be asked to write a research proposal before a major piece of writing such as an end of year project or a final year dissertation. The purpose of the proposal is to show how you intend to tackle the study and whether or not you have thought through the practicalities. Your lecturer will want to see that you have planned your research carefully in order to succeed.

The proposal will probably include the following:

- *Preliminary title*. What is the topic? What exactly is the research question?

- *What exactly do you hope to show?* What is the purpose of your work? Describe your research problem.

- *Why is the research important?* An argument as to why that problem is important, and what problems still need to be solved.

- *What do you already know about this topic?* The proposal should begin by giving the background to the subject area in which the research is situated. It will describe the important theoretical and practical issues it plans to address. This should be supported by some reference to recent literature. It should finish by indicating a problem that your research will solve.

- *How will the research be conducted?* A description of the proposed research methodology. A time line or Gantt chart may be required.

- *What resources will be needed?* What are the resource implications of the proposed research with regard to equipment, library resources, etc.?

- *How will the findings be used?* A description of how the research findings will be used and/or communicated to others.

- *A preliminary reading list*. This gives some idea of the reading you have already done and what you think you will need to do.

## Organisation of the research proposal

The typical stages involved in a research proposal would be as shown in Figure 12.3 on page 224.

### Activity 12.3 Understanding the structure of research proposals

Match the stages in Figure 12.3 to the text types described in various sections of this book. For example 'Explanation as to why it is important' is covered in Chapter 8, pp. 138–141.

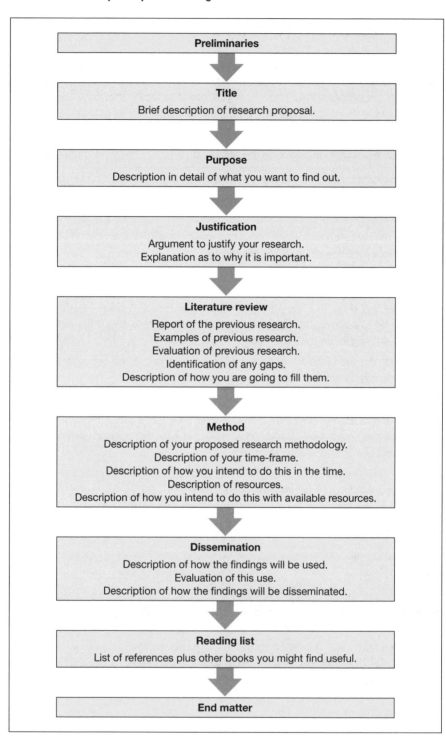

**Preliminaries**

**Title**
Brief description of research proposal.

**Purpose**
Description in detail of what you want to find out.

**Justification**
Argument to justify your research.
Explanation as to why it is important.

**Literature review**
Report of the previous research.
Examples of previous research.
Evaluation of previous research.
Identification of any gaps.
Description of how you are going to fill them.

**Method**
Description of your proposed research methodology.
Description of your time-frame.
Description of how you intend to do this in the time.
Description of resources.
Description of how you intend to do this with available resources.

**Dissemination**
Description of how the findings will be used.
Evaluation of this use.
Description of how the findings will be disseminated.

**Reading list**
List of references plus other books you might find useful.

**End matter**

Figure 12.3 **Typical stages involved in a research proposal**

# LITERATURE REVIEWS

Literature reviews can form part of a larger piece of work, such as an extended essay, report or dissertation; or they can stand alone. Look carefully at what exactly you have been asked to do.

Any study you carry out cannot depend completely on your own data, but must be situated in a context of what is already known about the topic in question. This context is provided in the literature review.

- First find the relevant information and studies.
- Then summarise the relevant studies, properly cited: who found out what, when, and how this developed the study of the topic. Remember that the reader will want to know *why* you have included any particular piece of research here.
- It is not enough just to summarise what has been said: you need to organise and evaluate it.
- You also need to justify its inclusion.
- You also review here methods that have been used that are relevant to your own study.
- Finish with a conclusion, explaining how your research will fill any gaps left by previous research.

The main purpose of the literature review is to justify your research. You do this by summarising the literature with the intention of showing that there is a gap in the knowledge, which you will fill.

TIP *If you are writing a report, check whether you need a separate literature review section.*

## Organisation of the literature review

A possible structure for a literature review is shown in Figure 12.4 on page 226.

### Activity 12.4 Understanding the structure of literature reviews

Match the stages in the outline above to the text types described in various sections of this book. For example, 'Description of the context' is covered in Chapter 7, pp. 117–124.

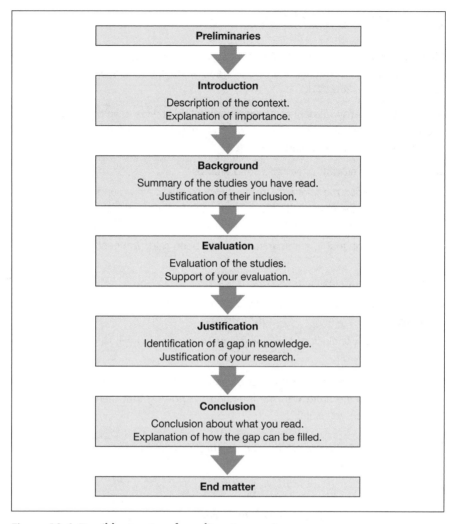

Figure 12.4 Possible structure for a literature review

# WRITING A REPORT

Reports are common in subjects like business and education. You will normally be expected to identify – or be given – a problem and carry out some kind of enquiry to solve it. To do that, you need to identify a problem and critically analyse it. Based on your knowledge and reading, you will offer different possible solutions. You will then need to carry out some kind of investigation to see which solution is best in your particular context. You therefore need to explain your method of investigation and describe your results. After that you will evaluate the different solutions and make a choice. You will have to justify your solution and make recommendations based on your study.

The report will probably be organised in the following way and it will have headings and subheadings to show the structure. It may use bullet points and numbered lists, and will probably include diagrams and charts.

- **Title page:** start by giving the title, the date and any other information you have been asked to provide.
- **Table of contents:** follow with a list of contents which shows the structure and content of the report.
- **Terms of reference:** these provide the background to the report by defining the problem. they summarise the researcher's understanding of the original brief.
- **Executive summary:** this summary or abstract summarises the main points of the report, including conclusions and recommendations.
- **Background:** this section introduces the problem and explains why the research was necessary.
- **Research methods:** this section explains how the research was carried out. One of its purposes is to persuade the reader that it was done well and the results should be believed.
- **Findings/results:** in this section, present the data you have collected.
- **Conclusions:** interpret the data and draw out the key points.
- **Recommendations:** in this section, identify any action arising from the conclusions and discuss what this involves in practice.
- **Appendices:** include here the fine detail (e.g. a copy of a questionnaire or raw data) that is not necessary for the main body of the report or that would clutter the report.
- **References:** list all the materials that you referred to in writing the report.

**TIP** *Departments differ in what they think should be in a report. Check what is required.*

## Organisation of the report

Looking at the main section from the point of view of the writing stages, you will find the stages shown in Figure 12.5 on page 228.

### Activity 12.5 Understanding the structure of reports

Match the stages in the outline above to the text types described in various sections of this book. For example, 'Description of the background' is covered in Chapter 7, pp. 117–124.

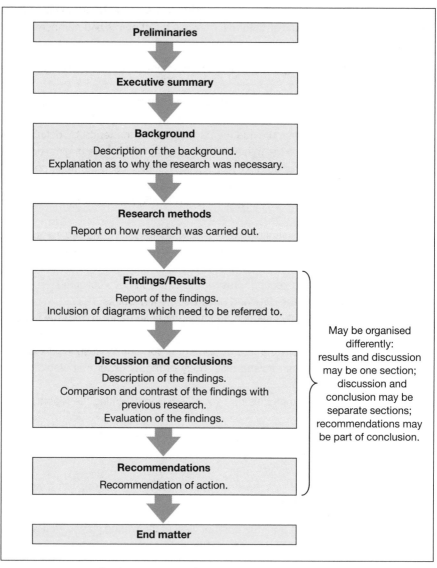

Figure 12.5 **Typical writing stages of a report**

# EXPERIMENTAL/RESEARCH REPORTS

Experimental research reports are common in subjects like engineering and psychology. You will normally be expected to identify a scientific problem and solve it by carrying out some kind of research. To do that, you need to identify a problem and critically analyse it by using your knowledge and reading. You will then need to carry out some kind of experiment or investigation to see which solution is best in your particular context. You therefore need to explain your method of investigation and describe your results. After that you will evaluate your findings and make a choice. Finally, you will have to justify any conclusions you come to.

The main section of most scientific or technical reports will probably be organised according to the IMRAD system. IMRAD is an acronym standing for:

- Introduction
- Methods
- Results And
- Discussion.

In a report, these sections are usually signalled with headings and subheadings. Diagrams and charts are used as necessary.

- **Introduction:** this section justifies the research by explaining why the study was undertaken and what its purpose was.
- **Methods:** this section reports on how the study was done. It normally includes procedures and materials. The two parts are sometimes given separate sections.
- **Results:** this reports what the study found.
- **Discussion:** this section discusses what the findings might mean, and why they matter, especially in relation to what other researchers have found. It clearly connects the results with your conclusion.
- **Conclusion:** this section, which may be part of the discussion, summarises the findings and points the research forward to the next stage.

> **TIP** *Some subjects, especially in life science, do not need much in the methods section as all the methods are well known. Check what is required.*

Of course the report will have a title page, an abstract, perhaps a contents page, references and possibly appendices.

## Organisation of the experimental report

A typical structure of an experimental report could be as shown in Figure 12.6 on page 230.

### Activity 12.6 Understanding the structure of experimental reports

Match the stages in the outline above to the text types described in various sections of this book. For example, 'Description of the background' is covered in Chapter 7, pp. 117–124.

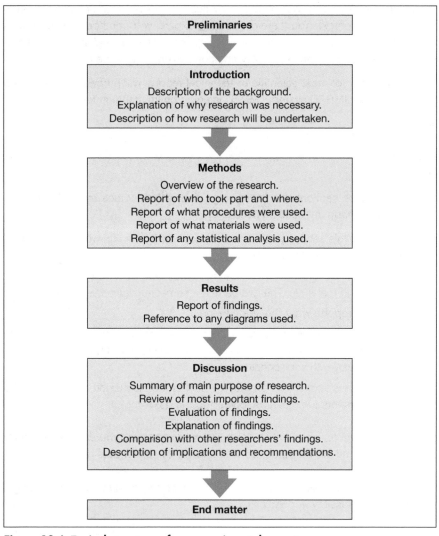

**Figure 12.6 Typical structure of an experimental report**

# BOOK REVIEWS

You may be asked to write a book review or a review of a journal article. This may be a simple summary of the discussion in a book or article but, it is more likely to be evaluative.

For a book review, you will probably include the stages below. A review or commentary on an article would include similar information.

- *What is the text about?* Introduce the book. What is the subject of the text? Who is it written for? What is the purpose of the book?

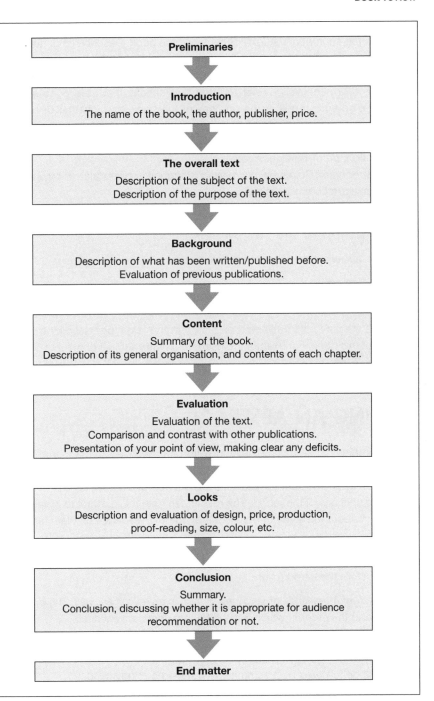

Figure 12.7 Stages of a book review

- *What has been written/published before?* Put the text in the wider context.
- *What is the content of the text?* Summarise the book. Describe its general organisation, and the contents of each chapter.
- *Is it any good?* Draw attention to parts of the book and comment on them positively and/or negatively – refer to other publications that have done something similar if you can. Look at the purpose of the book, and whether or not it succeeds. Is it appropriate for the audience, for example.
- *What about the design, etc.?* Make any other comments on, for example, price, production, proof-reading, size, colour.
- *Is it appropriate?* Conclude, discussing whether it is appropriate for the audience, and make a recommendation.

## Organisation of the review

The book review would have the stages shown in Figure 12.7 on page 231.

### Activity 12.7 Understanding the structure of reviews

Match the stages in the outline on page 231 to the text types described in various sections of this book. For example, 'Description of the subject of the text' is covered in Chapter 7, pp. 117–124.

# WRITING AN ABSTRACT

You will probably at some time have to write an executive summary or an abstract. The abstract can be part of a report or it can stand alone. For that reason it must be complete in itself. The abstract provides an overview of a study based on information from other sections of the report. The reader can read the abstract to obtain enough information about the study to decide if they want to read the complete report.

The abstract will have the title 'abstract', although in some subject areas, this section may be titled 'summary'. If it is part of a report, it usually comes after the title and before the introduction.

Abstracts from most fields of study are written in a very similar way. The information included and the order in which it is written are very conventional.

- Start by giving some background information to justify your study.
- Then describe the main purpose of your study.
- This will be followed by a summary of the methodology used.
- The key results will come next.
- Then evaluate these results.
- Finally, briefly describe the conclusions, which may include recommendations.

Notice that this is the same structure as the report.

# Organisation of an abstract

A possible structure for an abstract is given in Figure 12.8.

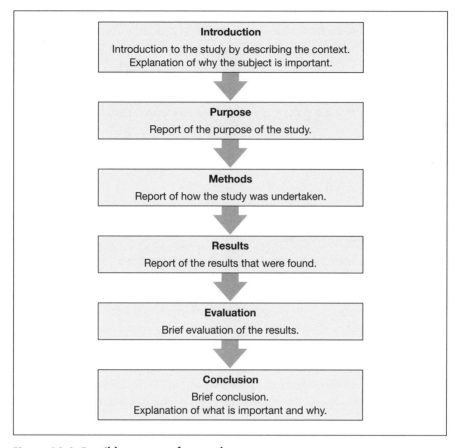

Figure 12.8 **Possible structure for an abstract**

**TIP** *Check with your department exactly how you should present your abstract.*

## Activity 12.8 **Understanding the structure of abstracts**

Match the stages in the outline above to the text types described in various sections of this book. For example, 'Explanation as to why the subject is important' is covered in Chapter 8, pp. 138–141.

# CASE STUDIES

A case study gives you a chance to study one aspect of a real-world problem in detail from many different viewpoints. It does not just restrict itself to a single research procedure such as a library search or interview data – but it could use any of them.

First, therefore, you need a problem to solve. You will then lead the reader through the stages of the investigation, which you will describe and evaluate, to the solution.

A case study can, for example, make use of the following methods:

- library research
- interviews
- questionnaires
- observation
- diaries
- historical documents
- collection of current documents.

A case study problem could, for example, be the introduction of a new working practice in a factory or office. After identifying and stating the problem you would then describe the new practice, what it is, how it works, why it was introduced. Then observe how it works, talk to people who are affected by it and talk to managers. Finally, you need to report on your findings, evaluate the results and come to a conclusion.

The way you would write up a case study depends on its purpose. Yin (1994: 4–6) identifies three different types of case studies, which you could choose from according to your purpose. They are exploratory, descriptive and explanatory case studies.

An *exploratory* case study is initial research that tries to look for patterns in the data and come up with a model within which to view this data. *Descriptive* case studies take this further and try to obtain information on the particular features of an issue. *Explanatory* research continues this even further by trying to analyse or explain why or how something happens or happened.

> **TIP** *Case studies can vary from subject to subject. Check what your subject requires.*

## Organisation of a case study report

The sequence shown in Figure 12.9 would probably be appropriate, with the sections changed round as necessary, depending on the type of study.

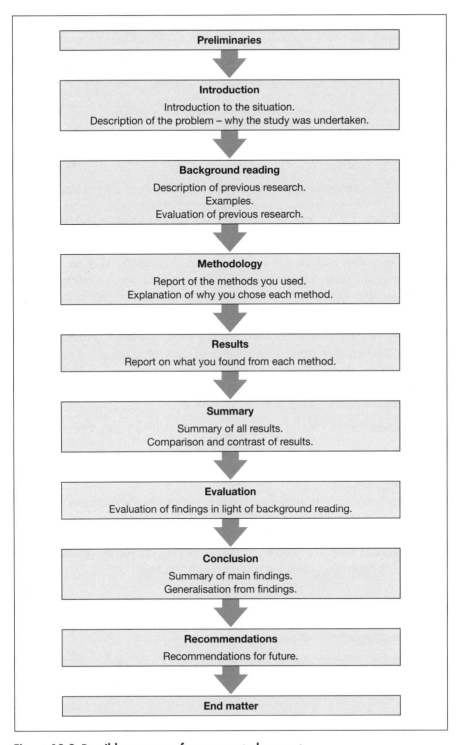

**Preliminaries**

**Introduction**
Introduction to the situation.
Description of the problem – why the study was undertaken.

**Background reading**
Description of previous research.
Examples.
Evaluation of previous research.

**Methodology**
Report of the methods you used.
Explanation of why you chose each method.

**Results**
Report on what you found from each method.

**Summary**
Summary of all results.
Comparison and contrast of results.

**Evaluation**
Evaluation of findings in light of background reading.

**Conclusion**
Summary of main findings.
Generalisation from findings.

**Recommendations**
Recommendations for future.

**End matter**

Figure 12.9 Possible sequence for a case study report

## Activity 12.9 Understanding the structure of case studies

Match the stages in the outline above to the text types described in various sections of this book. For example, 'Description of the problem' is covered in Chapter 7, pp. 117–124.

# REFLECTION

The purpose of reflective writing is to help you learn from a particular practical experience. It will help you to make connections between what you are taught in theory and what you need to do in practice. You reflect so that you can learn.

In reflective writing, you are trying to write down some of the thinking that you have been through while carrying out a particular practical activity, such as writing an essay, teaching a class or treating a patient. Through reflection, you should be able to make sense of what you did and why, and perhaps help yourself to do it better next time.

 See Chapter 9

You might reflect for many reasons and in many ways, for example in a diary or personal log. You are often asked to provide a record of what you did, a reflection of how you did it and how you are using what you are taught in your classes, and any practical experience you are gaining to do this. Your written reflection will also serve as a source of reference and evidence in the future.

Let us assume that you are reflecting on something that you have done in class.

- You will probably start by describing what you did.
- You might then want to write about exactly how you did the activity, what methods you used.
- You might then want to evaluate your performance. How well did you do?
- In order to do this, you need to consider what you have been taught. You might want to describe what the experts say.
- You may then need to consider your reactions. How did you/do you feel?
- You might finish by considering how you would do it next time.

 See Chapters 7–9

## Organisation of the reflective report

A possible structure of a reflective report is shown in Figure 12.10.

## Activity 12.10 Understanding the structure of reflective reports

Match the stages in the outline above to the text types described in various sections of this book. For example, 'Description of your situation' is covered in Chapter 7, pp. 117–124.

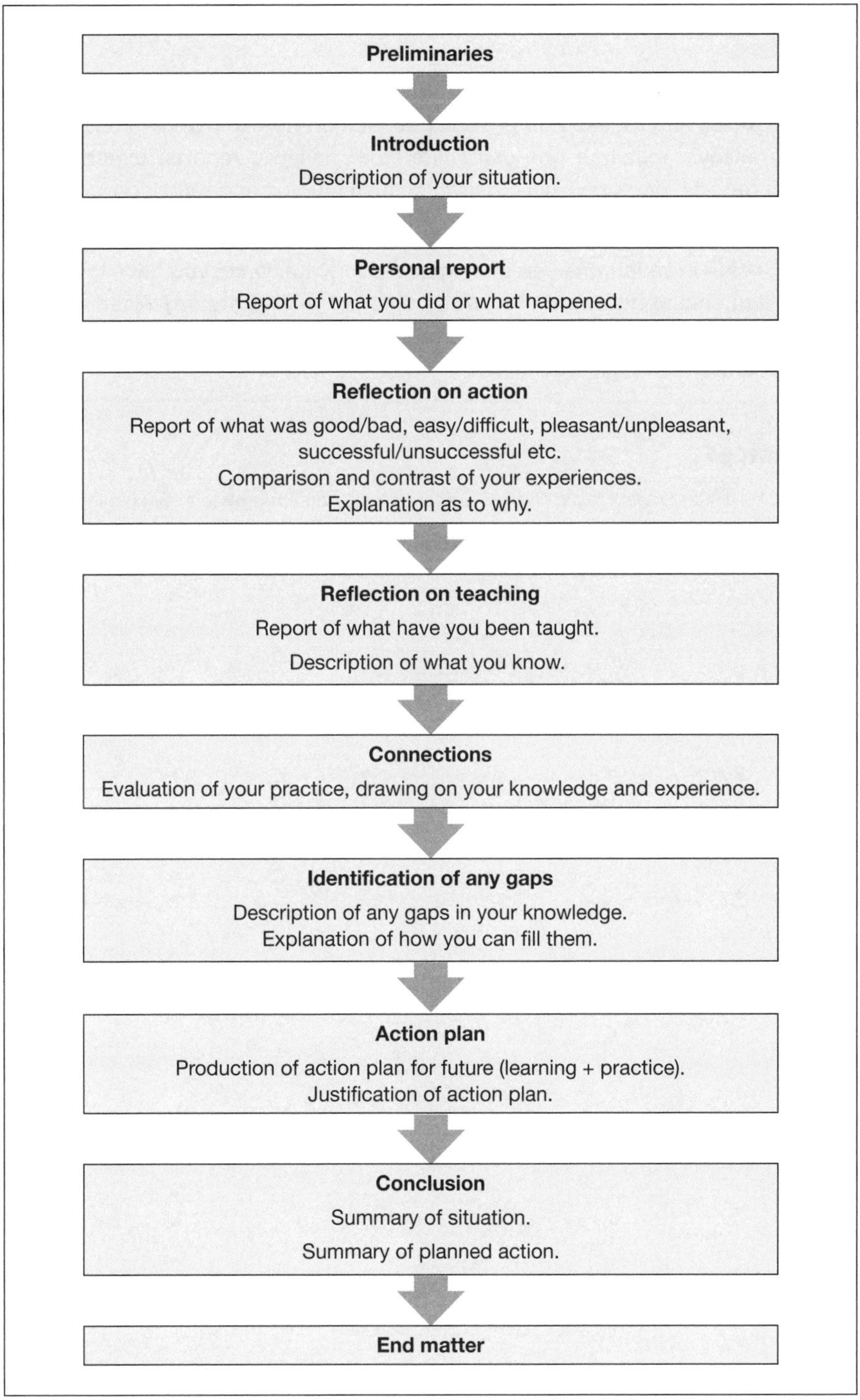

Figure 12.10 **Possible structure for a reflective report**

# SUMMARY

This chapter has tried to pull together the building blocks described in the previous chapters and focused on providing advice on how to use different genres, such as essays, research proposals, literature reviews, reports, experimental/ research reports, book reviews, abstracts, case studies and reflection.

You should now have some ideas about what the different genres are and know how to decide in which one you are expected to write. Once you have that information, you should be aware of how the different genres are organised and this should help in your writing. If you need more help on specific genres then access the other chapters in this book.

## References

Martin, J. R. (1992) *English texts: System and structure*. Amsterdam: John Benjamins.

Yin, R. K. (1994) *Case study research: Design and Methods* (2nd edn). London: Sage.

# 13 ▶ PRESENTING YOUR WORK

This chapter will consider how to make the most effective use of IT in the writing process (e.g. editing, spell checking, footnotes, text layouts and font sizes, use of 'white space' and other aspects of the printed page) as well as addressing situations where academic writing is carried out by hand (e.g. exams). It will then move on to consider other ways of presenting work (e.g. oral presentations, posters) and examine the interface between the original piece of writing and its derivative, suggesting effective ways of adapting a text.

This chapter will cover:

- using word processing packages effectively
- writing by hand
- adapting text for different purposes.

## USING THIS CHAPTER

# INTRODUCTION

By the time you get to hand in your written work, you will have spent considerable time researching relevant ideas, reading and evaluating texts, planning your content and organising your assignment. You may feel exhausted by all the effort you have put into addressing that assignment and the urge to just type it up and hand it in may be strong. Remember, however, that *presenting* the work you have created is equally important and one of the crucial final stages of the writing process. You need to ensure that you have adhered to the presentation guidelines and that your work is worth putting forward for assessment, not only in terms of content but also of presentation. The care you have taken over the entire text will be valued by your lecturer. This really is a case where first impressions count.

# USING WORD PROCESSORS EFFECTIVELY

Make sure you read the guidelines provided by your lecturers in the student handbook or assignment brief regarding the expected presentation of your written work. You may lose marks or, at worst, your work will not be read if it does not conform to the presentation requirements. These may include some or all of the following points:

- *Whether your text should be typed*. Typed texts are more legible.
- *The size of paper*. A4 is a standard size but check to make sure.
- *The type of font*. Do not choose a font you like over the one prescribed and avoid using different fonts in one text.
- *The font size*. It is often stated that if an assignment cannot be read it will be returned unmarked.
- *The left, right, top and bottom margins*. These help make your work more visually attractive and easier for the reader to access.
- *Text justification*. Unless your assignment brief has specifically requested left or right justification, do not change anything.
- *The line spacing*. This allows sufficient space for tutors to provide feedback. Spacing also helps the reader. The text should not appear cramped.
- *The page numbers*. Numbering pages ensures they will be read in the correct sequence if they become detached. Lecturers can also refer to the relevant page numbers when providing feedback.
- *The headers or footers*. Check whether these can or should be used and for what purpose.
- *The references*. Make sure you are using the specified referencing system.
- *The number of copies to be handed in*. Copies may be filed for future reference.
- *Whether work should be handed in electronically, physically, or both*. Electronic hand-in is often used as plagiarism detection software may be applied.

See
Chapter 10

The presentation requirements can be misunderstood as 'small points' not worth

240

much consideration with the content being more important, but if your work is to be assessed, it makes sense to provide your assessors with what they have asked for. Use the following checklist to help you:

- take the time to read the assignment guidelines
- on opening your document, choose the appropriate font and font size
- select the required line spacing
- do not adjust indents or change the colour of the text unless required to do so
- insert a header or footer as prescribed.

You are now ready to start typing your text. If you need to change any of the settings part-way through your document, just click on the relevant command, for example if you want to underline a word or make it bold. It is possible to make a number of changes to the settings to suit your needs but make sure they only affect the sections of the text you meant to change.

If you have already been using a document for brainstorming or organising your notes and you intended to copy, paste and expand the same document into your assessed piece of work, select all the text and follow the points above. The changes will then take effect automatically.

For the body of the text:

- Make sure your paragraphs are clearly marked with extra space as in this example (unless otherwise specified):

  **... The question which therefore arises is what can help ensure that students utilise the tutor feedback to improve their future assessed work?** (*end of one paragraph followed by line break*).

  **Students seem to rate tutor feedback quite highly but despite claiming to be aware of that feedback when tackling a later piece of written work ...**

- Use **bold,** *italics,* or <u>underline</u> text appropriately. Bold and underlining are normally used in headings and subheadings. Avoid using them to stress individual words in a paragraph as a way of telling your lecturer that you have included something important.
- Be careful when using bullet points or a number list. They tend to be unacceptable in essays whereas they may be included in reports. If they have not been mentioned in the requirements, ask your tutor. If you are unsure, it is best to avoid them.
- Make sure your spellchecker is on and pay attention to squiggly red or green lines under words and phrases (in Word). They indicate that something may be wrong. A word of warning however – do not always accept the suggestions offered by the computer for items it has underlined as they can sometimes be inaccurate! Do check your phrase or sentence carefully before deciding to accept or reject the suggested version. Remember also that the automatic spelling change offered may be American English (e.g. center (US) as opposed to centre (UK)) although this can be changed.

- Try to keep any illustrations and their accompanying text on the same page. You do not want the reader to be flicking backwards and forwards between pages to follow what you are describing.
- When including pictures, graphs or diagrams, allow white space around each item.

Compare the two examples below. Which is easier to read?

## Example 1

Have you ever had to choose your own essay/report topic or were you usually given a topic/choice of topics by your tutor?

### Table 1

|  | Own topic | Topic by tutor |
|---|---|---|
| Anna |  | Y |
| Dianne | Y |  |
| Mary | Y | Y |
| Jasmine |  | Y |
| Dinah |  | Y |
| Sarah |  | Y |
| Margaret |  | Y |

Table 1 shows findings which indicate that students do not tend to be particularly autonomous in their learning ...

## Example 2

Have you ever had to choose your own essay/report topic or were you usually given a topic/choice of topics by your tutor?

Table 1

|  | Own topic | Topic by tutor |
|---|---|---|
| Anna |  | Y |
| Dianne | Y |  |
| Mary | Y | Y |
| Jasmine |  | Y |
| Dinah |  | Y |
| Sarah |  | Y |
| Margaret |  | Y |

Table 1 shows findings which indicate that students do not tend to be particularly autonomous in their learning ...

The table used in Example 1, in conjunction with the white space around it, makes it easier for the reader to absorb the information rather than the dense text used in Example 2.

TIP *Always check the requirements for presenting your work and make sure you follow them.*

When you include figures such as graphs, diagrams or tables, you may like to choose a different typeface so the information stands out more. You must always ensure that your figures:

- have a title to help the reader know what they are about
- are all sequential
- are referred to in your text.

This is to ensure that there is a logical order to your figures and that you do not rely on them to put your message across. They need to be developed and explained by you.

## Activity 13.1 Identifying errors in layout

Part of the requirements in the assignment brief state the following:

Word-process your work on A4 paper using Times New Roman size 11. Use 1.5 line-spacing to allow for tutors' comments. Make sure the pages are numbered and your name appears in the header on every page. Do not indent text unless it is a quote over 5 lines long.

Using the above guidelines, identify what is wrong with the following extracts which are about to be handed in for assessment. There are at least two problems per extract.

### Extract 1

Research carried out by Lea and Street (1998, p.162) on native speaker students highlighted the problem of variety of expectations further. The students found that tutor expectations not only varied from department to department but more importantly from tutor to tutor within one module. Some tutors for example stipulated that the organisation of the essay should be shown in the introduction, whereas others were criticising the students for offering this information stating that they did not want to know what would follow.

### Extract 2

Lea and Street (1998: 164) found that the guidelines offered by the two universities they studied were providing ample advice on referencing, plagiarism and spelling criteria but nothing which reflected or answered the students' main problems such as an explanation of 'critical evaluation' which most tutors required but which the tutors themselves found difficult to express in terms of marking criteria.

→

**Extract 3**

7 Name: M.M-L.

Students seem to rate tutor feedback quite highly but despite claiming to be aware of that feedback when tackling a later piece of written work, they do not seem to have any strategies in place on how best to convert the feedback into an improved and more accurate piece of work (Curry and Hewings, 2003: 21).

> **TIP** *Printing your work and checking the layout before submitting it will help you spot spacing problems that you often cannot see on a computer screen.*

# WRITING BY HAND

There may be times in academic assessment when you do not need to, or indeed cannot, type your work, such as when you are writing a diary or journal, or when writing reports during practical sessions. Make sure you know what you are expected to do when keeping those records by looking at the brief and the handbook, and by asking your tutor. The content of these texts has been dealt with in other chapters in this book. Regarding the presentation of your work, the main points to consider are:

◀ See Chapters 1, 6–9, 12

- Keep your work tidy (e.g. avoid smudges and coffee stains).
- Write clearly and legibly.
- Use whitener to correct your work or cross out neatly with a single line.
- When referencing, underline the title (do not try and write in italics).
- Make use of white space. Avoid long chunks of text with no spaces.
- Use different colour pens to underline headings. This helps break text up.
- Draw shapes and diagrams using tools (e.g. ruler, protractor) to help you. Avoid drawing freehand unless you are an artist.

Make sure the last three points are acceptable to your tutors.

◀ See Chapter 2

Examinations are another time you will be required to write by hand as, clearly, you do not usually have the use of a computer when you are writing in an exam. Students often worry about whether to write in ink or pencil, what to do when they have made a mistake, and whether they are allowed to cross things out. Remember that you can always ask one of the exam invigilators at any time by raising your hand. Our suggestion, once again, is that you need to read the instructions carefully. If you can use calculators or if the exam writer intends for you to write using a pencil, then they will say so on the paper. If you are not allowed to rub or cross anything out, that will also be stated in the instructions. You can safely assume that if a requirement has not been stated by the invigilators or written in the exam instructions, it is not an issue to worry about.

Make sure you go into an examination with at least two pens that still have ink in them, and at least one pencil, eraser and sharpener. These are the minimum items you should have with you. Other items you can take into the examination room will depend on your subject and on what is allowed. Check requirements in advance.

**TIP** *Always check instructions before the exam day and always read the instructions on the paper on the day of the exam carefully.*

Other points you need to consider are:

- Try to keep your writing clear and legible.
- Cross out any errors. (This saves time. A strike-through line is sufficient.)
- Use white space around your paragraphs. (Do not write a continuous unbroken text.)

# ADAPTING TEXT FOR DIFFERENT PURPOSES

As part of your assessment, you may be required to present your work on slides or as a poster. You may be asked to work on these as a group and subsequently be marked as a group, but you may then be asked to produce an individual written assignment on the same topic. Other chapters in this book have looked at assignment writing extensively. This section will focus on the kind of features which help improve the visual attractiveness of presentation slides and posters.

## Presentation slides

The main point to remember when constructing presentation slides is to make use of plenty of white space. This means that there should almost be more space than words on each slide. The slide should provide enough information to make sense, but not so much that the text covers the whole slide. You do not want the audience to be reading your slides – you want them to listen to you. Your audience has not made the effort to attend your presentation in order to read information which could have been handed out to them instead.

In order to achieve a good balance of information and space, make sure you include your main points as cues, in a much shorter form. The cues will help prompt you and allow you to expand on them orally.

The following extract from an essay is used as an example. Read it and then look at the way the main points have been used as cues on the slides.

**Extract**

Unfortunately the new methods did not seem to improve learning and confusion ensued in the 70s and 80s as to how to proceed. Theoretical positions were changing quickly whereas practices were much slower. For example, Gattegno's Silent Way and Curran's Community Language Learning, both developed in the 60s, only became recognised in the 70s.

There was a shift from teaching methods to language teaching *objectives* which placed more emphasis on content and curriculum design.

The Threshold level syllabus (arrived at by an international group of scholars in the 70s) was used for a variety of languages (it was published for the English Language in 1975). It attempted to define a minimum level of general ability. It includes a lexicon of 1,500 items and the authors suggest that two thirds of that lexicon would be required for productive use.

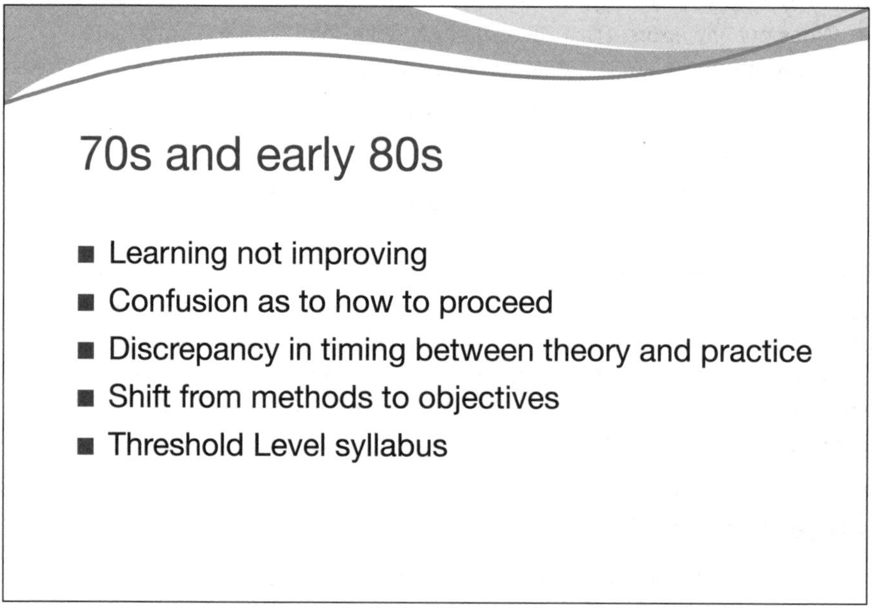

# 70s and early 80s

- Learning not improving
- Confusion as to how to proceed
- Discrepancy in timing between theory and practice
- Shift from methods to objectives
- Threshold Level syllabus

Figure 13.1 **Slide relating to extract**

If you now look at both the extract and the slide you will notice the following:

- The slide has a heading to help guide the audience as to its content.
- The points on the slide are not written in complete sentences.
- The first three points on the slide are a summary of the first paragraph.
- Only three words have been put on the slide for the whole of the third paragraph.
- The text is 138 words in total whereas the slide is only 28.

The above are suggestions only. You might have chosen different bullet points if you were preparing this slide. The point is that the majority of the information you would share with your audience would come from your oral input – not from the slide. If your slides are being assessed without an actual presentation taking place, hand them in with the accompanying text. There is also space at the bottom of each slide for you to write notes. You can use that space to give your lecturer further details on each item you have raised on your slides. Try not to make your slide too cryptic however by only writing one or two words per bullet point! As for designing the slide, experiment with fonts and colours until you find a design which works. Check that:

- the slide colour and the text colour do not clash
- the text size is large enough to be visible: an average text size would be 26 point (12 point for essays)
- any pictures, animations or diagrams you include are relevant
- you include bullet points if you need to, but do not overdo them
- you have not spent too much time creating beautiful slides whilst ignoring the importance of content.

**TIP** *Remember, always check the assignment brief to guide you.*

## Activity 13.2 **Turning text into slides**

The following extract has been taken from a text which is intended to be read as a report. Look at the slide that follows it and note the differences between them.

Cunningsworth (1995) stresses the importance of examining the type of activities in a coursebook in order to ensure that they serve a purpose. Wordlists and definitions do not have a place in coursebooks, neither do words out of context. The given activities should help raise students' awareness of the relationships between words. He divides these into 4 areas which he suggests good vocabulary activities should make use of:

1 semantic relations – word groups according to meaning, synonyms, hyponyms, opposites;
2 situational relationships – word sets associated with particular situations, eg *sport, transport, politics*;
3 collocations – words commonly found in association, eg *food and drink, for better or worse,* also noun + preposition links and phrasal verbs (verb + particle links);
4 relationships of form (often referred to as 'word building'), eg *long, length, lengthen*.

(Cunningsworth, 1995: 38)

---

## Good vocabulary activities

...should make use of:
- semantic relations
- situational relationships
- collocations
- relationships of form

(Cunningsworth, 1995: 38)

---

## Activity 13.3 Improving a slide

Look at the following slide and suggest any necessary changes to improve it visually.

---

### Nation's psychological conditions

- *Noticing* is defined as paying attention to the word. This can be achieved in a number of ways, such as use of bold, italics, inclusion in pre-teaching lists, written record on the board and in students' note-books and other such methods.

- *Retrieval* is used to strengthen the learning. In this case, either the form (or part of the form) OR the meaning (or part of the meaning) is visible to the learner. If the form is provided, for example, it acts as a memory aid for retrieval of meaning and vice versa. Retrieval is encouraged through meaning-focused use of the four skills. Activities such as re-telling, role-play and problem-solving are used for retrieval purposes where input is the basis of the production of the output. The word is retrieved when it needs to be used.

- *Elaborating* involves retrieval but adds strengthening to the process. It can occur through inclusion in contexts which are either new or unknown to the learner, or where rich instruction of the word is given. A good example in Tomlinson (ibid. p. 397), is use of the word 'adults'. Learners have read a short text on the weight of school bags for children with one sentence comparing it to adults. One of the comprehension questions after the text is 'At what age does a child become an adult?' This question extends the meaning of the word the learners have noticed and it also allows them to use it in a much different context.

---

## Posters

Many of the points raised for creating presentation slides are also relevant for posters.

The main point to remember when designing a poster is that you want people to choose to read it because it looks interesting. A poster needs to draw attention to itself. The following suggestions may help you achieve that:

- It should have a title – use the largest text on the whole poster for this.
- It should be visually attractive – make use of colour, diagrams, images and borders.
- The text size should be large enough for it to be read from a distance of at least 1 metre.
- It should include all the relevant information required but not in dense text.
- It should make good use of white space – avoid cramming in text and images to fill space.
- The sections should be spaced apart.
- Include headings in text larger than the sections but smaller than the title.

Posters which are created by simply printing out various parts of your assignment (without changes) and sticking them onto card are not successful. You need to strike a good balance between white space and the amount of information you give. Unlike presenting slides, where you are meant to offer further information on each point on the slide orally, posters need to provide adequate information by themselves. Ideally, if you are working off a text you have already written, you need to summarise the sections of your work over and over again until you are satisfied that the information you now have puts across your points succinctly. If you are creating a poster from scratch, you need to ensure that you elaborate on your points sufficiently to satisfy your audience. You can use a programme such as PowerPoint to help you design your poster.

**TIP** *Show your poster to a friend who is not involved in your work. If they cannot follow it, adjust it accordingly.*

Make sure you design your poster in a logical manner. If, for example, you are required to have sections such as methodology, results, conclusion and recommendations, bear in mind that people are likely to gaze at the top centre first to look for the title and get the overall feel of your poster. As they come closer, they are likely to let their eyes move across from left to right in a natural reading manner. It would be sensible, therefore, to have the methodology on the left and the recommendations on the right with the other sections progressing logically across the poster.

In an attempt to make their posters look more interesting, some students slant text left and right. This is fine as long as you do not overdo the slanting, resulting in people having to bend their heads left and right in an attempt to follow your text.

## Activity 13.4 **Evaluating posters**

Evaluate the following posters using the information in this section. Do you think they are successful or not? Give reasons for your opinions.

## Activity 13.5 **Improving posters**

What changes would you make to the following posters and why?

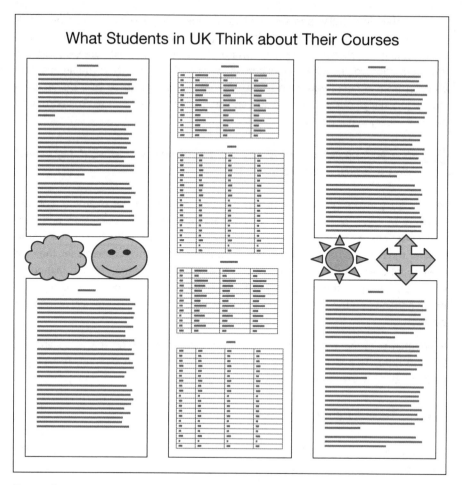

Poster 1

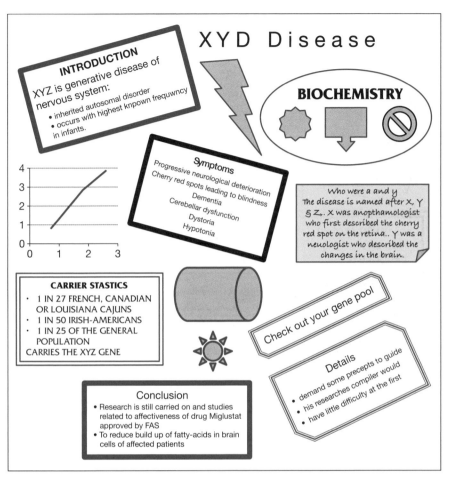

Poster 2

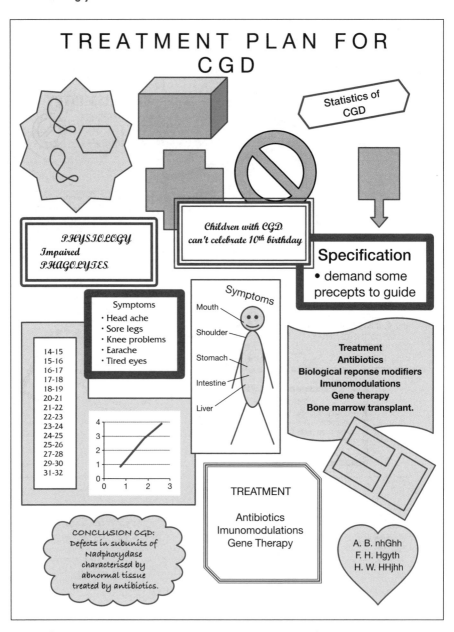

Poster 3

# SUMMARY

Presenting your work can be compared to presenting a cake. When baking a cake, you carefully mix the correct ingredients to make sure that the end result tastes delicious. When writing an assignment, be it an essay, a report, presentation slides or a poster, you carefully think about the content to make sure that the end result reads well. The final touches to a baked cake are added when you decorate it. You would not choose to throw on icing in lumps across the cake or decorate only half of it. Your guests would be put off by its appearance. In the same way you should finish off your academic work with pride. Always aim to keep your work clean, legible and ordered. You may not get extra marks specifically for appearance, but you may well lose some.

Throughout your education you have been receiving feedback on your work, either through comments on your school work, or through reports and exam results. This will continue in higher education and you must ensure that you make the most of that feedback right from the start of your studies. Responding to lecturer feedback on subsequent assignments by adapting your work appropriately can have a major impact on your marks. This chapter is aimed at increasing your awareness of feedback and improving your understanding of lecturer feedback comments.

This chapter will cover:

■ the purpose of feedback
■ formative and summative assessment and feedback
■ making sense of lecturers' feedback
■ contacting your lecturer
■ consequences of ignoring or not understanding feedback.

## USING THIS CHAPTER

# INTRODUCTION

Most of you recognise that the main reason lecturers give feedback on your assignments is to improve your work and help you achieve a higher grade by showing you your strengths and weaknesses. You may feel there are secondary reasons too, such as feedback is a justification for the mark or it is intended to improve your confidence. There may be some of you who feel feedback is unnecessary as the work has already been done and marked. We hope that by the end of this chapter you will learn to appreciate the importance of lecturer feedback and be armed with some strategies for using it to your advantage.

# THE PURPOSE OF FEEDBACK

We assume you are in higher education because you are interested in learning more about your subject as well as the overall experience. Whilst studying you need to show that you are indeed acquiring more knowledge and the way to prove that is through the assignments that you write and the tests that you sit. Lecturers also aim to increase your knowledge and your interest in the subject you are studying. They would like to see you succeed in your chosen path and therefore, in addition to the time they spend teaching you in class, they also try to give you more individual attention through tutorials and written feedback on your assignments. You may occasionally feel that they could be paying you more individual attention, but before you become overly critical, do consider the number of students they have to deal with on your programme. Lecturers are aware of their time constraints and they therefore devise ways of providing feedback which may at times seem rather generic (e.g. pro-forma feedback sheets with tick boxes). In most cases, nevertheless, further written feedback is provided on specific coursework. The overall aim of that feedback is to improve your future work. It is intended to help you build on your strengths and diminish your weaknesses. So, although the feedback given is usually on a completed, finished piece of work, the comments made by the lecturer should be taken on board for future assignments. It may be worth considering your current thoughts about feedback before continuing with the chapter. We clearly feel that feedback is extremely important, which is also why we are providing you with feedback on the activities in this book.

## Activity 14.1 Reflection on feedback

1 Do you know where your assessed work is?
- [ ] Yes, I know exactly where it is
- [ ] Yes, I could perhaps find it if I needed to
- [ ] Yes, I threw it away
- [ ] No, I don't know where it is

**2** How many times do you usually look at each piece of assessed work after it is marked? Circle one of the answers below

Never    Once    2–4 times    Over 5 times

**3** Why do/don't you look at your assessed work again?

**4** Have you ever had the opportunity to get comments on *drafts* of your work?

☐ No    ☐ Yes

**5** If yes, how useful did you find the comments?

_____

**6** In which of the following ways would you prefer lecturers to comment on your work? Tick ALL that apply:

☐ Written comments on a separate piece of paper (assignment cover sheet)

☐ Written comments throughout your work (e.g. on the relevant parts of the essay pages)

☐ Written comments at the bottom of the page of the submitted text

☐ Written comments throughout your work and on the assignment cover sheet

☐ Written comments with an opportunity to talk to lecturer

☐ Recorded (oral) comments

☐ Emailed written comments

☐ Would prefer to agree with individual lecturers on a specific method of receiving feedback

**7** i) What type of comments do you *expect* to get on your written work? Tick ALL that apply. ii) What type of comments would you *prefer* to get on your written work? Tick ALL that apply.

*Expect*  *Prefer*

☐  ☐  Praise. For example: 'Very good explanation!'

☐  ☐  Comments on your content and ideas.

☐  ☐  Comments on the organisation of your ideas in the text.

☐  ☐  Comments on your use of language e.g spelling, punctuation and grammar.

☐  ☐  Corrections of grammar and/or spelling.

☐  ☐  Naming of type of error with a correction. For example: 'Spelling: thrOUGH'

☐  ☐  Use of <u>underlining</u> to note errors but no correction.

☐  ☐  Questions about the error. For example: 'Why?' 'Where did you find this information?'

☐  ☐  Request for further information. For example: 'Further explanation required/needed here.'

☐  ☐  Ticks (✓)

☐  ☐  Use of a code to show what error has been made. For example, Gr = grammar, Sp = spelling, ? = unclear sentence/idea

☐  ☐  No comments. Only a mark.

→

**8** Would you like the opportunity to discuss with your lecturer the type of comments you would find useful?

☐ Yes
☐ No
☐ Not sure

Source: Martala and Parry (2008)

It is always worth spending some time reflecting on how you do things and why. Clearly, there are no correct answers to this exercise. Its main aim is to raise your awareness in terms of how you view feedback and how much further you are willing to embrace it. Compare your preferences and expectations to the actual feedback you receive and be prepared to discuss this with your lecturers. Research carried out at a university in Hertfordshire (Martala and Parry, 2008), for example, showed that the majority of students did not particularly like ticks whereas they expected written comments, especially on organisation, all over their work. They were, in fact, mainly receiving ticks on their work and feedback on assignment cover sheets. Moreover, whereas both students and lecturers had expressed an interest in negotiating feedback methods with each other, only a small proportion were given this opportunity. Feedback is intended as a two-way communication process but students need to approach their lecturers for this to occur. It is up to you to take that step towards improved communication methods with your lecturers.

**TIP** *Communicate your feedback preferences to your lecturers.*

## Negative issues of feedback

We feel that current terminology may conceal the benefit of feedback because of emphasis on the 'back'. When the word 'feedback' is mentioned, it is clear that the comments relate to a finished piece of work rather than a future one. Also, despite lecturers' efforts to give constructive criticism relating to your text, the work you have created is extremely personal to you and any criticism of it may inevitably be taken personally. You may feel disillusioned by negative remarks and problems with your writing and you may push the feedback aside and ignore it. That would unfortunately weaken your academic prospects.

## 'Feedforward' as a suggested solution

To help change your view of feedback, start thinking of the process as 'feed forward'. Many lecturers are already engaging with this concept which shifts the focus onto future rather than past assignments. The aim of feedforward is to suggest solutions which can be worked towards in future assignments thus making a direct link with the improvement of forthcoming work. Even if your lecturers are using the current feedback method, you may turn that into feedforward. An example may help. The lecturer comments: 'There are too many quotes on this page.' In feedforward terms you could interpret this as: 'I need to use fewer quotes by paraphrasing and summarising more.' Naturally if you want to improve your marks, you will need to make sure that you act on the feedforward. (Lecturer comments are 'interpreted' later in the chapter.)

# FORMATIVE AND SUMMATIVE ASSESSMENT AND FEEDBACK

You may be aware of the terms 'formative' and 'summative' assessment. These are ways in which your lecturers assess and feed back on what you are learning or have learned on your course. In broad terms 'formative' assessment is intended to help you improve though it may not necessarily carry a mark or contribute to your final grade. 'Summative' assessment is used for work that carries a mark which will contribute to your final score. The examples of both types of assessment can be the same. Therefore an essay, a multiple choice test, the writing up of an experiment, can all be ways of assessing you and providing feedback. With formative assessment however, the essay is more likely to be a draft and the test or experiment is more like 'mock exams'.

## Activity 14.2 Evaluating feedback on drafts and final scripts

Consider the writing of an essay as one example of both formative and summative assessment. The column on the left lists possible benefits of feedback. The other two columns are divided into 'draft essay' where formative feedback would be given, and 'essay' where summative feedback would be expected. Look at each proposed benefit and decide whether it would 'D = definitely', 'P = probably' or 'N = not likely' be of benefit to you for each type of essay. Circle the one you feel is appropriate.

| Benefits of feedback (Which of the following do you think can be achieved if you act on the feedback?) | Draft essay (Circle one letter) | Essay (Circle one letter) |
|---|---|---|
| An improved writing style | D P N | D P N |
| A better knowledge of the referencing system | D P N | D P N |
| More careful editing skills | D P N | D P N |
| A better structure with well-organised paragraphs | D P N | D P N |
| Wider reading to support your points | D P N | D P N |
| Adherence to assignment guidelines | D P N | D P N |
| An increase in your mark on subsequent essays | D P N | D P N |

## Activity 14.3 Rating the importance of feedback

Looking at your answers above, which of these two types of feedback do you think is the most important for your academic success: formative or summative?

If you have not circled any Ns then you feel that a number of benefits can be gained from both formative and summative feedback. However, if you have circled Ns you may feel that it is too late to change your essay now despite the feedback. Do remember, however, that any feedback you receive relies on you actually making use of it. You may not be able to increase the mark of your current essay, but the lessons you have learned through the feedback should help you in your future work. You may find that just better planning or editing alleviates the problem or that you need to do more reading and practise more with exercises such as those found in this and other books.

Hopefully you have seen that both forms of assessment and feedback are equally important. They are both valuable ways of gauging your progress and identifying areas you may need to improve. It is unfortunately true that many students are more likely to take part in summative activities (which carry marks) rather than formative ones (which do not), thus missing out on valuable opportunities for improvement. Students often only look at the mark on a returned assignment and do not always pay sufficient attention to useful comments provided by the lecturers. The marks given for an assignment should be seen as a useful form of feedback rather than the main focus of your studies.

## Activity 14.4 Feedback methods used in your context

It will help you to know the kind of formative and summative feedback methods utilised by your department. Look at the following list and tick all that apply. If you are not sure of some of the answers, try to find out by reading the course handbook and asking other students and your lecturers.

| Formative feedback methods | Yes | No | Not sure |
|---|---|---|---|
| Lecturer feedback on drafts – this process is integrated into the course | | | |
| Lecturer feedback on drafts – non-integrated, informal comments made to students who ask | | | |
| Peer feedback* on drafts – this process is integrated into the course | | | |
| Whole class feedback on typical areas of difficulty | | | |
| Personal feedback – you are asked to rate and comment on your own work | | | |

| Formative feedback methods | Yes | No | Not sure |
|---|---|---|---|
| Feedback provided by academic skills unit (or similar student academic support centre) | | | |
| Other | | | |
| **Summative feedback methods** | **Yes** | **No** | **Not sure** |
| Lecturer feedback written on assignment cover sheet | | | |
| Lecturer feedback provided all over the assignment | | | |
| Lecturer feedback given on template forms | | | |
| Lecturer feedback on pro-forma tick-box grids | | | |
| Written lecturer feedback with opportunity for tutorial | | | |
| Whole class feedback on typical areas of difficulty | | | |
| Peer feedback* | | | |
| Personal feedback – you are asked to rate and comment on your own work | | | |
| A mark and feedback on your course website | | | |
| A mark on your course website followed by comments on your hard copy | | | |
| Other | | | |

* Some students question the validity of peer feedback. In fact, peer feedback can be extremely valuable. A fresh pair of eyes may spot different things in the text. Moreover, if your peer cannot understand certain points in the text, it is highly likely that neither will your lecturer. At the same time, when *you* are reading a peer's work, you may pick up new ways of doing things.

TIP *Make sure you know what feedback methods are in place in your department.*

Knowing the various mechanisms in place better prepares you for the kind of help which is available. We would like to draw your attention to four areas, as follows.

# 1 Individual approaches to feedback differ

Despite the procedures in place for feedback, lecturers are all individuals and their approach may therefore be different. Some lecturers may make (coded) corrections on your text whereas others may only place ticks or write nothing. Some may only write on the assignment cover sheet whereas others may write on the top sheet, on the text, as footnotes and on a tick-box sheet at the back.

Our advice is therefore not to rely on there being one particular type of feedback. Whenever your work is returned to you, carefully examine the pages from start to finish as you may miss something important.

# 2 Look beyond the overall mark

We strongly urge you not to rely purely on the mark you may have already received, whether poor or excellent.

Make sure you pick up your hard copy and examine it carefully. We suggest you keep a small feedback notebook and you dedicate one page to one repeated feedback comment, adding to it every time one of your assignments is returned to you. The following is an example of a student's entries into a feedback notebook.

## Sample student notebook

| Page 1 | Page 2 | Page 3 |
|---|---|---|
| 28 Oct<br>Consult handbook for referencing conventions<br><br>17 Nov<br>Referencing conventions | 17 Nov<br>Make writing more cohesive – look at signalling words | 17 Nov<br>Use spellchecker |

Two things to note here are:

1 The feedforward terminology used in the notebook (e.g. not 'lack of cohesion', but 'make writing more cohesive'; not 'inadequate referencing', but 'consult handbook for referencing conventions'). If your lecturer has written feedback, change it into feedforward terminology. Think of it in terms of what you can do in future work.
2 The repetition of the same problem on page 1. If you find that one area is constantly reappearing as an issue, you need to make sure that you tackle it for future assignments. Ask your lecturer or an academic skills unit (if applicable) for help.

TIP *This notebook will also be particularly useful if you choose to use the academic skills service, if one is available. The service will then be in a position to focus on the specific areas you need to improve.*

TIP *If you really want to impress, add a page at the start of your next assignment asking the lecturer to look at one particular area of your work which you are trying to improve on.*

## 3 Analyse positive and negative comments

Some lecturers may like to emphasise the positives whilst others may seem more critical.

Look through the positive comments with a fine-tooth comb. Some lecturers are so concerned about hurting students' feelings that they may 'cloud' the areas which need improvement with too many encouraging remarks. This may make you feel good, but it is not helping you much. For example:

*Wide-ranging and interesting essay – well written and researched, covering the main points well, although perhaps lacking the necessary depth for analysis. But encouraging start.*

Pat yourself on the back for the five areas done well, by all means, but do not over-look the sentence 'lacking the necessary depth for analysis'. As this is being mentioned, aim to do something about it whilst also continuing the good work.

On the other hand, when you read what seem overly critical remarks, do not take them to heart. Use the feedforward strategy we looked at earlier and choose one or two points to deal with in your next assignment rather than trying to fix everything at once. Most importantly, do not take the remarks personally. For example:

*It is a shame you have restricted the majority of your discussion to information from lectures. You do not demonstrate your own understanding of the subject by simply regurgitating other people's examples. You must also use references throughout your work to acknowledge the sources of information/facts you discuss. You should also use more books/journals (academic sources) and fewer web references. This work does not reflect the 22-hour time burden.*

Take a deep breath and appreciate that the lecturer has actually given you a great deal of useful feedback despite the negative language used. Rather than only mention two points in order to soften the blow, they seem to have covered every area that needs attention. This approach has probably saved you from poor marks in your future work as long as you make sure you carefully consider each point. Ask yourself if you would rather be marked down on five subsequent assignments for making mistakes you were not aware of. If you do not like the negative way in which this has been written, change it into feedforward language as described earlier.

## 4 Turnaround time

A specified turnaround time for assessed work forms part of university regulations. Five weeks is a common turnaround time, but you should check your institution's regulations. If the deadline has passed and you are still waiting, and as long as there has been no illness or other extenuating circumstances, you are entitled to ask your lecturer when your work will be returned.

If the work you are waiting for is in the form of a draft, then a one to two-week turn-around time is more appropriate.

# MAKING SENSE OF LECTURERS' FEEDBACK

Often the problem lies not with a lack of appreciation of feedback, but with a lack of understanding of what the feedback means and how to put it to use. This section attempts to clarify this.

We mentioned earlier that the mark alone is insufficient. Nevertheless, the mark also carries meaning as it is a quick indicator of excellent, good or poor work. (For grades and their meanings please refer to your course handbook. As a general guide, an 'A' = 70+, a 'B' = 60+, a 'C' = 50+, a 'D' = 40+, an 'E' = 35+ and an 'F' is a clear fail.) Regardless of your mark, you should then read the feedback. Feedback on excellent work will encourage you to use similar strategies in the future and feedback on poor work will pinpoint the areas you need to work on to improve your future grades.

## Lecturers' comments

Provided you can decipher the lecturer's handwriting, common comments found on assignment cover sheets and on your text itself can be seen in Table 14.1. The comments are taken from actual student work. Reading through the comments you will begin to see the type of issues picked up by lecturers when marking your work, which may help you avoid making the same mistakes.

Table 14.1 **Common comments**

| Lecturers' comments (usually found on assignment cover sheet) | What they mean (in feedforward terms) | What you need to do |
|---|---|---|
| *Good understanding apparent* | Keep up the good work. | Maintain the reading you are clearly doing. |
| *Good attempt to apply theory* | You are on the way to achieving good critical writing. | Read Chapters 10 and 11 on incorporating authors' ideas and on finding your own voice for further suggestions. |
| *A highly critical account* | Make sure you maintain this level of critical writing. | Keep reading critically (see Chapter 5) and make sure your own voice continues to come through in your work (see Chapter 11). |
| *Well-written* | Put the same effort into future work. | Continue to organise your work and to write well-structured, cohesive text. See Chapter 6. |
| *Lack of integrated references*<br><br>*Please use an appropriate referencing style*<br><br>*There are clearly two very different writing styles in this assignment*<br><br>*You are in great danger of plagiarism due to lack of references* | Make sure you always acknowledge the authors whose words or ideas you are using. | You must never copy text from a source. You must always include the reference in the text and in the reference list at the end. Copied text tends to stand out from student writing. To avoid plagiarism issues, never include unreferenced material in your work. Check the referencing conventions used in your faculty. See Chapter 10. |
| *Try not to rely on quotes to make your points*<br><br>*Stronger link between your point and the reference needed* | Incorporate authors' ideas into your writing. Make sure your voice is heard and your opinion is supported by a referenced source. | Try to construct your paragraph so it includes your point with support from a source, or use the idea from the source first and link it to your point. See Chapters 10 and 11. |

→

## Table 14.1 continued

| Lecturers' comments (usually found on assignment cover sheet) | What they mean (in feedforward terms) | What you need to do |
|---|---|---|
| *Your work became descriptive in places*<br><br>*Need to increase the critical element*<br><br>*You seem to lack critical review*<br><br>*Needed to have shown critical depth*<br><br>*Need to develop an analytical ability* | Your ideas and opinions (your voice) must be made clearer in your writing. Question what you read. | Make sure you read sources with a questioning, critical mind which is consequently reflected in your writing. Ask questions such as 'how' or 'why' and weigh the strengths and weaknesses of an argument in your reading as well as in your writing. Avoid stringing ideas from sources together to make your point. See Chapters 5, 10 and 11. |
| *There is a lack of evidence to substantiate your arguments*<br><br>*Some wild assumptions made without back up evidence*<br><br>*A very opinionated piece of work* | Ensure that you have evidence from sources to support your points. | Do not make statements which are not backed up by evidence from sources. They will not be accepted. You need to balance ideas from sources with your own opinions. See Chapters 8, 10 and 11. |
| *Your understanding of the theories is limited*<br><br>*Limited reading*<br><br>*You need to use a range of sources. Don't rely on one author*<br><br>*You have restricted your discussion to information from the lectures* | Read more sources to develop more ideas and arguments in your work. These include: books, journals and all relevant academic publications. | You should always read extensively on the subject and incorporate ideas from the relevant sources into your own thinking to form a valid argument. Do not regurgitate. Do not accept only one author's point of view. The lecturer's notes are not enough. See Chapters 4, 5, 10 and 11. |
| *Fewer web references!* | You should use more books and academic journals. | If the web references are of an academic nature the lecturer will be happy. Wikipedia and Google references are usually frowned upon. See Chapter 4. |

**Table 14.1 continued**

| Lecturers' comments (usually found on assignment cover sheet) | What they mean (in feedforward terms) | What you need to do |
|---|---|---|
| *Plan?!*<br><br>*You need to include structure of essay in intro*<br><br>*Paper should have a better structure* | Write a plan. Group relevant ideas together and make sure the order they appear in is logical. Include structure in the introduction. | Your work would benefit from a plan before you start. You must attempt to organise your ideas more logically. Indicate the structure of the essay in the introduction and follow that structure in your text. Use signalling phrases to guide your reader. See Chapters 2, 3, 6 and 12. |
| *You need to improve your sentence structure* | Shorten your sentences. Avoid complicated sentences with subclauses. | When your spellchecker puts a squiggly line under a sentence, read it carefully and make any essential changes (not necessarily those offered by the program). Make use of appropriate conjunctions. See Chapters 6 and 15. |
| *Take pride when handing in work* | Imagine your work is a piece of art. Handle it accordingly. | Check your work thoroughly for spelling mistakes, correct order of pages, printing clarity and other proof-reading issues. See Chapter 15. |
| Lecturers' comments (usually found within the text) | What they mean (in feedforward terms) | What you need to do |
| *Circled or underlined words*<br><br>*Poor sentence structure*<br><br>*Spelling!* | Make sure you edit your work. Read everything carefully before handing it in. | Avoid use of informal language (including contractions, e.g. 'don't', or abbreviations, e.g. 'etc.'. Choose your words more carefully. Always keep the spellchecker switched on. It will help with correct spelling and grammar. Always allow yourself time to edit your work. See Chapters 6 and 15. |
| *Ref?*<br><br>*Source?*<br><br>*Page (number)?* | Use appropriate citation. | Make sure you provide references in the text when using someone else's ideas or words. Always remember to include the author, year of publication and the relevant page number of your quoted source. See Chapter 10. |
| ✓ | Good point. Well done. | This is good. Keep thinking like this. |

→

**Table 14.1 continued**

| Lecturers' comments (usually found within the text) | What they mean (in feedforward terms) | What you need to do |
|---|---|---|
| **?**<br>*This doesn't make sense.*<br>*I don't follow/understand.*<br>*Why is this relevant?*<br>*How does this relate to the essay topic?* | Make sure you edit your work. Read everything carefully before handing it in. Group relevant ideas together and make sure the order they appear in is logical. | Make sure your points are relevant and your argument is clear to a person other than you. Provide a good link between your point and the assignment topic and make the links between ideas more obvious. Imagine you are explaining to someone outside your field. See Chapters 6, 10 and 11. |
| *Stay focused*<br>*Rambling* | Make sure your points are relevant and your argument is clear to a person other than you. | Do not veer off the topic in an attempt to increase your word count. Is this piece of information vital to your argument? |
| *Why? / How?*<br>*Explain*<br>*Examples*<br>*Such as?*<br>*More details needed* | Provide evidence from sources to support your points. | When you make a point, you must support it with examples and evidence. Use these lecturers' questions and apply them to your points when you proof-read your work. Make sure you have provided relevant answers. See Chapters 10 and 11. |
| *No!* | Make sure you have your facts straight before making any claims. | Read sources carefully and make sure you understand the point they make before you use it in your work. See Chapter 5. |

The majority of the authentic feedback shown in Table 14.1 seems to relate to one of the following areas:

- reading
- planning and text organisation
- critical writing
- referencing
- editing.

We have attempted to cover these areas in this book to help you succeed in your studies. Try the activities in the suggested chapters and search for other material which may help you further as early in your course as possible.

# CONTACTING YOUR LECTURER

It is essential that you see your lecturer if you do not understand the feedback. You should not use that time to try and haggle with the lecturer in order to increase your mark as you will be wasting your time (and the lecturer's). Many lecturers indicate their availability in one or more of the following ways:

- in the course handbook
- on their doors (often there is a grid for you to write your name for an appointment)
- on the course website
- by specifying 'open door policy'.

In case none of the above is applicable, talk to your lecturer after the lecture and arrange a suitable time to meet. Do appreciate however that the lecturer may be going to another lecture and may not have time for you at that moment.

## Emailing your lecturer

It is always best to email your lecturer in order to make an appointment. Ask for confirmation as sending the email does not necessarily mean it has been received or opened and you would not want to have made a wasted trip. Also make sure that your email explicitly states the reason for requesting an appointment, for example: 'I would like to see you regarding the feedback on my assignment, TITLE OF ASSIGNMENT. There are a few areas I would like to clarify and I would appreciate your time' (or words to that effect). Make the subject line pertinent too. Subject lines with 'hi' or 'urgent' or 'question' or 'CN I C U?' are both inappropriate and often considered SPAM and so trashed; 'coursework feedback' should be acceptable.

## At the meeting

Make sure you go prepared with exactly what you want to say. Take your feedback notebook with you both to remind you of areas you would like to discuss and to make notes of any advice. If you have been allocated a 15-minute slot for example, you do not want to waste the first few minutes trying to formulate your thoughts or expecting your lecturer to play a guessing game. You could perhaps say one of the following:

'I would like to prioritise my areas of improvement and wanted to check with you which ones affect my work most.'

'I am not sure I understand this comment fully. Does it mean...?'

'I'm sorry, I can't quite read your writing here. Does it say...?'

Do not leave the room until you have fully understood what you need to do with your future assignments (clearly within reason).

# CONSEQUENCES OF IGNORING OR NOT UNDERSTANDING FEEDBACK

Clearly, if you ignore the lecturer's feedback, the main consequence will be that you will continue to produce work of a similar standard. In Chapter 3 we asked you to decide what kind of marks you are happy with. (If you are excelling, congratulations; keep up the good work.) Do look at the feedback all the same as it will identify what you do well and you can therefore do the same in future. Look out for lecturers' feedback which uses words such as 'almost', 'mostly', 'somewhat', 'an attempt' as they indicate that further improvement is needed.

If you are averaging 'C' and 'B' grades and would like a higher mark, utilising the feedback will help you improve.

If passing is sufficient for you and you are managing to pass, you may be able to get away with not taking any feedback on board. As feedback also forms part of your personal and working life however, failing to use it does question your whole attitude to study and work.

# SUMMARY

We have tried to show you that marks are not a sufficient indication of how you are progressing with your studies. You need to know the reasoning behind a particular mark if you want to learn from it. The feedback you receive both explains and justifies the mark with a view to helping you improve your future work. Clearly, in order for you to improve, it is essential that you understand the feedback and that you respond to it in your later assignments. Keeping a record of that feedback for you to refer to may be a useful aid to your future academic success.

## References

Martala, M. and Parry, J. (2008) *Lecturers' Written Feedback and Students' Use of Feedback – A Match Made in Heaven?* Hatfield: The University of Hertfordshire.

# 15 ▶ EDITING YOUR WORK

Making sure that your work has met with all the requirements you were given and that it is a finished product is an essential step in the process of academic writing. We suggest that as you read through this chapter you check the advice in it with an assignment that you have to give in shortly. Alternatively you could find one that you have recently completed and reflect on how it compares to the standards we suggest.

This chapter will cover:

- using a checklist to edit your work
- checking for grammar and proof-reading
- using a draft to edit your work.

## USING THIS CHAPTER

# INTRODUCTION

Editing involves looking at your work with a critical eye, measuring it against certain standards and then changing it to meet those standards. Before you start to edit your work you should feel satisfied with its overall shape, confident that you have answered the question set and are ready to hand your work in on time. If you can leave yourself enough time (a few days perhaps) between finishing the work and the deadline to review your work you will find this really beneficial. It will mean you can look at what you have produced more objectively, notice anything that may be missing and spot mistakes.

Editing is best done in stages, in which you check for different things. The more times you can read through your work, focusing each time on a different aspect and correcting where necessary, the better it will become. You can choose any order that suits you to do this, what matters is that you read your work more than once.

# THE PROCESS OF EDITING

As we have said before in this book, academic writing has certain qualities that mark it out from other kinds of writing. These qualities could be summed up as:

- structured and complete
- relevant
- well communicated
- unbiased
- economical
- owned by you
- fully referenced.

You can use these seven qualities as a checklist, to decide what and how much editing is needed for any piece of work that you do.

# STRUCTURE

There is always an expectation that academic writing guides the reader through the text, not only by developing ideas and arguments in a logical manner but also by ordering the material. This means that you need to check for two kinds of structure: internal and external.

## Internal

Make sure that:

See
Chapter 6
- there is a logical flow to your writing

- all your paragraphs link together
- all ideas are developed fully in the paragraphs or sections
- the text does not jump from one idea to another and then back again.

## External

ter 13 If your assignment includes a table of contents you can use it to check the structure of your work. Otherwise make sure that:

- all sections of the assignment are present and in the right order
- your pages are numbered and in the right order
- your name is on the document
- any appendices are in the right order
- your references are included.

In addition, ensure that:

- you have a title page (if required)
- all headings and subheadings (if required) are numbered
- you have included headers and footers (if required).

## Activity 15.1 Correct the table of contents

Highlight the mistakes in the table of contents below. Look at the order of the chapters, the page numbering and the subheadings.

→

(Wilson et al., 2008: v)

# RELEVANCE

See
Chapters 1
and 12

Your work has to carry weight and authority if readers are to trust in what you write. You must therefore ask yourself the following questions and make corrections if any of your answers are 'no'. If they are, these corrections are likely to be major ones, and you would need time on your side to make them.

- Have I answered the assignment brief?
- Have I used the right format/genre?
- Are my facts correct?
- Is all the material relevant?

# COMMUNICATION

Your reader will find it more difficult to understand your meaning if your language falls short of certain standards. Although this is to some extent a matter of style, which is a personal thing, there are some rules you can follow to make sure your language is appropriate. Form and content must work together and not against each other.

## Is the language appropriate?

See
Chapter 6

This means that, unless you are quoting from the original text or writing reflectively, your writing should not use any:

- contractions (e.g. 'hasn't', 'didn't', 'they're'): instead write 'has not', 'did not', 'they are'
- text speak (such as 'l8r' instead of 'later')
- colloquial speech (such as 'footie' instead of 'football')
- exclamation marks
- unfinished sentences
- repetition of phrases
- questions (such as 'Who would have thought that. . .?').

# Has the grammar been checked?

Your use of grammar depends on your knowing and understanding the rules of the language you are writing in. If you feel unsure of these, get hold of a grammar book and check. Some of the most common mistakes are with:

- tenses
- irregular verbs
- subject/verb agreement.

## Tenses

You need to make sure that you use the right tense for your verbs. If, for example, you start a sentence with the words 'Last year', make sure that any verb that follows is in the past tense.

> *Example:* Last year China **hosted** the Olympic Games.

## Irregular verbs

A regular verb in English ends in '-ed' (such as the word above, where 'hosted' is the past tense of 'host'). Irregular verbs have a variety of forms, some of the most common being:

> *go* – past tense is 'went' (go – went – gone)
> *see* – past tense is 'saw' (see – saw – seen)
> *take* – past tense is 'took' (take – took – taken).

If you are not sure what the past tense of a verb is, look it up. You will find that dictionaries often include a list of the most common irregular verb forms.

## Subject/verb agreement

Check that the verb is in the singular or plural, according to the subject.

> *Example:* In the UK a general election normally **takes** place every four or five years.

## Activity 15.2 **Spot the mistake**

Each of the following sentences has a grammar mistake in it and one of them has two. Highlight all the errors and correct them.

1 Last month the government introduces new regulations for small businesses.
2 Investors who bought shares in the dot.com industries saw there value fall over time.
3 Historians disagrees over the origins of communism.
4 Under-age drinking are a major problem today.
5 You're work has to carry weight and authority if readers are to trust in what you write.

## Is the punctuation correct?

Punctuation acts to break sentences into units that allow you to understand meaning. Although punctuation is to some extent a matter of style, there are some basic rules that do not change.

- **Full stops (.)** – to show the end of a sentence. A capital letter must follow a full stop. For example:

    This year there was snow in London in October. This is the first time this has happened since 1934.

- **Commas (,)** – to separate parts of sentences. The three examples below show the effect of commas on meaning. In the first example there are no commas. The addition of commas in the second means that the sentence reads more fluently and makes more sense. In the third example, the commas are in the wrong place and the sentence makes little sense.

    *Without commas*: The rules of a particular sport such as the off-side rule in football or the rules of a club are designed to bring order to a particular activity.                                        (Keenan and Riches, 2007: 3)

    *With commas*: The rules of a particular sport, such as the off-side rule in football, or the rules of a club, are designed to bring order to a particular activity.

    *Commas in the wrong place*: The rules, of a particular sport, such as the off-side, rule in football or the, rules of a club are, designed, to bring order to a particular activity.

- **Apostrophes (')** – to show possession, for example:

    Great Britain's power as a colonial ruler.

    The twentieth century's most important invention.

Be careful not to put an apostrophe where it is not needed. It is ungrammatical to write:

    The strength of the law lies in it's power to protect the individual.

- **Quotation marks (' ')** – to show that you are using the words of someone else. For example:

    As Shakespeare said: 'Neither a borrower nor a lender be.'

- **Colons (:)** – to add extra information after a clause. For example:

    We need three kinds of support: economic, moral and political.

- **Semi-colons (;)** – to separate items in lists, especially if these are long and complicated and already contain commas. For example this text is discussing the Council of the European Union:

    In the latter case each country has a certain number of votes (France, Germany, Italy and the UK have 29 votes each; Spain and Poland have 27 each; Romania 14 votes; the Netherlands 13 votes; Belgium, Czech Republic, Greece, Hungary and Portugal have 12 votes apiece; Austria, Sweden and Bulgaria 10 votes; Denmark, Ireland, Lithuania, Slovakia and Finland seven votes; Cyprus, Estonia, Latvia, Luxembourg and Slovenia have four votes each and Malta has three).        (Keenan and Riches, 2007: 29)

- **Capital letters (A, B, C)** – to start a sentence or for a proper name. For example:

  English, Berlin, December.

## Activity 15.3 Correct the punctuation

The following paragraph has no punctuation. Make all the corrections you think it needs.

> the current cultural context in which we find ourselves located allows little opportunity for silence and appears to place little value on it our shopping centres offices cars and homes are full of sound some might say noise and the invention of email mobile phones and ipods means people are constantly in communication with each other and are able should they choose to to talk or listen to someone or something all the time under these circumstances silence is an unfamiliar phenomenon therefore when it is encountered it can be unnerving and potentially be perceived as threatening and deskilling yet we would argue it should not be and need not be                                        (Wilson *et al.*, 2008: 310)

## Is everything written out in full?

An acronym is when the first initials of a group of words are used to make another recognised word. If you use an acronym write it in full the first time, followed by the shortened version. After that, you can use the shortened version each time. For example:

United Nations (UN)

You should not use an abbreviation in a piece of academic writing, unless you are quoting from the original text.

## Correct spelling?

It is important that words are spelt correctly. Good spelling makes a good impression and helps make the meaning clear. The following two examples demonstrate the effect spelling can have on first impressions.

*Correct spelling*: There are 365 days in a year. There are 52 weeks in a year and 7 days in a week. There are 24 hours in a day and 60 minutes in an hour.

*Incorrect spelling*: Their are 365 daze inn a yere. There are 52 weaks in a yeare and 7 daze in a weak. Theyre are 24 ours in a day and 60 minits in an hour.

Sometimes it is difficult to know the correct spelling for a word. For example:

'Exaggerate' not 'exxagerate'

'Committee' not 'comittee'

'Management' not 'managment'

'Necessary' not 'necissary'

If you know you are not a good speller, use a dictionary and make use of the spell-checking facilities provided by your computer. Try also to learn the correct spelling for as many words as you can.

## Activity 15.4 Correct the spelling

In Activity 15.2 you corrected some mistakes in grammar. Now correct the spelling mistakes.

1 Last month the governement introduced new regulashions for small businesses.
2 Investores who bought shairs in the dot.com industries saw their value fall over tyme.
3 Historyans disagree over the origins of comunism.
4 Under-age drinnking is a major problam today.
5 Your work has to carry wait and authority if reeders are to trust in wot you write.

# Proof-reading

Word processors can do much of the hard work of proof-reading so make sure you use the grammar and spell check. The system is not foolproof, however, as the following two examples show. The first is an example of what happens when you hit the wrong key.

### Example 1: typing mistake

the Hundred Years Waf

instead of:

the Hundred Years War

'Waf' is not a word, so will be flagged up by the spellchecker. It is not safe to assume, however, that the right word will be the first one on the list of suggestions offered. The correct word 'War' is fourth on the list in the most common word processing package, Word. It comes after 'waft', 'wave' and 'wait'.

### Example 2: mis-typing a word

**Technology has produced many fine, tin fabrics.**

instead of

**Technology has produced many fine, thin fabrics.**

If as in this example you type 'tin' instead of 'thin', a word processor will not correct it. You could then have a sentence that would not be picked up by the spellchecker but would make no sense at all.

So, remember that you will always need to read your work through, either to check for sense or for common mistakes such as 'their' (the possessive pronoun) instead of 'there' (adverb of place).

**TIP** *If you have time, read your work aloud to yourself. It should help you to decide if there are mistakes in your grammar or if you have mis-typed a word.*

## How good is the look and feel?

pter 13 The final area where communication is helped is in how your writing looks on the printed page. Chapter 13 gave you detailed advice on presentation: look back at it and think about the following:

- the typeface (an assignment will often give guidance on this, but avoid elaborate or unusual fonts)
- the layout – how much space is there between paragraphs and lines?
- paragraphs – are they more or less of equal length or do you have too many short paragraphs?
- your use of white space (margins, at the top and bottom of a page)
- charts – these must all be clearly labelled
- graphs – make sure the scale is good enough for them to be understood.

# BIAS

Another expectation of academic writing is that it is not one-sided, that is to say it considers both sides of an argument. If you are given an essay title that asks you to discuss the advantages and disadvantages of an issue, you will be expected to give equal treatment to each side. If you are asked to consider the causes of a particular event, you will be expected to explore each cause you write about in equal measure. This is something to think about when you are reading through your work. If you feel that it is one-sided then you need to try and correct the imbalance.

# ECONOMY

When you write an assignment you will almost certainly be given a word limit. Often you will be given a range to work within (that is, a minimum and maximum word length). Alternatively, you may be told what the tolerance is, such as 10 per cent over or under the word limit. Pay attention to this information, as you do not want your work to lose marks if you write too much or too little.

## Have you written too much?

If you find that you have gone beyond the acceptable word limit you will need to cut out some of your writing. Try to make the decision rationally. You could perhaps:

- use fewer examples in your discussion
- check that you have not repeated yourself and made the same point several times over
- remove any material that you think is not central to the assignment.

## Have you written too little?

If you find that you are under the acceptable word limit you will need to expand your writing. This problem is often linked to not exploring an issue fully enough or providing enough detail in the analysis. Try to develop your writing in a structured way:

See Chapters 2 and 6

- Look back at your original plan and check that you have included all the points.
- Look through the notes you made. You may be able to expand on some of the points.
- Look at the topic sentence in every paragraph. Have you developed each one fully enough?
- Have you given enough examples to support the points you are making?

If you do have to cut out material, bear in mind that your work must still make sense, read logically and keep its structure.

# OWNERSHIP

Your writing must demonstrate that you are the originator of and are in sole control of the words. You want to avoid the charge of plagiarism at all costs and need to ask yourself these questions:

See Chapters 10 and 11

- Have I used my own words except for when I have quoted something?
- Is it always clear when I am quoting or citing another writer?
- Can the reader tell this is my own piece of work?
- Does my own voice come through?

If you have access to anti-plagiarism software, use it to check that you have not accidentally copied words or failed to use quotation marks. If you submit your work electronically you may in any event find that your work is automatically checked for plagiarism.

# REFERENCING

The final area to consider is your use of referencing, to ensure that your work has the completeness it needs for a piece of academic writing. You need to check that you have acknowledged all your sources, both in the text and in your reference list, and that your references are accurate. Well-written references are always appreciated by the marker and you are likely to be marked down if they are wrong or of poor quality.

## Activity 15.5 Improve this referencing

Read this paragraph and then look at the references that follow it. The writer has made several mistakes in the list of references. Highlight them and make the corrections using the referencing guidelines in Chapter 10.

> The multi-layered nature of the problems experienced make decisions both about how to intervene and where to intervene very problematic and can lead to workers choosing either to 'condemn or condone' as opposed to sitting on the fence somewhere (Kroll and Taylor, 2000). In addition social workers have to be able to separate recreational drug use from problem drug use (Harbin and Murphy, 2000) without over-reacting to the former and under-reacting to the latter (Gilman, 2000). As mentioned previously, this means it is important to treat each case individually and without preconceived notions of the quality of care drug users can provide. If this is not the case, then again, as pointed out by Taylor and Kroll (2004, p.1117):
>
> > there is the danger of either making unfounded connections and assumptions between chronic substance misuse and parenting or of under-reacting and failing to identify the maltreatment that a significant minority of children experience.
>
> **References**
>
> Harbin and Murphy. Background and current context of substance misuse and child care. In F. Harbin and M. Murphy (eds), *Substance Misuse and Child care: How to Understand, Assist and Intervene When Drugs Affect Parenting,* (pp.109–155) Lyme Regis: Russell House
>
> Giman, M. (2000) Social exclusion and drug using parents. In F. Harbin and M. Murphy (see above for details).
>
> Kroll, B. and Taylor, A. (2004) Working with parental misuse: Dilemmas for practice. *British Journal of Social Work, 34*,1115–32
>
> (Wilson *et al.*, 2008: 602)

**281**

## Using a draft

See Chapters 1, 6 and 14 Often you are able to hand in a draft to your lecturer for comments. Whether you have been given formal feedback on it or not, editing a draft version is one way of improving your work. You should compare your draft with the following items:

- the assignment brief
- the assignment marking criteria
- the plan you wrote for the assignment
- the notes you made
- the feedback you received on the draft.

### Activity 15.6 Comparing your draft

Find the documents mentioned above.

1 Read the assignment brief and marking criteria again. Now check your draft. Does it meet the instructions and criteria?
2 If not, make corrections.
3 Read the plan you made and the notes you wrote. Does it follow them and include all the information you wanted to put in?
4 If not, make corrections.
5 Read the feedback. Have you addressed the comments?
6 If not, make corrections.

# SUMMARY

Any piece of academic writing needs to go through the process of being edited. This book has been edited. Editing work is something that you have to make space for if you want to hand in a piece of work that does justice to your efforts. It is part of the debate you will have with yourself (consciously or unconsciously) about whether you want just to pass or to do well in your academic studies. It allows you to understand yourself as a writer and provides you with tools for developing your skills in handling the written word.

## References

Details of highlighted references can be found in the Introduction on page xxii.

# A LAST WORD

At the beginning of this book we referred to writing as a process as well as a product. We hope that we have shown you effective techniques for both of these: how to prepare for an assignment through planning, researching and reading, and then how to write one, following the demands of the assignment. We have shown you how to write in a variety of genres, to help you conform to the discipline you are studying in. We have also given you examples of text types that you can use as building blocks in your writing. We hope too that you have seen the value of using feedback to help you improve your writing at every stage of the process.

We wanted to show you that academic writing is not just what your lecturers and textbooks produce. We believe that it is something you can learn how to do, something you can improve on all the time and that there are tools to help you do both of these things. As we have said before, academic writing is different from other forms of writing. It belongs to a community that you join once you start studying in higher education. That community expects you to respect the style and conventions of an academic text, to develop your analytical and critical skills over a period of time, and to demonstrate them through your writing. This is why we have balanced a chapter on working with other people's ideas with one on using your own voice: we think it is important that you own the academic writing that you produce and that allowing your voice to come through in your writing is one of the ways you prove your membership of the academic community.

We also believe that it is important that you do not just think of academic writing as a means to an end. Many of the chapters in this book could serve two purposes: most importantly to help you to write an assignment, but also to show you how to communicate well, with accuracy and depth. Communication is not just about giving facts and opinions, it is about presenting yourself as a professional. The chapter on writing reflectively comes at a time when more and more professions are expecting that you will be able to reflect upon your practice and to write about achievements and personal development. To this end, we hope that this book will help you to progress beyond your studies, where you can carry the skills you have practised here into a wider setting.

We wish you all the best with your studies and your future writing.

*Andy Gillett, Angela Hammond and Mary Martala*

# FEEDBACK ON ACTIVITIES

## Chapter 1 UNDERSTANDING THE TASK

### Activity 1.1 Your subjects of study

Was it easy to decide which main area your subject falls into? If you look through the Intute website (http://www.intute.ac.uk) you will find the listings, along with a lot of useful material for each subject.

### Activity 1.2 Understanding learning outcomes

Learning outcomes are linked to the levels of learning in Bloom's Taxonomy. If you do not understand the learning outcomes for your particular modules, make sure you ask one of your lecturers for an explanation.

### Activity 1.3 Understanding the assessment criteria

Do you understand all the criteria? What do you need to do to make sure you get a good mark for this assignment?

## Chapter 2 OVERCOMING THE BLANK PAGE

### Activity 2.1 Understanding the title (1)

(a) Key words in the title: English language test, your teaching context, use theories, evaluate test.

(b) Possible questions:
- What is the teaching context I am familiar with?
- Which test should I use, e.g. progress, placement?
- Which test theories should I consider?
- Is this a good test for my context or not? Why/why not?

(c) Relevant ideas to include in the answer (ticked):
- ☑ language learning theories
- ☑ a description of your chosen teaching context
- ☑ test design theories
- ☑ an outline of different test design methods
- ☑ a description of the test
- ☑ a list of the different teaching contexts
- ☑ a copy of the test

## Feedback on activities

☐ a review of existing English language tests

☐ an answer key for the test

☑ a decision on the usefulness of this test in your teaching context

### Activity 2.2 Understanding the title (2)

(a) Key words in the title: resource utilisation, financial resources, business strategies, create value, illustrate with cases.

(b) Turning the key points into questions.
- What does 'resource utilisation' mean?
- What strategies are available to companies?
- How can financial resources be used to create more value for a company?
- What examples of cases are there?
- Does resource utilisation work? If yes, how? If not, why not?

(c) Relevant ideas to include in the answer (ticked):

☑ an explanation of the term 'resource utlilisation'

☑ an assessment of how valuable the term 'resource utlilisation' is

☑ a short description of the different kinds of resources a business can draw on

☐ details of the various ways a business can create value

☑ an outline of the financial resources available to a business

☐ an in-depth discussion of the different strategies available to a business

☑ examples of specific cases which can be used as evidence

### Activity 2.3 Understanding your own title

There is no set answer here as you are working with your own titles. Use the guidelines in the chapter to check your procedure. Working with a peer may also help you focus your points more.

## Activity 2.4 Evaluating plans

| Strengths | Weaknesses | Changes |
|---|---|---|
| Correct **key words** chosen | | |
| **Instruction verb** identified | | |
| Mainly relevant points in **introduction**. | 1 History of WWW more appropriate than of Internet.<br>2 Order of introduction.<br>3 It omits the users. | 1 Provide history of WWW.<br>2 Re-order introduction points to history, development and functions.<br>3 Include the users. |
| Relevant points in **central section**. | E-commerce and e-learning should be expanded. | 1 Better definition of communication.<br>2 How did people communicate before the WWW? |
| **Conclusion** includes personal view. | Security and accessibility should be in central section, not in conclusion. | Include security and accessibility in central section. |
| | **References** are not sufficient. | Improve references. |

## Activity 2.5 Improving the plan

This would depend on which points you wanted to concentrate on as well as the required length of the essay, but when writing a plan you should ensure that your introduction provides background information on the subject, that only relevant information is included in the essay overall and that the main points raised are treated equally. You should always read other sources to help you substantiate your ideas and you should not add new ideas in the conclusion. Look at the third column above for further additions.

## Activity 2.6 Experimenting with blank pages

There is no set answer here. The purpose of this activity is for you to try out some of the techniques offered in the chapter on how to overcome the blank page and identify those you can work with.

## Activity 2.7 Evaluating techniques

There is no set answer here. The purpose of this activity is for you to try out the techniques offered in the chapter and identify those you can work with.

## Chapter 3 PLANNING YOUR WORK

### Activity 3.1 Understanding the assignment brief

If you find that some information is missing or is not clear enough, make sure you ask someone: either your lecturer or someone else on your course. Thinking about what you already know about the subject of the assignment will help you decide how much time you need to spend preparing for it, so it is a useful tool to help you plan.

### Activity 3.2 Practicalities

It is important to know the practical details to avoid losing marks on, for example, going over word length, handing work in late or emailing work rather than handing in a printed copy.

### Activity 3.3 Understanding the assessment criteria

The assessment criteria should explain how many marks the different parts of the assignment carry and give an idea of the standard expected for each grade or level. Make sure you are completely clear about each criterion.

### Activity 3.4 Checklist

There may be other things you want to include in this checklist, in which case you could draw up your own. If you have marked the 'Perhaps' column for anything, you need to decide whether that should be 'Yes' or 'No' before you really get down to work.

### Activity 3.5 Needs analysis

You may not find that there is a very big difference between what you already know about the subject of your assignment and what you do not know (and therefore need to find out). The extent of the gap will affect the amount of time you give to this stage of preparation.

### Activity 3.6 Prioritising your work

This activity suggests you put your work in order of the deadlines for each assignment. You could however put them in order of difficulty as that will also affect the amount of time you spend on each one.

### Activity 3.7 Planning your week

Although you should try to block out more than one hour at a time – the example shows two-hour slots – try to think of how you could use a single hour at a time for perhaps sorting through your notes or reading an article that you have decided is useful. Adapt the example for hourly or 90 minute slots if that is what suits you.

### Activity 3.8 **Planning the tasks**

The level of detail you include in each of the main headings is your decision, but the more you add the clearer you should be about how much time the assignment is likely to take. Try to build in contingency and allow a bit of extra time for the various tasks.

## Chapter 4 CARRYING OUT THE RESEARCH

### Activity 4.1 **Sources you have used before**

There is no right or wrong answer for this activity. While each type of source (traditional and electronic) has its own value there will be times when one is more suited to a particular kind of assignment. The activity is designed to make you reflect upon the way you have used sources in the past so that you make sure you use a full range of them.

### Activity 4.2 **Investigating your subject gateway**

- **Pinakes**. Notice how this subject gateway provides links to a variety of subjects including the four Intute subject divisions.
- **Intute**. Did you notice which of the four areas provided resources in each of these two main genres of academic writing? The results are of course linked to the requirements of different disciplines.

### Activity 4.3 **Deciding the type of sources**

Examples of sources you could use are:

- the organisation's website
- company report(s)
- government legislation
- journals and newspapers
- a book on how to write a case study.

### Activity 4.4 **Deciding the topic key words**

Examine the influence of sporting personalities on public attitudes towards overall fitness.

| | |
|---|---|
| Examine | ☐ |
| Influence | ☐ |
| Sporting personalities | ☑ |
| Public attitudes | ☑ |
| Overall | ☐ |
| Fitness | ☑ |

## Feedback on activities

When you are deciding on key words you need to look for major ideas or concepts to search on. In this example key concepts are 'sporting personalities', 'public attitudes' and 'fitness'. 'Influence' and 'overall' are not ideas in themselves, they are linked to the judgement you have to make in the assignment. 'Examine' is of course an instruction word.

So your search for information will be based on these key words:

Examine the influence of **sporting personalities** on **public attitudes** towards overall **fitness.**

## Activity 4.5 Identifying extracts from a text

| Abstract | No, not in a book |
| --- | --- |
| Acknowledgments | No |
| Appendix | No |
| Author | Eddie McLaney and Peter Atrill |
| Blurb | Yes |
| Date of publication | 2008 |
| Details about author | Yes, freelance academic and author with good experience |
| Edition | 4th – successful book |
| Foreword | No |
| Glossary | No |
| Index | Yes |
| ISBN | 978–0–273–71136–0 |
| List of contents | Yes |
| List of references | Not on extract |
| Place of publication | Harlow, Essex, UK |
| Preface | No |
| Publisher | Pearson |
| Reviewers' comments | No |
| Subtitle | An introduction |
| Title | Accounting |

## Activity 4.6 Looking at your own material

This depends on whether you look at a textbook or a journal.

290

## Activity 4.7 Using the index

- Accounting scandals – just one page near the beginning, probably just a quick reference.
- Auditors – several pages, definition on page 678 (in bold type).
- Balance sheets – many pages, treated very fully, definition on page 678 (in bold type).
- Classification of assets – two or three pages, probably useful.
- E. I. Altman – mentioned on page 263, probably a reference.

# Chapter 5 READING AND NOTE-TAKING

## Activities 5.1 and 5.2 What do you read? and How do you read?

You probably read newspapers every day. You might read a magazine once a week etc. You might read menus occasionally.

| What do I read? | How often do I read it? | What is my purpose in reading the text? | In what way do I read the text? |
|---|---|---|---|
| Newspapers | Every day | To find out what is happening in the world; to get sports results; to see what's on TV. | Scan through the paper, find something interesting, read carefully. |
| Textbooks | Every day | For assignments, to get knowledge. | Read carefully, try to remember. |
| Magazines | Once a week | For enjoyment, to get information. | Scan through to find something interesting, read carefully, miss out boring bits. |
| Menus | Lunchtime | To find out what there is to eat, find prices. | Quickly to see what there is. |
| Recipes | Evening | To find out how to cook something. | Carefully – you don't want to get it wrong. |
| Novels | Weekends | For pleasure. | Read slowly, miss out the boring bits. Start at the beginning. |
| Emails | Every day | To keep in touch. | Skim through quickly to get main information. |
| Text messages | Most of the time | To keep in touch. | Skim through quickly to get main information. |

## Activity 5.3 Understanding titles

It depends on what questions you have asked. You will usually be able to find the answers and by doing so you will have a rough idea of what the text is about.

## Activity 5.4 Using titles

Probably these would be the best.

> Brassington, F. and Pettitt, S. (2006) *Principles of Marketing* (4th edn). Harlow: Pearson Education.

> Kotler, P., Armstrong, G., Wong, V. and Saunders, J. (2008) *Principles of Marketing* (5th edn). Harlow: Pearson Education.

If you are a law student, you might check:

> Keenan, D. and Riches, S. (2007) *Business Law* (8th edn). Harlow: Pearson Education.

It is possible that you might be interested in the psychological aspects of marketing:

> Martin, G. N., Carlson, N. R. and Buskist, W. (2007) *Psychology* (3rd edn). Harlow: Pearson Education.

## Activity 5.5 Making use of text structure

1 Solicitors usually need a degree in any subject to start.
2 They also need to continue their education throughout their careers.

## Activity 5.6 Scanning a text

1 What kinds of businesses are there?
   - sole proprietorship
   - partnership
   - limited company.

2 Can you find a definition for each of these?
   - Sole proprietorship is where an individual is the sole owner of a business.
   - A partnership exists where at least two individuals carry on a business together with the intention of making a profit.
   - Limited companies can range in size from quite small to very large; unlimited number of owners; liability of owners is limited.

3 What kind of businesses are the following?
   - electrical repair shops – probably sole proprietorship
   - solicitors – probably partners
   - easyJet – limited company.

## Activity 5.7 Skimming a text (1)

The following text is constructed from the first sentences of the longer text. It gives a good general summary of the text and could well be enough.

Financial ratios provide a quick and relatively simple means of assessing the financial health of a business or of different businesses. Ratios can be very helpful when comparing the

financial health of different businesses. By calculating a small number of ratios it is often possible to build up a good picture of the position and performance of a business. Ratios help to
highlight the financial strengths and weaknesses of a business, but they cannot, by themselves, explain why those strengths or weaknesses exist or why certain changes have
occurred. Ratios can be expressed in various forms, for example as a percentage or as a proportion. There is no generally accepted list of ratios that can be applied to the financial
statements, nor is there a standard method of calculating many ratios.

## Activity 5.8 Skimming a text (2)

It depends on what you have asked. You will usually be able to find the answers and
by doing so you will have a rough idea of what the text is about.

## Activity 5.9 Skimming a text (3)

Here are the first and last paragraphs in the following text. It gives you a good idea
of what a Queen's Counsel is.

**Queen's Counsel**
After ten years in practice, a barrister may apply to become a Queen's Counsel, or QC (sometimes called a silk, as they wear gowns made of silk). This usually means they will be offered
higher-paid cases, and need do less preliminary paperwork. The average annual earnings of a
QC are £270,000, with a small group earning over £1 million a year. Not all barristers attempt
or manage to become QCs — those that do not are called juniors, even up to retirement age.
Juniors may assist QCs in big cases, as well as working alone. Since 1995, solicitors can also
be appointed as QCs, but there are currently only eight QCs who come from the solicitor profession.

The Government's current view is that the badge of QC is a well-recognised and respected
'kitemark' of quality both at home and abroad. The existence of QCs helps enhance London's
status as the centre of international litigation and arbitration.

## Activity 5.10 Skimming a text (4)

The headings in the text give you a good idea about the meaning of the text.

**When can custom be a source of law?**
To be regarded as conferring legally enforceable rights, a custom must fulfil several
criteria:

- time immemorial
- reasonableness
- certainty and clarity
- locality
- continuity
- exercised as of right
- consistency
- obligatory
- conformity with statute.

The correct answers are (b) consistent and clear, and (d) reasonable.

## Activity 5.11 Taking notes

These are notes in list format. You may feel that another format suits the text better.

NOTES

Traditionally – lawyers – white middle-class, male – seen as unapproachable for many people

Recently – wider range of people

Women ↗ since 1950s; now 41% solicitors ♀
      Still probs with pay, promotion, working conds
            ♂ £ < ♀
            Only 23% ♂ partners; 50% ♀
            2003 – 9 ♂ made QC; 112 ♀
      Law career ≠ motherhood

Ethnicity – No. from ethnic minority grps ↗ – 4% 1995; 2003 8%
      Racism in bar oral exams
      but 23% partners; 39% white

Class – biggest obstacle – only 20% ← working class
      33% ← private schools
      £ prob. for poorer students – part-time study possibility

Disability – significant barriers to entry
      Old court buildings ≠ disabled access – steps being taken

## Chapter 6 FEATURES OF ACADEMIC WRITING

### Activity 6.1 Identifying formality

**(a)** 1 = academic essay; 2 = text message (I have a question for you. Who ate my pizza? See you later. Love); 3 = spoken argument.

**(b)** Excerpt 1 uses formal vocabulary and the passive, and is written in cautious and objective language with references. Excerpt 2 uses texting language. Excerpt 3 uses subjective, emotive language with rhetorical questions and contracted forms (e.g. don't).

## Activity 6.2 Identifying formal and informal features

1

|  | Excerpt 1 is a formal text | Excerpts 2 and 3 are informal texts |
|---|---|---|
| **Formal vocabulary** | assessor, described, posing, positioning, exercising, stimulating, assessed, oblige, consider, perspectives, deem, acceptable, achieve | **Excerpt 3**, proposal, issue |
| **Cautious language** | may, often | **Excerpt 3** clearly, would |
| **Objective language** | Author does not use 'I think or I believe'. Whole extract is objective | |
| **Subjective language** | | **Excerpt 3** I don't think; I believe |
| **Emotive language** | | **Excerpt 3** at all, ludicrous, better off |
| **Use of questions** | | **Excerpt 2** Who 8 my pizza? **Excerpt 3** How could anyone imagine . . .? |
| **Passive voice** | described by Ivanic; will be assessed | |
| **Contracted forms** | | **Excerpt 3** don't |
| **References** | Ivanic and Simpson (1992: 146) | |

2  See answers to Activity 6.1b.

**NB**. *Answers to Activities 6.3 to 6.9 are suggestions only. Other alternatives are also possible.*

## Activity 6.3 From informal to formal

1 indicates  2 discovered  3 unacceptable  4 many  5 causes
6 attempted  7 donated  8 such as  9 needs to  10 sufficient.

## Activity 6.4 Finding synonyms

1 consider  2 performed  3 deteriorated  4 discover  5 investigated
6 increasing  7 continuing/persisting  8 divided  9 survive  10 attended.

## Activity 6.5 Writing passive sentences

(a) Prices are stable and have been maintained in this way over generations.
(b) Tropical forests are defined here as 'evergreen or partly evergreen forests'.
(c) The discussion will be confined to general principles of treatment.
(d) Many genes were transcribed and many proteins synthesised.
(e) These findings were replicated.

## Activity 6.6 Constructing passive sentences

All of the following are possible.

1 This surgeon is considered to be a brilliant practitioner.
   It is considered that this surgeon is a brilliant practitioner.
2 The drug is claimed to have produced no undesirable side effects.
   It is claimed that the drug produced no undesirable side effects.
3 Only a small fraction of the nitrous oxide emitted to the atmosphere each year is
   thought to come from fossil fuel use, primarily coal.
   It is thought that only a small fraction of the nitrous oxide emitted to the atmosphere each year comes from fossil fuel use, primarily coal.
4 The only problem with daytime sleep is believed to be that it is too short.
   It is believed that the only problem with daytime sleep is that it is too short.
5 Although the patient is expected to pay for his treatment, he will be reimbursed
   via the state medical insurance scheme.
   It is expected that although the patient will have to pay for his treatment, he will
   be reimbursed via the state medical insurance scheme.

## Activity 6.7 Subjective language

Everybody, everyone, our (×3), we (×3), as far as I am concerned, I believe, their, I
also think.

## Activity 6.8 Objective style

Here is a suggested answer:

The threat of global warming to the earth has generally been established. Gases constantly
pollute the atmosphere and waste which could be recycled is put into landfill. There seem to
be two main ways in which people can help combat this pollution. Firstly, by increasing the use
of public transport and reducing the number of private cars on the roads. Secondly, by recy-
cling more plastic and glass bottles. Equally, left-over food could be composted rather than
thrown away.

## Activity 6.9 Substituting questions

1 The jury has symbolic importance. As jury trial represents judgement by one's
   peers, the jury is seen as a major control over abuse of state power.
2 Suctioning is associated with several complications. Several techniques can be
   used to minimise or decrease these complications. These include hyperinflation
   and hyperoxygenation.

3 The overall variation of the impedance can be shown as follows: for frequency $f_1$, the inductive reactance AB and the capacitive reactance AC are equal in magnitude so that the resultant reactance is zero. Consequently, the impedance is then only the resistance AD of the circuit.
4 The main objective of a business is financial. A business is normally set up with a view to increasing the wealth of its owners.

## Activity 6.10 Identifying features of critical writing

The answers for this activity are provided in the text as a learning tool (see p. 98).

## Activity 6.11 Ensuring you write critically

Use the checklist provided to guide you when writing critically.

## Activity 6.12 Dividing a text into paragraphs

The first paragraph clearly begins with the topic sentence 'Respiration is the act of breathing' and ends with 'the cells of the body tissues'. This paragraph explains the meaning of respiration by describing the gases and organs used in external and internal respiration.

Paragraph 2 now adds to the respiration theme by talking about inhalation, exhalation and ventilation. It begins with 'Inhalation or inspiration . . .' and ends with ' . . . out of the lungs'.

The final idea introduced in paragraph 3 is costal and diaphragmatic breathing. The paragraph begins with 'There are basically . . .' and continues to the end of the passage.

Clearly all three paragraphs relate to breathing. Each paragraph, however, develops a particular aspect associated with breathing. Breaking down these ideas into paragraphs rather than writing them all in one paragraph helps the reader follow the organisation of the text and, as a result, understand the text much more easily.

## Activity 6.13 Evaluating supporting sentences

The paragraph develops the topic sentence by explaining that the consequence of eating fast food is a tendency to become addicted to it. What makes this consequence alarming is also explained: the addictive nature of the sugars and fats in fast food affect the brain in a similar way to drugs. The two questions asked of the topic sentence are therefore answered by the subsequent supporting sentences.

## Activity 6.14 Identifying suitable topic sentences

1 The correct answer is (b). Sentence (a) is too general and (c) is too detailed.
2 The correct answer is (a). Sentence (b) is too general and (c) raises too many points.
3 The correct answer is (b). Sentence (a) is too general and (c) has already started to develop the point.

## Activity 6.15 Matching topic sentences to supporting sentences

Answers: 1 (c), 2 (e), 3 (f), 4 (a), 5 (d). Topic sentence (b) was not required.

## Activity 6.16 Writing topic sentences

Suggested answers:
1  People vary in their attitudes towards the natural world.
2  Media planners consider many factors when making their media choices.
3  Social interactions are different for different people.

## Activity 6.17 Developing supporting sentences

(a)  Partial dictation may be considered as an alternative. *What is partial dictation? Why can it be an alternative?*
(b)  Plug gauges are one of the most common types of fixed gauges. *What are plug gauges? How are they used?*
(c)  The intensity of the north–south exchange is shown in many, often unexpected, ways. *What is the north–south exchange? Why is it intense? In what ways is it shown to be intense? Why are these ways often unexpected?*

## Activity 6.18 Writing supporting sentences

There are no correct answers for this activity provided the supporting sentences are relevant to the questions.

## Activity 6.19 Writing concluding sentences

These will depend on your topic and supporting sentences. Make sure your concluding sentence is not a repeat of the topic sentence but includes a summary of your paragraph. The following are suggested answers based on our answers to Activity 6.16.

1  Clearly, people's attitudes to nature vary.
2  If these factors are not considered, the planners' choices will not be well informed.
3  Hereditary differences thus cause differences in social interaction.

## Activity 6.20 Identifying signalling expressions

The numbers in brackets indicate the line number in which the expressions occur.

Indeed (2), This process (5), as a result (5), as (7), Prior to this (8), with the idea (10), However (11), although (11), because of (12), These ideas (13), therefore (13).

## Activity 6.21 Using suitable signalling expressions

The inappropriate words have been crossed out and suitable replacements are shown in bold.

Research (Slotte & Lonka 1999) on student note-taking methods ~~usually~~ suggests that there are specific ways of reading a textbook which can maximize learning. ~~As a matter of fact,~~ half of the research sample were asked to review their notes during note-taking; the other half were not given any explicit instructions. ~~Besides,~~ analysis of the quality and quantity of notes ~~similarly~~ **then** indicated that reviewing notes during essay writing was associated with good performance on questions that required comprehension of the text and deep, ~~and what is more,~~ detailed knowledge. ~~Moreover,~~ **However**, reviewing these notes did not ~~naturally~~ help with drawing original conclusions about the text. ~~In comparison~~ **Importantly**, it was noted that students summarising the text in their own words, ~~apart from this,~~ with their own subheadings and structure, performed better than those students who took verbatim notes or, ~~in short,~~ took notes in the exact order in which the material appeared in the text. ~~Actually,~~ this finding suggests that deeper understanding (and better performance) comes from having read and understood material in a text and ~~finally~~ expressing it in your own words.

### Activity 6.22 Evaluating the importance of links between paragraphs

Extract 2 leads the reader from paragraph to paragraph. Linking phrases such as 'a greater advantage' signal to the reader that a further positive point will be explored. This way, the reader does not have to rely solely on the information in the paragraph in order to deduce whether the point is a positive or negative one. The easier a text is to follow, the more likely it is to be marked higher.

### Activity 6.23 Identifying links

There are many advantages

A greater advantage . . . is . . .

The efforts . . . cannot be overemphasised.

Having considered the advantages . . . setbacks will be discussed.

A further drawback is . . .

The final disadvantage worth considering is . . .

### Activity 6.24 Adding links between paragraphs

**Another common use of STs** is to help pupils . . .

**Finally**, STs may also be members of staff . . .

### Activity 6.25 Checking for paragraph links in your own work

Use the questions in this activity to guide you when checking your paragraph links.

## Chapter 7 WRITING DESCRIPTIVELY

### Activity 7.1 Writing definitions

Here are suggested definitions of the following terms

## Feedback on activities

**Accrued expense:**
An accrued expense is an expense that is outstanding at the end of an accounting period.

**Brand:**
A brand is a name, term, sign, symbol or design, or a combination of these that identifies the goods or services of one seller or group of sellers and differentiates them from those of competitors.

**Contingency fee:**
A contingency fee is a fee payable to a lawyer in the event of him/her winning the case.

**Fixed cost:**
A fixed cost is a cost that stays the same when changes occur to the volume of activity.

**Renewable energy:**
The term renewable energy describes the energy flows that occur naturally in the environment, such as solar radiation, the wind, the tides and the waves.

**Retailer:**
A retailer is a business whose sales come primarily from retailing.

**Small claims track:**
This is a procedure used by the county courts to deal with claims under £5,000.

(Definitions based on Hughes, 2008; Elliott and Quinn, 2008; McLaney and Atrill, 2008; Kotler *et al.*, 2008)

## Activity 7.2 Adding descriptive detail

Below is the original text. You will have written something very different but it may be useful to compare what information has been included.

Banding is the placing of pupils within a class into ability groupings. It is common in primary schools and is also used in secondary schools, where it describes a slightly different teaching arrangement – a large year group is sometimes divided into two or more groupings. Pupils can be of equal ability or differentiated on criteria similar to streaming.

(Davies, 2006: 12)

## Activity 7.3 Writing descriptions

You will have written something very different but it may be useful to compare your text with the one given below. Notice how the description starts with a general sentence, pointing out the main parts. It then describes each of the parts in more detail.

Each tooth has three parts: the crown, the root and the pulp cavity [see Figure 7.1]. The crown is the exposed part of the tooth, which is outside the gum. It is covered with a hard substance called enamel. The ivory-coloured internal part of the crown below the enamel is the dentin. The root of a tooth is embedded in the jaw and covered by a bony tissue called cementum. The pulp cavity in the centre of the tooth contains the blood vessels and nerves.

(Kozier *et al.*, 2008: 276)

## Activity 7.4 Describing how something works

It is unlikely that you will have written anything like the example shown below. We do hope, though, that in a similar way you have attempted to describe the physical structure of the wind turbine and said something about how it works.

Most modern wind turbines are now broadly similar: the three-bladed, horizontal-axis upwind design championed by Danish turbine manufacturers. Horizontal-axis wind turbines (HAWT) have the main rotor shaft and electrical generator at the top of a tower housed in the nacelle.

Since a tower produces turbulence, the turbine is usually pointed upwind of the tower. Small turbines are pointed into the wind by a simple wind vane, whereas large turbines generally use a wind sensor coupled with a computer-controlled servomotor to face into the wind, so that the blades can collect the maximum amount of energy. The rotor blades, generally made from glass-reinforced polyester (GRP) or laminated wood, drive a generator through a speed-increasing gearbox, converting the slow rotation of the blades into the high rotational speed more suited to electricity generation. Most machines use induction generators which generate electricity at a relatively low voltage (typically 690 V) and high current which is then delivered to the local distribution network via a step-up transformer.     (Hughes, 2008: 812)

## Activity 7.5 Describing processes

Make sure you have described the sequence in the present tense and that your sequence is clear.

### Cleaning

The following steps are usually followed when cleaning an object in a hospital.

First the article is rinsed with cold water to remove organic material. Hot water is not used as it coagulates the protein of organic material and tends to make it adhere. Next, the article is washed in hot water and soap. Soap is used as the emulsifying action of soap reduces surface tension and facilitates the removal of substances. Washing dislodges the emulsified substances. A stiff-bristled brush is used to clean the equipment with grooves and corners. After that the article is rinsed well with hot water. The article is then considered to be clean. Finally the brush and sink are cleaned with disinfectant.     (Kozier *et al.*, 2008: 214)

## Activity 7.6 Describing an operation

Although you are unlikely to have written exactly the same as what is presented below, comparing your texts may be useful.

The braking system of a car is a good example of how a hydraulic system works. When the brake pedal is pressed a piston operates which forces brake fluid out of the master cylinder and along four narrow pipes to the slave cylinders attached to the brake drums or discs so that the same pressure is applied to the brakes in each wheel. This brings the car to a smooth halt. Provided the system is kept filled with brake fluid, hydraulic brakes work instantly because liquids cannot be compressed to any great extent.

If air leaks into the system, the brakes become much less efficient. This is because, unlike liquids, gases are compressible and some of the movement of the brake pedal is taken up in squeezing the air bubble.

(*The Penguin Book of the Physical World* (1976) London: Penguin p. 52)

## Activity 7.7 Describing changes 1

Although you will not have written exactly the same as in the example below, make sure you have included an explicit reference to the figure, described some of the changes shown in the graph and made some comment.

Figure 7.5 shows the changes in the rate of inflation between May 1999 and May 2001. In May 1999, inflation stood at 10%. After a slight drop to 8% in August and September of that year, it rose steadily over the next 7 months to reach a peak of 30% in May 2000. There was then a slight drop to 28% in June and July before inflation increased again to return to the peak of 30% in August. There was then a slight fluctuation over the next 5 months before it started to improve and fall steadily to reach a low point of 17% in January 2001. Inflation then started to rise again and predictions for the future suggest that it will continue to do so in the immediate future. If it does continue to increase, the government will need to bring in economic measures to control it.

## Activity 7.8 Identifying classification

The classification is based on sea level, whether or not it is under water.

## Activity 7.9 Describing changes 2

For example

Legal changes can be divided into two broad categories according to their causes. The first type of legal change is caused by the law responding to changes taking place in society. Political, social and economic changes, technological advancements and changing moral beliefs all lead eventually to changes in the law. Indeed, the law must be responsive to new circumstances and attitudes if it is to enjoy continued respect. The second type of legal change arises from the need to keep the law in good working order. Like any piece of sophisticated machinery, the law machine must be kept in a neat and tidy condition, maintained on a regular basis, with essential repairs undertaken when necessary.

(Keenan and Riches, 2007: 13)

## Activity 7.10 Distinguishing between instructions and descriptions

Make sure you have reported in the past tense and that your sequence is clear.

### Cleaning

The following steps were followed when cleaning an object in a hospital.

First the article was rinsed with cold water to remove organic material. Hot water was not used as it coagulates the protein of organic material and tends to make it adhere. Next, the article was washed in hot water and soap. Soap was used as the emulsifying action of soap reduces surface tension and facilitates the removal of substances. Washing dislodges the emulsified substances. A stiff-bristled brush was used to clean the equipment with grooves and corners. After that the article was rinsed well with hot water. The article was then considered to be clean. Finally the brush and sink were cleaned with disinfectant.   (Kozier *et al.*, 2008: 214)

## Activity 7.11 Reporting an experiment

Have you written something similar? Make sure you have used the past tense, the passive and have referred to the time sequence when necessary.

Two thin flexible steel rods were taken.

### Experiment 1

First one of the rods was bent in order to feel how how tough and springy it was. Then the rod was held in a Bunsen burner flame and heated until it was bright red. It was then dipped very quickly into cold water. Finally the rod was bent as before and the results were recorded. It was found that the rod had become brittle and broke easily.

### Experiment 2

The second rod was taken and heated in the Bunsen burner flame until it was red hot. The rod was then kept in the heat for about fifteen seconds after it had turned red. Next it was removed from the heat very slowly and allowed to cool gradually. Finally the rod was bent as before and the results were recorded. It was found that the rod was relatively easy to bend without breaking.

# Chapter 8 WRITING CRITICALLY

## Activity 8.1 Identifying explanations

Situation: traffic accidents occur mainly between four and six o'clock in the morning.
Reason: sleepiness and fatigue of drivers.

## Activity 8.2 Writing explanations

Here is an example:

Of the main dune types identified in Figure 12.11, star dunes usually attain the greatest size. This is because they develop in the depositional centres of sand seas, where net sediment accumulation and sand-transporting wind directional variability is greatest.

(Holden, 2008: 458)

## Activity 8.3 Explaining why

### Why do new products fail?

There are several reasons why so many new products fail. One reason is that, although an idea may be good, the company may overestimate market size. There just was not the demand for the product. For example electronic books (e-books) promised to deliver vast amounts of reading materials in a single lightweight package so that travellers would not have to haul large paperbacks around on vacations and business trips. Like many publishers, Random House UK made a foray into e-books at the turn of the decade. However, the product did not catch on. According to the company's interactive director, 'It was not for lack of thought or interest – it is just because the consumer market did not happen.'

Another reason is that the actual product may be poorly designed. There may be techno-logical drawbacks. In the case of e-books, readers tend to read fiction in particular ways – curled up on a couch or sitting on a bus or train. E-books need a digital display, but readers rarely want to sit in front of a PC of carry a cumbersome laptop.

It may also be a 'me too' product which is no better than products that are already estab-lished in the marketplace. Or it might be incorrectly positioned in the market, launched at the wrong time, overpriced or advertised and promoted badly. A high-level executive might push a favourite idea despite poor marketing research findings. Sometimes the costs of product development are higher than expected and sometimes competitors fight back harder than anticipated.

(Kotler *et al.*, 2008: 552–3)

## Activity 8.4 Identifying arguments

The claim being made is that there is a connection between intelligence and nutri-tion.

## Activity 8.5 Identifying degrees of caution

Pupils are normally keen to see how teachers perform and will want to settle so that they can weigh them up. (Davies, 2006: 130)

The elderly may also have difficulty in comprehending and initiating grammatically complex sentences (Kemper, 1992). (Martin *et al.*, 2007: 491)

Oceans are very important in controlling the climate of the Earth. (Holden, 2008: 59)

The main practical difference between these is that a public company can offer its shares for sale to the general public, but a private company is restricted from doing so. (McLaney and Atrill, 2008: 119)

## Activity 8.6 Writing cautiously

The missing words are: vastly; particularly; perhaps; primarily.

## Activity 8.7 Identifying points of view

There has been much discussion over recent years as to whether the professions will eventually fuse. (Elliott and Quinn, 2008: 185)

Others have suggested that common law barristers have a better chance of surviving competition from solicitors. They cater for the needs of ordinary high street solicitors, who generally have a wide-ranging practice, and spend much of their time seeing clients and gathering case information. (Elliott and Quinn, 2008: 185)

Alternatively, it has been suggested that the Bar might survive, but in a much reduced form, and there is much debate about which areas would suffer most. (Elliott and Quinn, 2008: 185)

Some studies, however, have shown that it is not necessarily distraction that is responsible for reducing pain but rather the emotional quality of the distractor. Positive stimuli, such as humour and laughter, are known to reduce pain perception (Cogan *et al.*, 1987; Rotton and Shats, 1996) but increasing the attention required to complete cognitive tasks (distraction without emotion) does not (McCaul and Malott, 1984). (Martin *et al.*, 2007: 376)

## Activity 8.8 Identifying evaluative phrases

Mental health problems are intensely personal experiences for both the person who is directly affected, but also for those close to them. However, the causes of mental health difficulties are not just personal but also social and political, or as is sometimes said, 'psycho-social'. (Wilson *et al.*, 2008: 566)

The main disadvantages of these early classifications is that the emphasis on geological inheritance and sea-level history leaves only limited concern for the hydrodynamic processes. The morphology of depositional coastal environments (those consisting of mud, sand and gravel, rather than eroding rocky shores) responds to the relative dominance of river, wave and tidal factors (Boyd *et al.*, 1992). (Holden, 2008: 480)

## Activity 8.9 Identifying advantages and disadvantages

*Advantages*:
- The environmental impact is low.
- There is little visual impact.

- The impact on coastlines is minimal.
- Chemical pollution is also minimal.
- Wave energy devices present no problems for marine life.
- Economies can be achieved by installing them in groups.
- Installation, maintenance and operating costs are then spread over a much larger total generating capacity.

*Disadvantages*:
- Wave energy may present some hazard to shipping.
- Peak power is generally only available far from land.
- Near the shore waves lose energy due to friction between the water and the seabed.
- The typical wave frequency is difficult to couple to a generator frequency of 50 or 60 Hz.
- The capital costs are high.                                   **(Hughes 2008: 818)**

## Activity 8.10 Describing disadvantages

Some disadvantages exist. Visual impact is a matter of much debate. It is determined by the size, the colour, the blade design and the number of wind turbines in a wind farm. In particular, it is very dependent on the particular landscape in which the wind farm is placed. It can also be exacerbated by the need for long distribution and transmission lines required to bring the wind generation capacity from remote locations to consumers.

Acoustic disturbance is a possible problem, though modern designs are quieter and, in fact, noise levels are considerably lower than those produced by cars. One of the difficulties is that wind turbines are often sited in remote locations which would normally be very quiet. Other considerations might concern site clearing, the need for access and the possible impact on birds and wildlife in sensitive habitats.                **(Hughes, 2008: 814)**

## Activity 8.11 Writing about advantages and disadvantages

This is the original source document for you to compare with your text.

### The franchisor's perspective

*Benefits*
Both small and large companies can expand through franchising. The two main benefits are financial and managerial. From a financial point of view, rapid growth in market coverage and penetration can be achieved using the resources provided by the franchisees. To open a new directly owned outlet would involve an investment both in capital assets (shop fittings, equipment, property, etc.) and in working capital for stock and other operating costs. There would also be the risk of failing to achieve sales targets and financial projections. Many of these risks are effectively borne and financed by the franchisees through their start-up capital investment, licence fees and any other royalty payments.

The franchisee also represents a committed management resource. The franchisee becomes the legal owner of the business and will therefore suffer from failure or benefit from success. By applying entrepreneurial skills within the framework of the franchise agreement, the franchisee will have to manage the local operation, promote sales and control resources. It would be very hard for the franchisor to motivate salaried staff to make the same effort, because they would not be running the same personal risks as a franchisee (Barrow, 2001).

There are other benefits from franchising. Of particular importance is the ability to develop economies of scale in purchasing, marketing and corporate image and branding without having a large organisation. Indeed, a small enterprise seeking to expand quickly can gain these benefits on the basis of the franchisees' capital. The important benefit of a business format franchise system, however, is that it can divorce service design and planning from

## Feedback on activities

service delivery and operations. The skill for a successful franchisor might therefore lie in opportunity assessment, system design and franchisee recruitment rather than in the technical area of production.

*Disadvantages*

There are, nevertheless, also problems associated with franchising a business. Some of them relate to handling difficult, ineffective or remote franchisees, especially as they become highly experienced in trading in the system area. This could lead to some questioning of the franchise relationship, if poor or ineffective support is being provided by the franchisor (Pettitt, 1988). Furthermore, if the franchisor is felt to be abusing its power, franchisees might start to group together to negotiate on more equal terms with the franchisor. Reputable and better-established franchisors often welcome the formation of formal franchisee groups, as a means of generating feedback and working together to develop a more effective franchise system.

**(Brassington and Pettitt, 2006: 1086–7)**

## Activity 8.12 Comparing

In the late 1980s and early 1990s, a series of studies reported significant differences in non-verbal IQ between schoolchildren who received vitamin and mineral supplements (VMS) and those who received a placebo (Benton, 1992; Haller, 1995; Eysenck and Schoenthaler, 1997). Those who received the supplements scored significantly better.    **(Martin *et al.*, 2007: 486)**

## Activity 8.13 Contrasting

There is a wealth of research to demonstrate that disabled children are more vulnerable to abuse and neglect than their non-disabled peers (Kelly, 1992; Miller, 2003). In addition to this, research also demonstrates that disabled children are not protected from harm to the same extent as their non-disabled peers (Edwards and Richardson, 2003; Marchant and Page, 2003; Cooke, 2000).    **(Wilson *et al.*, 2008: 566)**

## Activity 8.14 Discussing differences

Some examples are:

■ With respect to attainment at GCSE, children from the higher professional socio-economic class obtain higher qualifications than children from other classes.

■ Overall, students from professional classes obtain more GCSE passes than children from non-professional backgrounds.

■ Very few children from the higher classes obtain no GCSEs.

## Activity 8.15 Identifying evidence

1 The surface of the ocean gains heat by radiation from the Sun, particularly in lower latitudes, and by conduction and convection from warm air flowing over the waves. Heat is lost by evaporation, by reradiation to space and by conduction to cold air above (Barry and Chorley, 2003).

2 More heat is gained than lost at the low latitudes.

3 More heat is lost than gained at the high latitudes.

4 Water acts as a major store of the energy of the Sun.

5 The movement of ocean currents from the low latitudes to the high latitudes is very important in transferring energy to the colder regions and thus maintaining the Earth's temperatures in the present range.

6  When ocean circulation changes occur, such as during El Nino events, then they can have a dramatic effect on the climate of the Earth.                    **Based on Holden (2008: 59)**

## Activity 8.16  Identifying examples

River maintenance is needed where human use of rivers does not allow natural fluvial processes to be fully maintained or where the channel dynamics are in conflict with human use. For example, river flow regulation by dams can cause sedimentation and siltation of gravels below tributary junctions due to the reduced frequency and magnitude of floods. This, in turn, can have adverse impacts on aquatic organisms such as salmon, which require uncovered gravels to spawn.                                                        **(Holden, 2008: 406)**

Where there is a plentiful supply of material, and the process which moves it can only move a limited amount for a short distance, the rate of transport is limited by the transporting capacity of the process, which is defined as the maximum amount of material which the process can carry (Kirkby, 1971). A transport process like this, such as rainsplash, is described as transport limited.                                                        **(Holden, 2008: 302)**

## Activity 8.17  Adding support

The marketing information system primarily serves the company's marketing and other managers. However, it may also provide information to external partners, such as suppliers, resellers or marketing services agencies. For example, Tesco gives key suppliers access to information on customer buying patterns and inventory levels, and Dell creates tailored Premium Pages for large customers, giving them access to product design, order status and product support and service information.                    **(Kotler *et al.*, 2008: 326)**

## Activity 8.18  Supporting arguments

There are many reasons why hydroelectric power should be taken seriously by governments (Hughes, 2008). Firstly it is renewable and therefore has no cost. Secondly, it produces no waste and therefore is very clean and cheap to run. Unlike the wind, for example, the water flow does not vary so the power produced is constant. Finally, hydroelectric plants last a long time and the lakes which hold the water can be used for water sports.

## Activity 8.19  Writing conclusions

Post-graduate international students at UK Institutions of Higher Education often find difficulty dealing with discussion. An attempt was made to help students with this by utilising the group discussion facility of a university Virtual Learning Environment (VLE). However, as most of the students were from East Asia, who may consider education as essentially a passive process, it was felt necessary to investigate whether they would undertake such an activity seriously and how well they would do. Our studies over the last two years clearly show that as long as the online discussion was clearly integrated into the course structure (aims, objectives and assessments), East-Asian students understand the purpose and take it seriously – like all students. The students do, though, need explicit teaching and help in using appropriate and relevant language. This is not something that is specific to our East Asian learners, but something all students need. We see here a new role for EAP.          **(Gillett and Weetman, 2006)**

# Chapter 9  PERSONAL AND REFLECTIVE WRITING

Remember there are no right or wrong answers for the activities in this chapter. Here are some suggestions for things to consider.

### Activity 9.1 Phrases to encourage reflection

You will have thought of your own phrases, but in case you cannot think of many here are some suggestions:

With hindsight . . .
My own view is that . . .
Another problem that I came across was . . .
From my perspective . . .
Now that I look back on the last year/month/week . . . .

### Activity 9.2 Questions that call for reflective writing

Although all five questions are about learning and study 1 and 2 are phrased in an impersonal way, suggesting you could write without any reference to your own situation. On the other hand, questions 3, 4 and 5 ask you to discuss learning and study as it relates to you and expect you to draw on your own experience for evidence and examples. Question 3 is about the process of learning, question 4 about learning habits and preferences and question 5 about your own abilities.

### Activity 9.3 SWOT analysis (individual)

Whatever you have put in the four boxes you have hopefully been realistic and honest with yourself. The idea behind the SWOT analysis is that over time you should work hard to convert weaknesses and threats into strengths and opportunities, as well as to maximise strengths you do have and opportunities already facing you.

### Activity 9.4 SWOT analysis (subject)

You could try doing a SWOT analysis on a subject you are having trouble with, so helping you pinpoint the difficulties and think of ways of tackling them.

### Activity 9.5 Placing your skills in a wider context

This activity asks you to think not just about your studies but beyond them to the world outside, so helps you think about your employability. It suggests you think of plans to improve any skills you feel you should work on.

### Activity 9.6 Using the learning cycle

Did you write about all four stages of the cycle? They are:

1 Describe
2 Review
3 Conclude
4 Plan.

The learning cycle relates to the expression you sometimes hear people use when they have gone through a difficult experience and say, 'I've learnt my lesson – next time I'll do things differently.'

### Activity 9.7 Three examples of a template to record your thoughts

If these do not interest you or do not seem relevant, why not draw up some of your own? Try to use the templates on a regular basis, to draw up a picture of your development over time.

## Chapter 10 WORKING WITH OTHER PEOPLE'S IDEAS AND VOICES

### Activity 10.1 Finding and correcting referencing errors

1 'School readiness is a term that refers to a child's ability to go to school ready to learn, having already gained ... skills that will prepare them for class learning beforehand' (Davies, 2006: 47).
2 'Biogeography is an important area of science and informs global environmental policy as well as local land management practice' (Hilary S.C. Thomas, 2008: 241).
3 According to McLaney and Atrill, 'the relevant/marginal cost approach deduces the minimum price for which the business can offer the product for sale' (2008: 420).
4 'In practice, airlines are major users of a relevant/marginal costing approach' (McLaney and Atrill, 2008: 420).
5 'Damage to the **amygdala**, a cluster of neurons located deep in the temporal lobe, affects emotional behaviour ...' (Martin, *et al.*, Psychology. 3$^{rd}$ ed. London: Pearson Education. 2007: 157).

### Activity 10.2 The mechanics of quoting

For example:

1 Martin, Carlson and Buskist (2007), state that 'one of the key features of the visual system is that it is organised hierarchically at the neural level' (p.197).
2 'Market leaders can expand the market by developing new users, new uses and more usage of its products' (Kotler *et al.*, 2008: 475).
3 According to Davies 'since 1999 LEAs have had specific duties to combat bullying. Schools *must* have anti-bullying policies and LEAs must ensure that their schools comply with their duties' (2006: 269).

### Activity 10.3 Summarising unfamiliar text

Read the text as many times as you wish in order to understand it. Provided you understand the text you read, you should be able to summarise the main points.

### Activity 10.4 Noticing features in summarised text

| Features you identify | Original version | Summarised version |
|---|---|---|
| Length of text | | Shorter than the original |
| Numbers | Contains five instances of numbers | Only contains one number |
| Language | | With the exception of the names of the oceans, the words have been changed from the original |
| Amount of information | | Details have been omitted |

# Feedback on activities

### Activity 10.5 Evaluating summarised text

Summary 1 is better. It is shorter than the original; the style is different to the original; the details have been removed; the main points have been summarised.

### Activity 10.6 Summarising short texts

There is no one correct version of this text. Make sure you have referenced the source, you have not copied any text, you have kept the meaning the same as the original, you have written the summary in your own style and you have shortened the text. The following is only a suggestion:

Prisoners serving short sentences benefit from a home detention curfew introduced in 1998. This allows their early release with a special licence which has curfew conditions. These include being at a specific location between 7pm and 7am for electronic monitoring. This consists of an ankle tag, which connects to a device in the phone system which in turn connects to a central computer. Any violations of curfew can thus be reported to the Prison Service. The prisoner can also be recalled if he is a danger to the public.           (Elliott and Quinn, 2008)

### Activity 10.7 Summarising longer texts

The same applies as for Activity 10.6. When summarising a longer text, you should use the same technique as for a short text. The following is only a suggestion:

Urine collects in the bladder until stretch receptors are stimulated. The receptors send signals to the second to fourth sacral vertebrae of the spinal cord which trigger the relaxation of the internal sphincter. The conscious part of the brain assesses the appropriacy of the location and either relaxes the external sphincter for urination to occur, or causes the urge to diminish until later. This voluntary control is only possible provided there has been no harm to the neural region of the cord and brain or to the motor zone of the cerebrum.           (Kozier *et al.*, 2008)

### Activity 10.8 Using your own texts

There are obviously no set answers for this activity. Its purpose is to encourage you to work with texts relevant to you. Check your work with the help of the summarising tips.

### Activity 10.9 Evaluating paraphrased text

Paraphrase 1 is the better example. The author has made a better attempt at finding synonyms, changing the structure of the sentences, retaining meaning and not copying text.

### Activity 10.10 Paraphrasing text

There is no one correct version of these texts. Make sure you have referenced the source, you have not copied any text (unless technical terms are included), you have kept the meaning and the length the same as the original and you have written the paraphrase in your own style. The following are suggestions only:

**Text 1**
One study compared results between children adopted from an at-risk background and those who had returned home or were fostered. The results of the at-risk children were worse. There

is no clear reason for this. Perhaps adoptive parents of children who are more popular are assessed more stringently. **(Martin *et al*., 2007)**

**Text 2**

Marketing communications have been greatly influenced both by segmented marketing and by the dramatic development in ICT. Mass media communications was previously the result of mass marketing. Now, a new marketing communications model is developing as a result of targeted marketing and a shifting communications setting. **(Kotler *et al*., 2008)**

## Activity 10.11 and 10.12 Using your own texts

There are no set answers for these activities. Their purpose is to encourage you to work with texts relevant to you. Check your work with the help of the summarising and synthesising tips.

## Activity 10.13 Finding and correcting errors on reference list

Thompson, G. (2001) Interaction in Academic Writing: Learning to Argue with the Reader. *Applied Linguistics,* 22, 58–78. (Thompson's initial is missing. Title of article should not be in italics. Journal name should be in italics.)

Davies, S. (2006) *The Essential Guide to Teaching.* Harlow: Pearson Education. (Capital letters needed in title. Publisher's name is missing.)

Jeffries, S. (2008) The Ice Age. *The Guardian,* 21 August, pp 4–6. (Date and month should follow newspaper's name which should be in italics.)

Brassington, F. and Pettitt, S. *Principles of Marketing.* 4th edn. Harlow: Pearson Education. (Edition should not be in brackets. Capital letter needed in title.)

Holden, J. (ed.) (2008) *Physical Geography and the Environment* 2nd edn. Harlow: Pearson Education. (Publishing place is missing. Title should be in italics.)

## Activity 10.14 Find the overall error

The references are not in alphabetical order.

## Activity 10.15 The mechanics of referencing

Davies, S. (2006) *The Essential Guide to Teaching.* Harlow: Pearson Education.

Kotler, P., Armstrong, G., Wong, V. and Saunders, J. (2008) *Principles of Marketing* 5th European Edition. Harlow: Pearson Education.

Martin, G. N., Carlson, N. R. and Buskist, W. (2007) *Psychology* 3rd edn. Harlow: Pearson Education.

NB. These are in alphabetical order.

## Activity 10.16 Identifying acceptable referencing methods

Most people would agree that the only really acceptable ones are 3 and 7. Number 5 would need quotation marks and acknowledgement. None of the others would be acceptable without acknowledgement. Number 4 would never be acceptable.

## Chapter 11 FINDING YOUR OWN VOICE

### Activity 11.1 Recognising voices

You found the ideas of the writer as well as the ideas of other researchers.

### Activity 11.2 Identifying voices (1)

You will have come up with something like this:

| Text | Voice |
|---|---|
| The definition of communication used by social workers needs to be wide and open. | Writer's voice. |
| Marchant and Page (2003) point out that, sadly, the biggest barrier to communicating with disabled children continues to be the attitudes and behaviour of professionals and the failure to follow guidance. | Marchant and Page's indirect voice – summary. |
| They state, 'We see it as vital that communication is understood as more than the use of speech and language and that all professionals' working definition of communication includes the wide range of ways [disabled] children make their wishes and feelings known' (Marchant and Page 2003: 60). | Marchant and Page's direct voice – quotation. |
| Morris (2002) points out that as the majority of people use spoken language to communicate, disabled children who use other means of communication often find their way is undervalued and unrecognised. | Morris's indirect voice – summary. |
| This can apply equally to disabled adults. | Writer's voice. |

You identified three different kinds of voice:

1 the author's voice
2 other people's voices, heard directly, through a quotation
3 other people's voices, heard indirectly, through a summary.

## Activity 11.3 Identifying voices (2)

The voices are shown in the second column.

| | |
|---|---|
| Infants also exert control over what their carers talk about. | Writer's voice. |
| The topic of conversation usually involves what the infant is playing with or is guided by what the infant is gazing at (Bohannon, 1993). | Bohannon's indirect voice – summary. |
| This practice means that infants hear speech that concerns what they are already paying attention to, which undoubtedly facilitates learning. | Writer's voice. |
| In fact, Tomasello and Farrar (1986) found that infants of mothers who talked mostly about the objects of their infants' gazes uttered their first words earlier than other infants and also developed larger vocabularies early in life. | Tomasello and Farrar's indirect voice – summary. |

## Activity 11.4 Showing confidence

The highlighted words and phrases in the following texts show the writer's stance.

| Modal verbs | e.g. **will, may, might, could** |
|---|---|
| The behaviour of ocean waves can be estimated using linear wave theory. (Holden, 2008: 474) | |
| **Modal adverbs** | e.g. **certainly, definitely** |
| This certainly occurs in large-scale, worldwide industrial markets, such as chemicals, oil and pharmaceuticals. (Brassington and Pettitt, 2006: 76) | |
| **Modal adjectives** | e.g. **certain, definite** |
| It is accompanied by much more definite and often more valuable criticism of earlier schemes. | |

(If you have selected 'more valuable', you are correct that it is an expression of the writer's stance but it is not related to confidence.)

## Activity 11.5 Making relationships clear

The highlighted words and phrases in the following texts show the writer's position.

Ultimately, competitive edge is the name of the game.     (Brassington and Pettitt, 2006: 34)

Similarly, Salthouse (1992, 1993; Craik and Salthouse, 2000) has argued that the elderly perform more poorly at cognitive tasks because they become slower at performing them.
(Martin et al., 2007: 491)

## Activity 11.6 Identifying the strength of claims

The highlighted words and phrases in the following texts show the writer's position.

| Introductory verbs | e.g. **seem, indicate, suggest** |
|---|---|
| In other words, materialism still seems to play a big part in influencing perceptions and attitudes towards others. (Brassington and Pettitt, 2006: 61) | |
| Reporting verbs | e.g. **believe, find, discover, show, confirm, suggest** |
| A study by Dittmar and Pepper (1994) showed that adolescents, regardless of their own social background, generally formed better impressions of people who own rather than lack expensive possessions. (Brassington and Pettitt, 2006: 61) | |

## Activity 11.7 Identifying evaluative statements

The highlighted words and phrases in the following text show the writer's position.

| Evaluative adjectives | e.g. **important, misguided, wrong, inaccurate, incorrect** |
|---|---|
| Often a 'tsunami' is referred to as a 'tidal wave'. However, this term is inappropriate because tides and tsunami differ from each other in many respects. (Holden, 2008: 481) | |
| Evaluative adverbs | e.g. **accurately, unsatisfactorily** |
| The practice has grown up in recent years of referring, however inaccurately , to a mistress as a 'common law wife'. | |
| Evaluative nouns | e.g. **difficulty, problem, crisis** |
| There is also the danger that R & D and engineering may become focused on the product for the product's sake. (Brassington and Pettitt, 2006: 26) | |
| Adverbs of frequency | e.g. **often, sometimes** |
| Services often depend on people to perform them, creating and delivering the product as the customer waits. (Brassington and Pettitt, 2006: 31) | |
| Modal nouns | e.g. **assumption, possibility** |
| The difficulty lay in the fact it was characterised as classless and free of exploitation. | |

## Activity 11.8 Understanding how voices are used

The highlighted words and phrases in the following text show the writer's positon.

There is a clear, obvious and important link between intelligence and nutrition. Brown and Pollitt (1999) claimed that malnutrition can impair brain function and IQ in the long term; and iodine deficiency during pregnancy may lead to retardation and cretinism. In the late 1980s and early 1990s, a series of studies reported large differences in non-verbal IQ between schoolchildren who received vitamin and mineral supplements (VMS) and those who received a placebo (Benton, 1992; Haller, 1995; Eysenck and Schoenthaler, 1997). Those who received the supplements scored considerably better.

In non-verbal IQ between schoolchildren who received vitamin and mineral supplements (VMS) and those who received a placebo (Benton, 1992; Haller, 1995; Eysenck and Schoenthaler, 1997), those who received the supplements scored significantly better.

(Martin *et al.*, 2007: 486)

# Chapter 12 FEEDBACK ON ACTIVITIES

## Activity 12.1 Identifying genres

The genres you write will depend very much on your subject. Read your assignment briefs carefully, though. You may not need to write an essay, but you will almost certainly need to write a critical discussion at some point in your studies.

## Activity 12.2 Understanding the structure of essays

| Preliminaries | See |
|---|---|
| **Introduction**<br>Description of the situation<br>Explanation as to why it is particularly important<br>Explanation of essay organisation | Chapter 7, pp. 117–124<br>Chapter 8, pp. 138–141 |
| **Main idea**<br>Presentation of the main idea<br>Support with examples and evidence<br>Evaluation of main idea | Chapter 7, pp. 117–124<br>Chapter 8, pp. 154–8<br>Chapter 8, pp. 145–150 |
| **Further ideas**<br>Presentation of further ideas<br>Support with examples and evidence<br>Evaluation of further ideas | Chapter 7, pp. 117–124<br>Chapter 8, pp. 154–8<br>Chapter 8, pp. 145–150 |
| **Conclusion**<br>Summary of the ideas<br>Evaluation of the ideas<br>Statement of your own point of view with reasons | Chapter 10, p. 199<br>Chapter 8, pp. 145–150<br>Chapter 8, pp. 142–5<br>Chapter 8, pp. 154–8 and<br>Chapter 8, pp. 158–160 |
| **End matter** | |

## Activity 12.3 Understanding the structure of research proposals

| Preliminaries | See |
|---|---|
| **Title**<br>Brief description of research proposal | |
| **Purpose**<br>Description in detail of what you want to find out | Chapter 7, pp. 117–124 |
| **Justification**<br>Argument to justify your research<br>Explanation as to why it is important | Chapter 8, pp. 138–141<br>Chapter 8, pp. 145–150 |
| **Literature review**<br>Report of the previous research<br>Examples of previous research<br>Evaluation of previous research<br>Identification of any gaps<br>Description of how you are going to fill them | Chapter 7, pp. 129–132<br>Chapter 8, pp. 154–8<br>Chapter 8, pp. 145–150<br>Chapter 7, pp. 117–124 |
| **Method**<br>Description of your proposed research methodology<br>Description of your time frame<br>Description of how you intend to do this in the time<br>Description of resources<br>Description of how you intend to do this with available resources | Chapter 7, pp. 117–124 |
| **Dissemination**<br>Description of how the findings will be used<br>Evaluation of this use<br>Description of how the findings will be disseminated | Chapter 7, pp. 117–124<br><br>Chapter 8, pp. 145–150<br>Chapter 7, pp. 117–124 |
| **Reading list**<br>List of references plus other books you might find useful | Chapter 10, pp. 180–199 |
| **End matter** | |

## Activity 12.4 Understanding the structure of literature reviews

| Preliminaries | See |
|---|---|
| **Introduction**<br>Description of the context<br>Explanation of importance | Chapter 7, pp. 117–124<br>Chapter 8, pp. 142–5<br>Chapter 8, pp. 138–141 |
| **Background**<br>Summary of the studies you have read<br>Justification of their inclusion | Chapter 10, p. 199<br>Chapter 8, pp. 142–5<br>Chapter 8, pp. 138–141 |
| **Evaluation**<br>Evaluation of the studies<br>Support of your evaluation | Chapter 8, pp. 145–150<br>Chapter 8, pp. 154–8 |
| **Justification**<br>Identification of a gap in knowledge<br>Justification of your research | Chapter 7, pp. 117–124<br>Chapter 8, pp. 142–5<br>Chapter 8, pp. 138–141 |
| **Conclusion**<br>Conclusion about what you have read<br>Explanation of how the gap can be filled | Chapter 10, p. 199<br>Chapter 8, pp. 142–5<br>Chapter 7, pp. 117–124<br>Chapter 8, pp. 158–160 |
| **End matter** | |

## Activity 12.5 **Understanding the structure of reports**

| Preliminaries | See |
|---|---|
| **Executive summary** | Chapter 10, pp. 185–189 |
| **Background**<br>Description of the background<br>Explanation as to why the research was necessary | Chapter 7, pp. 117–124<br>Chapter 8, pp. 138–141 |
| **Research methods**<br>Report on how research was carried out | Chapter 7, pp. 129–132 |
| **Findings/Results**<br>Report of the finding<br>Inclusion of diagrams which need to be referred to | Chapter 7, pp. 129–132<br>Chapter 7, pp. 124–7 |
| **Discussion and Conclusions**<br>Description of the findings<br>Comparison and contrast of the findings with previous research<br>Evaluation of the findings | Chapter 7, pp. 117–124<br>Chapter 8, pp. 150–154<br>Chapter 8, pp. 145–150<br>Chapter 8, pp. 158–160 |
| **Recommendations**<br>Recommendation of action | Chapter 8, p. 160 |
| **End matter** | |

## Activity 12.6 Understanding the structure of experimental reports

| Preliminaries | See |
|---|---|
| **Introduction**<br>Description of the background<br>Explanation of why research was necessary<br><br>Description of how research will be undertaken | Chapter 7, pp. 117–124<br>Chapter 8, pp. 138–141<br><br>Chapter 7, pp. 117–124 |
| **Methods**<br>Overview of the research<br>Report of who took part and where<br>Report of what procedures were used<br>Report of what materials were used<br>Report of any statistical analysis used | Chapter 7, pp. 129–132 |
| **Results**<br>Report of findings<br>Reference to any diagrams used | Chapter 7, pp. 129–132<br>Chapter 7, pp. 124–7 |
| **Discussion**<br>Summary of main purpose of research<br>Review of most important findings<br>Evaluation of findings<br>Explanation of findings<br>Comparison with other researchers' findings<br>Description of implications and recommendations | Chapter 10, p. 199<br>Chapter 8, pp. 145–150<br>Chapter 8, pp. 150–154<br>Chapter 8, pp. 138–141<br>Chapter 7, pp. 117–124<br>Chapter 8, pp. 158–160<br>Chapter 8, p. 160 |
| **End matter** | |

## Activity 12.7 Understanding the structure of reviews

| Preliminaries | See |
|---|---|
| **Introduction**<br>The name of the book, the author,<br>publisher, price | |
| **The overall text**<br>Description of the subject of the text<br>Description of the purpose of the text | Chapter 7, pp. 117–124 |
| **Background**<br>Description of what has been<br>written/published before<br>Evaluation of previous publications | Chapter 7, pp. 117–124<br>Chapter 8, pp. 145–150 |
| **Content**<br>Summary of the book<br>Description of its general organisation, and<br>contents of each chapter | Chapter 10, p. 199<br>Chapter 7, pp. 117–124 |
| **Evaluation**<br>Evaluation of the text<br>Comparison and contrast with other<br>publications<br>Presentation of your point of view, making<br>clear any deficits | Chapter 8, pp. 145–150<br>Chapter 8, pp. 150–154<br><br>Chapter 8, pp. 142–5 |
| **Looks**<br>Description and evaluation of design,<br>price, production, proof-reading, size,<br>colour, etc. | Chapter 7, pp. 117–124<br>Chapter 8, pp. 145–150 |
| **Conclusion**<br>Summary<br>Conclusion, discussing whether it is<br>appropriate for audience<br>Recommendation or not | Chapter 10, p. 199<br>Chapter 8, pp. 158–160<br><br>Chapter 8, p. 160 |
| **End matter** | |

## Activity 12.8 Understanding the structure of abstracts

| Introduction | |
|---|---|
| Introduction to the study by describing the context | Chapter 7, pp. 117–124 |
| Explanation of why the subject is important | Chapter 8, pp. 138–141 |

| **Purpose** | |
|---|---|
| Report of the purpose of the study | Chapter 7, pp. 117–124 |

| **Methods** | |
|---|---|
| Report of how the study was undertaken | Chapter 7, pp. 129–132 |

| **Results** | |
|---|---|
| Report of the results that were found | Chapter 7, pp. 129–132 |

| **Evaluation** | |
|---|---|
| Brief evaluation of the results | Chapter 8, pp. 145–150 |

| **Conclusion** | |
|---|---|
| Brief conclusion | Chapter 8, pp. 158–160 |
| Explanation of what is important and why | |

## Activity 12.9 Understanding the structure of case studies

| Preliminaries | See |
| --- | --- |
| **Introduction**<br>Introduction to the situation<br>Description of the problem – why the study was undertaken | Chapter 7, pp. 117–124 |
| **Background reading**<br>Description of previous research<br>Examples<br>Evaluation of previous research | Chapter 7, pp. 117–124<br>Chapter 8, pp. 145–150 |
| **Methodology**<br>Report of the methods you used<br>Explanation of why you chose each method | Chapter 7, pp. 129–132<br>Chapter 8, pp. 138–141 |
| **Results**<br>Report on what you found from each method | Chapter 7, pp. 129–132 |
| **Summary**<br>Summary of all results<br>Comparison and contrast of results | Chapter 10, p. 199<br>Chapter 8, pp. 150–154 |
| **Evaluation**<br>Evaluation of findings in light of background reading | Chapter 8, pp. 145–50 |
| **Conclusion**<br>Summary of main findings<br>Generalisation from findings | Chapter 10, p. 199<br>Chapter 8, pp. 142–5<br>Chapter 8, pp. 158–160 |
| **Recommendations**<br>Recommendations for future | Chapter 8: Recommendations, p. 160 |
| **End matter** | |

## Activity 12.10 Understanding the structure of reflective reports

| Preliminaries | See |
|---|---|
| **Introduction**<br>Description of your situation | Chapter 7, pp. 117–124 |
| **Personal report**<br>Report of what you did or what happened | Chapter 7, pp. 129–132 |
| **Reflection on action**<br>Report of what was good/bad,<br>easy/difficult, pleasant/unpleasant,<br>successful/unsuccessful, etc.<br>Comparison and contrast of your<br>experiences<br>Explanation as to why | Chapter 7, pp. 129–132<br>Chapter 8, pp. 150–154<br>Chapter 8, pp. 138–141 |
| **Reflection on teaching**<br>Report of what have you been taught<br>Description of what you know | Chapter 7, pp. 129–132<br>Chapter 7, pp. 117–124 |
| **Connections**<br>Evaluation of your practice, drawing on<br>your knowledge and experience | Chapter 8, pp. 145–150 |
| **Identification of any gaps**<br>Description of any gaps in your knowledge<br>Explanation of how you can fill them<br>Generalisation to future | Chapter 7, pp. 117–124<br>Chapter 8, pp. 138–141 |
| **Action plan**<br>Production of action plan for future<br>(learning + practice)<br>Justification of action plan | Chapter 9, p. 169 |
| **Conclusion**<br>Summary of situation<br>Summary of planned action | Chapter 10, pp. 199<br>Chapter 8, pp.158–160 |
| **End matter** | |

# Chapter 13 PRESENTING YOUR WORK

## Activity 13.1 Identifying errors in layout

**Extract 1**

Two problems: (1) the font used is illegible; (2) the line spacing used is only single, there is therefore no room for tutor comments.

**Extract 2**

Three problems: (1) the size of font used is far too large; (2) the left margin is too wide; (3) single-spacing has been used.

**Extract 3**

Two problems: (1) the initials in the header are not sufficient as a full name is required; (2) the page number appears too close to the name and may be misunderstood.

### Activity 13.2 Turning text into slides

The differences are:

- The slide has a title.
- The introductory text does not appear on the slide at all. The speaker will include it in the presentation but does not need to write it on the slide.
- The points on the slide are not complete sentences; they are key words to prompt the speaker.
- The examples in the text have not been added to the slide.

Remember that the speaker should always be expanding on the points shown on the slide. You do not want a slide full of information that you will read word for word.

### Activity 13.3 Improving a slide

A possible improvement would be to delete the examples from the text. The slide would then look something like this:

---

## Nation's psychological conditions

- *Noticing* is defined as paying attention to the word. Use of bold, italics, inclusion in pre-teaching lists, written record on the board and in students' note-books.

- *Retrieval* is used to strengthen the learning. In this case, either the form OR the meaning (or parts of either) is visible to the learner. One acts as a memory aid for retrieval of the other. Meaning-focused use of the four skills: re-telling, role-play and problem-solving.

- *Elaborating* involves retrieval but adds strengthening to the process. It can occur through inclusion in contexts which are either new or unknown to the learner, or where rich instruction of the word is given.

---

Alternatively, you could delete even more text and only show this:

---

# Nation's psychological conditions

---

- *Noticing* – defined as paying attention to the word

- *Retrieval* – used to strengthen the learning

- *Elaborating* – involves retrieval but adds strengthening to the process

---

## Activity 13.4 Evaluating posters

### Poster 1

- *Negative points.* The poster is far too busy. Information has been taken from the original printed text and stuck onto the poster. This results in people having to read the information as if it were an essay. The tables in the middle section are provided without any explanations and there are too many of them. The pictures do not complement the subject.
- *Positive points.* Some pictures have been included to add variety and the title is easier to read from a distance.

### Poster 2

- *Negative points.* Poorly organised. There seems to be no connection between some of the areas, with pictures being included but with no reference as to why. Too many varieties of font are used.
- *Positive points.* The amount of written text is acceptable. There is adequate white space. Text and images are quite balanced.

### Poster 3

- *Negative points.* The poster does not give sufficient information regarding this topic. It has concentrated far too much on appeal rather than substance. The pictures and text seem to have been stuck on without much thought.
- *Positive points.* A great deal of white space is easier on the eye. By cutting patterns on the paper, an attempt has been made to provide variety.

## Activity 13.5 Improving posters

You could follow the guidelines provided in this chapter in addition to the comments in Activity 13.4. Remember that although you want the poster to be visually attractive, you must also make sure that a person looking at it, who may not perhaps know much about the subject, is being given sufficient detail to understand the message.

## Chapter 14 WORKING WITH FEEDBACK

### Activity 14.1 Reflection on feedback

**1** Knowing where to find your assessed work may indicate how important the feedback on that work is to you. However, the work may have had no or poor written feedback in which case you did not see a reason for keeping it.

**2** Once again, this depends on the work and the feedback received. Clearly the more times you consult the feedback, the more likely you are to take it on board for subsequent assignments.

**3** Perhaps you need to reconsider your practice based on the information in this chapter.

**4** You may have seen more value in receiving feedback on drafts as the final mark of the same piece of work would be influenced by your actions on the feedback.

**5** This would depend on the lecturer, but it is worth considering whether your marks improved as a consequence.

**6** This merely acts as an example of the various ways in which lecturer feedback can be given. It is worth considering what you have received already, which method you prefer and why, and whether your preferences are matched by your lecturers'. You may approach your lecturers with your views.

**7** Different lecturers mark in different ways, but once again, evaluate what you would prefer against what you receive and discuss this with your lecturers.

**8** This is a valuable student–lecturer exchange which should take place more frequently. Once again, see if you can approach your lecturers to discuss your preferences.

### Activity 14.2 Evaluating feedback on drafts and final scripts

There are no correct answers for this activity as individuals will rate each type of feedback differently. Look at the feedback provided with Activity 14.3 for an explanation of your answers.

### Activity 14.3 Rating the importance of feedback

Feedback is provided as part of the activity.

### Activity 14.4 Feedback methods used in your context

The answers will vary based on your learning environment. We feel that it is important for you to know the existing mechanisms in your department, so with this activity we hope to increase your awareness of the kind of help that is available.

### Activity 14.5 Preparing for writing in a feedback notebook

**1** Read more books, journals and academic publications to develop more ideas and arguments.

**2** Write a plan. Group relevant ideas together in your text and make sure the order they appear in is logical.

**3** Make your ideas and opinions (your voice) clearer. Question what you read.
**4** Acknowledge the authors whose words or ideas you are using.
**5** Make sure you edit your work before handing it in.

## Chapter 15 EDITING YOUR WORK

### Activity 15.1 Correct the table of contents

The table has the following mistakes:

**INTRODUCTION**
The chapters should be numbered 1 and 2.

**Part One**
There is no page reference for Chapter 4.
Chapters 5, 6 and 7 are in the wrong order.
The title of chapter 8 is missing.

**Part Two**
Details of chapters 11–13 are missing.

**Part Three**
The words 'Part Three' are missing from the subheading.
Details of chapters 15–19 are missing.

**Index**
This must be put at the end.

### Activity 15.2 Spot the mistake

The correct words are in bold type.

**1** Last month the government **introduced** new regulations for small businesses.
**2** Investors who **bought** shares in the dot.com industries saw **their** value fall over time.
**3** Historians **disagree** over the origins of communism.
**4** Under-age drinking **is** a major problem today.
**5** **Your** work has to carry weight and authority if readers are to trust in what you write.

### Activity 15.3 Correct the punctuation

The correct punctuation is:

The current cultural context in which we find ourselves located allows little opportunity for silence and appears to place little value on it. Our shopping centres, offices, cars and homes are full of sound, some might say 'noise', and the invention of e-mail, mobile phones and iPods means people are constantly in communication with each other and are able, should they choose to, to talk or listen to someone or something all the time. Under these circumstances, silence is an unfamiliar phenomenon. Therefore, when it is encountered, it can be unnerving and potentially be perceived as threatening and deskilling. Yet, we would argue, it should not be and need not be.

## Activity 15.4 Correct the spelling

The correct words are in bold type.

1 Last month the **government** introduced new **regulations** for small **businesses**.
2 **Investors** who **bought shares** in the dot.com industries saw **their** value fall over **time**.
3 **Historians disagree** over the origins of **communism**.
4 Under-age **drinking** is a major **problem** today.
5 Your work has to carry weight and authority if **readers** are to trust in **what** you write.

## Activity 15.5 Improve this referencing

1 In the first reference the writer has left out the initials of the two authors and has forgotten to include the year of publication (2000).
2 In the second reference the writer has spelt the name of the author incorrectly (Gilman, not Giman). They have given the names of the editors of the book the chapter comes from, but have left out all other details. It is not enough to put, as this writer has, 'see above for details'. The information must be given in full.
3 In the third reference the writer has reversed the order of the surnames of the two authors. This cannot be done, the details must match exactly.
4 The writer has forgotten to include one of the references (Kroll and Taylor, 2000).

## Activity 15.6 Comparing your draft

Chapter 14 gave you advice on how to use feedback in a positive way to act on comments you receive on your work. Each time you write an assignment you need to make sure you act on the feedback you receive to avoid losing marks for the same problem.

# INDEX

329

# Index

# Index

# Index